HURTING FOR LOVE
Munchausen by Proxy Syndrome

Unfortunateley there
will be cases popping
up even in your
own backyard —
They are worthy of
study — and can teach
us much about the
rest of us —

Best —
Herb Selman

HURTING FOR LOVE
Munchausen by Proxy Syndrome

Herbert A. Schreier
Judith A. Libow

THE GUILFORD PRESS
New York   London

© 1993 The Guilford Press
A Division of Guilford Publications, Inc.
72 Spring Street, New York, NY 10012

Printed in the United States of America

This book is printed on acid-free paper.

Last digit is print number: 9 8 7 6 5 4 3 2

Library of Congress Cataloging-in-Publication Data

Schreier, Herbert A.
    Hurting for love : Munchausen by proxy syndrome / Herbert
A. Schreier, Judith A. Libow.
       p. cm.
    Includes bibliographical references and index.
    ISBN 0-89862-121-6
    1. Munchausen syndrome by proxy. 2. Munchausen Syndrome
by Proxy—diagnosis. 3. Munchausen Syndrome by Proxy—
therapy. I. Libow, Judith A. II. Title.
    [DNLM: WM 170 S378h 1993]
RC569.5.M83S37 1993
616.85'8223—dc20
DNLM/DLC
for Library of Congress   92-48483
                                             CIP

*To Jake and Judy, and
in memory of my parents, Nathan and Hilda*
—H.S.

To Carl and to my parents, Lynne and Ben
—J.L.

*And to our wonderful coworkers at
Children's Hospital Oakland
who truly are there for the children*

Foreword

The case histories at the beginning of this book provide a vivid picture of the weird and extravagant ways by which some mothers abuse their children. Those who have encountered Munchausen by Proxy syndrome abuse will be familiar with its potential severity, and some will have seen even more horrific cases. Some readers may recall a child with a mystifying and serious illness for whom no solution could be found and, in retrospect, will now realize the probability that the illness was false, fabricated by the mother. Others will recognize for the first time that a child with apparent chronic illness, for whom they are the primary physician, probably has false illness and that the child can be restored to normal health with speedy intervention.

I encountered my first case of Munchausen by Proxy syndrome more than 15 years ago. As the regional pediatric nephrologist I had been failing to help a girl with disabling urinary tract problems. Her symptoms and signs escalated in severity and at the end of one holiday weekend, during which several senior specialist colleagues and I had performed a range of complex investigations to identify the cause, we were no nearer to understanding it. That night I spoke to the mother, who was living in the hospital with her child, in the mother's sitting room by the ward. I was tired and unhappy, mainly because of my failure to solve the problem, despite putting the 6-year-old girl through a mass of unpleasant procedures. The mother pointed me to a comfortable chair and brewed me a cup of tea. She told me how grateful she was for all my efforts, and how much she admired me for trying so hard. She told me not to worry so much.

That night I could not sleep. The diagnostic problems churned in my mind, at the back of which was my awareness of the incongruity of the mother being less worried about her child than I. At about 3:00 A.M. I suddenly realized the reason, and for the first time suspected a mother of fabricating a prolonged illness in her child. This solution to my dilemma was so obvious that it allowed everything to fall into place. In the middle of the night I telephoned one of my close colleagues who had assisted me with the case that weekend and merely said, "I know the reason why we couldn't make a diagnosis: her mother is causing the illness and tampering with the samples." My colleague immediately replied, "It's absolutely obvious." It *was* absolutely obvious once one deduced what was actually happening and once one realized that mothers could behave in that way. Before I returned to sleep that night, I recalled two other problem cases in which, now that I looked back on them in the light of this case, the illness had almost certainly been false.

While Munchausen by Proxy syndrome abuse can be obvious for those who have encountered it, it can be very difficult to identify for those who have not. Goethe wrote, "We see only what we know." There may be disbelief, which is likely to be a particular problem in any community, child-care service, or legal system without previous experience with the syndrome. One of the most lonely and difficult periods of my life was in the early years of defining the syndrome; often my accounts of fabricated illness were met with disbelief or ridicule. Frequently I did not have the precise forensic proof of abuse that would be demanded by criminal lawyers. Even when I could amass significant circumstantial evidence of fabricated illness, I often failed to convince social service agencies or the legal system that a child was being abused. I know from discussion and correspondence with colleagues in other countries that the same initial reaction of disbelief, followed by a process of accommodation on the basis of local experience, seems to be necessary in each country before satisfactory ways are devised for recognizing and managing factitious illness abuse.

Understanding the mothers affected by Munchausen by Proxy syndrome is difficult, in part because their own explanation of what they did and why they did it once their activities are exposed are often clearly designed to mask real actions and true motivations. I have had the opportunity to talk with mothers many years after the abuse they committed and I am impressed by the slow process of revelation. Early on, when the fabrication is detected, they usually deny any wrongdoing. This is particularly likely if the police are involved in concurrent criminal investigations. Although a partial confession may emerge during child-care proceedings, frequently there is not even a partial admission of guilt, particularly if the spouse and the grandparents are denying the possibility of abuse. At that stage some mothers acknowledge that the evidence (for example, a video recording of their abusive actions or toxicological analysis) does support the diagnosis of abuse, but they continue to deny conscious agency ("I must have done it, but I can't remember a thing"). Later, there may be more recollection, but as one mother who had suffocated her child said, "It was only about 6 years afterward that I really thought hard about what I'd done and was willing to talk about it, even though I'd always remembered every detail all the time."

Cases in which both mother and father are jointly, and knowingly, involved in Munchausen by Proxy syndrome are rare. Much more common are cases in which the father is a passive colluder, turning a blind eye on what is happening and failing to help his child, or support his partner. But if we incriminate the fathers as passive colluders, we must also incriminate doctors as passive colluders or even, some might say, active colluders. In most cases the mother merely invents a false illness story concerning her child. Rather than actively harming the child physically herself, it is the doctors who harm the child with their venepunctures, prescriptions of drugs, investigations, and surgical procedures. Munchausen by Proxy syndrome abuse is nearly always an example of misdiagnosis, and sometimes a misdiagnosis that has been sustained over a period of many years. Most of us medical professionals feel rather guilty when we identify the syndrome in one of our patients.

Although the invention of factitious illness in children by their parents is likely to have occurred in past ages, it may well be more frequent in the era of modern medicine. The modern doctor is much more likely to order tests or to make referrals to specialists than to spend time listening to the mother. For many physicians it is easier to request an investigation, even one that is costly and itself takes several hours, than to spend time talking with the mother. Few medical professionals would doubt that most surgeons would much prefer to do three operations on children, each lasting 4 hours, than to spend even 1 hour talking with each of the three mothers of these children. The increased specialization of modern medicine is a further aid to factitious illness abuse. Children see an endocrinologist for their growth, a nephrologist for a urinary tract problem, and a neurologist

because of alleged seizures. There is a shortage of experienced gener-
alists who look at the child as a whole, let alone as an individual
playing a complex part within a family.

I have seen several cases of Munchausen by Proxy syndrome
abuse in which the child has accumulated three or four volumes of
carefully written hospital records, all emanating from prestigious
European and North American hospitals. Doctors' notes record in
detail the many examinations, investigations, and procedures, yet
amid 100 pages of notes there is no reference to family circumstances
or any inquiry about the mother's health or background. If a child
with recurrent life-threatening events (which occur only in the presence of the mother) is extensively investigated over a period of 18
months in six prestigious medical centers, and no one thinks to
examine the mother's medical record, which would reveal three
laparoscopies (with normal findings), six operations for a "frozen
elbow" (with normal findings), and two entries by different doctors
concerning an unusual lesion on her hand ("as though hit with a
hammer"), are not the doctors at fault? What is the correct diagnosis:
Munchausen by Proxy syndrome abuse or medical negligence?

It will be some time before there is reliable information about
prognosis. As the authors of this book indicate, it is all too easy to gain
an overly pessimistic impression of the prognosis from the published
case reports, because they tend to highlight extreme cases and disasters.
However, overall, my colleagues and I were dismayed by our long-term
findings 1 to 14 years after diagnosis of Munchausen by Proxy syndrome abuse. Bearing in mind that it was the milder cases with an
anticipated more favorable prognosis who were reunited with natural
parents, the outcome for the children who were either reunited with
their parents or placed in alternative care was disappointing. Of 54 index
children, half the outcomes were considered as "unacceptable"; sim-
ilarly, 56 of their 90 siblings had outcomes that were rated as unacceptable.

Drs. Schreier and Libow have provided a wealth of carefully
researched information, which they have analyzed thoughtfully and
presented in a most stimulating way. Familiarity is said to lead to
boredom, but there are some subjects about which the more one
knows the more fascinating and difficult they become. Munchausen
by Proxy syndrome abuse is an example of that and remains a major
challenge for all those who try to help children and their families.

Professor Roy Meadow
Leeds, England

𝕮𝖜

Preface

During a single year (1984–1985) at Children's Hospital in Oakland, California, where we both work in the department of psychiatry, we encountered several cases of Munchausen by Proxy syndrome (MBPS). This syndrome applies to a group of patients, usually mothers, who systematically fabricate information about their childrens' health or intentionally make their children gravely ill.

Unfamiliar with the problem, we initially focused on understanding the intricacies of the clinical manifestations of this very perplexing disorder. Our study led us to write a paper entitled "Three Forms of Factitious Illness in Children: When Is It Munchausen Syndrome by Proxy?," published in the *American Journal of Orthopsychiatry*. We took a strong position even then that this syndrome did not apply to parents who simply needed help with a difficult home situation or who wanted some attention. Our ongoing study of this disorder convinces us that we were right and that there is a discontinuity between MBPS parents and this latter group. After the paper's publication in 1986 we were surprised to find ourselves in the position of de facto experts, asked to consult on cases by a variety of perplexed health care professionals around the country.

The first part of this book tries to clarify the most salient commonalities in these cases based on our own clinical experience and a careful reading of the literature. We owe a great deal to the pioneering work of Dr. Roy Meadow, a pediatrician in England, who has accumulated more clinical experience with this disorder than any other observer. He has been a careful and perceptive commentator from the begining, when he first called our collective attention to this problem in 1977.

The very dramatic and remarkable similarities in the way the MBPS parents behave inspired our efforts to understand the psychodynamic issues involved in the syndrome. For a number of reasons, understanding proved more difficult than our initial straightforward clinical investigations. Few cases were discussed in the psychological literature and still fewer treatment regimes were reported. We treated only a few patients ourselves, and we were usually called in late in the process, by which time we could not investigate with the depth and detail that a study of the syndrome requires. Through the years, however, we have been able to accumulate enough early childhood and family material to put together what we feel are interesting and reasonably sound hypotheses concerning the psychology of this confusing and devastating disorder.

In the vast majority of cases, the Munchausen by Proxy parent is the mother. Our psychodynamic investigations led us into the areas of female psychological development, work on impostors, and recent thinking on "female forms" of perversions to try to explain the incredible ability of the women affected by the syndrome to simultaneously appear intensely caring for their children while slowly (at times over years) poisoning or in other ways harming (through their own agency or through the unwitting agency of a physician) them. Unlike the other forms of child abuse in which men are more often involved, and where there are usually obvious signs of intense rage on the part of the parent and disordered parent–child interactions, the mothers involved in MBPS look to all the world like wonderful parents and appear to have very close relationships with their children, as do their children with them. Our interest in feminist thought and systemic theory also sensitized us to the significant issues involved in a disorder in which a less powerful class of people attempts to gain recognition from a more powerful and patriarchal societal system.

As intensely interesting as the dynamic issues in this form of mothering "imposturing" was the finding that fathers and husbands could be completely oblivious (and, more rarely, actively supportive) of the process that involved numerous office visits and hospitalizations of their own children. Their role in this disorder remains poorly understood, for almost nothing has been reported about the early histories of these "absent fathers" and their relationships with their wives and children.

Aside from data on the mothers, our interviews and interactions with MBPS families and their physicians and nurses provided us with information about their contradictory behaviors and their effects on caregivers. Our research led us to try and understand the role played by the doctor in this phenomenal and deadly masquerade. For both of us, trained as we were during the heyday of systems theory and psychodynamic psychotherapy, the data concerning physicians afforded us an opportunity to examine the complex dialectical process that takes place between these two real and symbolic caretakers, mothers and doctors, caught in a frighteningly destructive "dance" and often in an overt power struggle.

As we began to understand the needs of a young girl growing up undervalued and even ignored (our own data and published reports on the mothers' early histories did not frequently show much direct abuse), we could begin to see why as grown women they turned to the powerfully parental and nurturant image of the physician. A striking feature of the syndrome is how these mothers manufacture whole new lives for themselves through their interactions with doctors and hospitals.

Early on we recognized that these women did not present themselves as wholly passive in their relationships with medical professionals, but instead often gained control of these very powerful but ultimately disappointing parental figures. This vision led us not just to the individual dynamics and family histories of these women and the contribution of their physicians, but also pushed us to attempt to place this syndrome in the context of the destructive and unfulfilling roles assigned women during the era of modern medicine. The use and abuse of medical care to gain a bit of personal salvation by MBPS patients has been disastrously costly to all involved.

Family violence, though with us throughout history, has received increasing (and well-deserved) attention in the past 30 years. The literature emphasizes "violent assault as the archetypical problem" (Gordon, 1988, p. 6) though as Linda Gordon points out, child *neglect*, less dramatic, more ambiguous, and calling forth much less outrage, is vastly more common. Unfortunately, neglect is often transmitted from generation to generation. Our contact with MBPS mothers has convinced us that even the much less overt forms of neglect these mothers experienced as they were growing up can have tragic consequences, including the acting out of a revenge fantasy employing an infant's body in an intense sadomasochistic transferential relationship with the child's doctor. One of the inspirations for this book is the desire to protect countless other potential victims, both children and their parents, from becoming ensnared in this disorder.

As with other forms of child abuse, this "abuse done by women . . . [is] a product of the sex/gender order of society" (Gordon, 1988, p. vii). Also, the *reaction* this disorder engenders cannot be separated from the ordering of power in our society. "Discovered" as it was in the early years of the second wave of feminism, when male authority and the social construction of mothering were in tumultuous disequilibrium, the ability to "see" intensely bad mothering varied dramatically and very much with the social agenda of the observer.

Usually one does not find attempts at social analysis in a book in which clinical descriptions, epidemiological research, legal precedents, and management strategies form the mainstay. Since this is the first book-length study devoted to the subject of MBPS, we wanted to be as encyclopedic as possible in drawing together information on this syndrome. A clinical/medical study would focus too much on the syndrome specifics and woman/mother as abuser and would likely end up seeming to blame mothers for yet another "failure" in the family. A psychodynamic study would focus too narrowly on individual/family dynamics, even if it included the dynamics of the physicians' contributions. We are now much more aware of the dangers of taking such formulations out of their social and historical context. While *nowhere* near as common as more typical forms of child abuse, MBPS is not a trivial problem, even in terms of its numbers. The fact that it is so frequently a problem of women who masquerade as good mothers, who base their identity on "mothering," and who can fool professionals (medical and legal) for years or even decades, forces us to reflect on our conceptualizations of social categories such as mother, doctor, and judge.

For those who would argue that this dangerous behavior represents an extreme end of a continuum, we point to the family data we have collected that belie this idea.

Why an individual would use her own child to manipulate the medical establishment is the subject of this book. Whatever the attraction medical institutions hold for many, only a relative few, and we will argue a *seriously* wounded and disturbed few, offer their children up in just this way. The difficulties in detecting their actions, too often too late to save a child's health, is an equally interesting and complex story worthy of study and one we will also address.

This book is an attempt to examine in detail the detection, definition, dynamics, and management of this disorder. We hope we have offered enough descriptive material to be practically useful and at the same time enable readers to arrive at their own hypotheses. Clearly, our dynamic formulations are open to different interpretations. We thus strive not to be definitive, but rather to open up discussion about this perplexing and troubling disorder, an effort which we hope will ultimately lead to clearer understanding and help for all involved.

We will argue that MBPS behavior is rooted in the young girl's need for but lack of recognition from others in her formative years, and is undoubtedly aided by individual constitutional givens. The relatively common family life histories uncovered in the lives of the mothers have outcomes so disastrous that we are compelled to reexamine our assumptions about "normative" behavior and its meaning.

There is a precedent in our field, as well as in education, history, and the social sciences, of being unable to "see" certain dynamics and their outcomes even as they virtually stare us in the face. We hope, in our attention to the details of these dynamics as well as their social context, to provide the element often missing from clinical texts: that of leading the way toward an understanding that will then provide the means for prevention.

Acknowledgments

One of the greatest pleasures that has come from our experience writing this book over the past years has been the opportunity to discover a network of wonderful colleagues around the country. The fact that Munchausen by Proxy syndrome crosses so many worlds—medicine, law, child protection, psychology, psychiatry—has afforded us many exciting interchanges with dedicated professionals. Our special thanks to the many who immeasurably added to our book by sharing ideas, observations, and personal experiences of MBPS, including Dr. William Byrne, Dr. J. Reid Meloy, Dr. Christopher Bools, Dr. David Beck, Dr. Joel Singerman, Dr. Ann Petru, Dr. Jean Sarris, Dr. Donna Rosenberg, Dr. David Golub, Dr. Mark Usatin, Dr. Kathy Mason, Dr. Pat Siegel, Dr. Deidre Conway Rand, Dr. Alan Valcov, Dr. Bernard Kahan, Dr. Klaus Minde, Dr. Anthony Urquiza, Dr. Lisa Canin, Dr. Mary Sanders, Mark Mendelow, Ann Crean, Beatrice Yorker, Dr. Carrie Fitzsimmons, Dr. Drew Westen, Dr. Roger Williams, Rachel Fahrer, Kathy Methfessel, Dr. Kathleen Faller, and so many others.

Many generous friends and colleagues have contributed their time to read and critique sections of the manuscript over countless revisions. We particularly wish to thank Dr. Robert Wallerstein, Dr. Owen Renik, Dr. Diane Ehrensaft, Dr. Judy Stacey, Dr. Steve Portuges, Dr. Steve Seligman, Dr. Carl Gacono, Dr. Roy Meadow, Dr. Alan Shonkoff, and Dr. Virginia Goldner, as well as the editors at *The Bulletin of the Menninger Clinic*, Joyce Lindenbaum, Tom Laqueur, Robert Post, and Nancy Scheper-Hughes. Their generosity, expertise, and candor have gone a long way in helping guide us as this book took shape.

We have found that one of the best, most unexpected pleasures of authorship in a project of this kind has been the opportunity to develop ongoing friendships with recently discovered colleagues who share our commitment to understanding this fascinating disorder. We look forward to a long and continuing collaboration with many of these new friends including attorneys Jacqueline Rypma, Cathy Cook, and Kelly Hargreaves, law student Sherilyn Kempf, Dr. Lynne Sturm, Dr. Mark Usatin, Detective Mike Gorman, and Pauline Canny, formerly of NBC News. All have shared with us a great deal of excitement about our project and have been an ongoing source of encouragement. Thank you all.

Of course this book would never have happened without the long and tireless efforts of our local support network. Special thanks to Dr. Terry Kupers whose dogged encouragement made the project seem possible. And thanks to Jake Stacey-Schreier who patiently made it through a second book written in his household in his young life—the first, by his mother, Judy, set the standard for writing excellence for the family.

Many important friends have been an ever-present source of inspiration and confidence, especially Marsha Mirkin, Debra Levinsky, and Bev Lesch. Thanks always to Carl Olson for serving as the voice of reason and to Lynne and Ben Libow for their constant, loving support.

Our thanks also to our research assistant, Lynne Calonico, for her many hours spent tracking down obscure references. Len Shapiro, Marjorie Pineo, Annie Kinn, and Josh Devlin from the Medical Library at Children's Hospital Oakland have always been there when help was needed. Our gratitude and appreciation also to our editor, Kitty Moore, for her experience, her advice, and most of all for sticking with us and always maintaining her sense of humor. Anna Brackett at The Guilford Press was truly a pleaure to work with. And we are exceedingly grateful to Kathy Horikoshi, our typist, for her tolerance, efficiency, and uncanny ability to make order out of chaos. You have all been wonderful to work with on this book.

Finally, thanks also must go to Helene Davis, Ulli Hanley, and Doreen Reed for their help and support through this long project. Our appreciation as well to the staff and the trainees in the Department of Psychiatry at the hospital for their patience in listening to little but Munchausen by Proxy syndrome for the last 3 years.

The following publishers have generously given permission to use extended quotations from copyrighted works:

From "Hyperthermy in a Man up to 148°F." by A. Jacobi, 1895, *Transactions of the Association of American Physicians, 10,* 159–191. Copyright 1895 by the Association of American Physicians.

From "Munchausen Syndrome: Its Relationship to Malingering, Hysteria, and the Physician–Patient Relationship" by B. Cramer, M. R. Gershberg, and M. Stern, 1971, *Archives of General Psychiatry, 24,* 573–578. Copyright 1971 by the American Medical Association.

From "Chronic Factitious Fever in Puberty and Adolescence: A Diagnostic Challenge to the Family Physician" by J. H. Herzberg and S. M. Wolff, 1972, *International Journal of Psychiatry in Medicine, 3*(3), 205–212. Copyright 1972 by Baywood Publishing Co.

From "Web of Deceit: A Literature Review of Munchausen Syndrome by Proxy" by D. Rosenberg, 1987, *Child Abuse and Neglect, 11,* 547–563. Copyright 1987 by Pergamon Press Ltd.

From *The Death Shift: The True Story of Nurse Genene Jones and the Texas Baby Murders* by P. Elkind, 1989. Copyright 1983, 1989 by Peter Elkind. Used by permission of Viking Penguin, a division of Penguin Books USA Inc.

From "Projective Identification as a Mode of Perception and Behavior in Families of Adolescents" by J. Zinner and R. L. Shapiro, 1972, *International Journal of Psycho-Analysis, 53,* 523–530. Copyright 1972 by the Institute of Psycho-Analysis.

From "How 'Mild' Is Mild Munchausen Syndrome by Proxy?" by D. Roth, 1990, *Israel Journal of Psychiatry and Related Sciences, 27*(3), 160–167. Copyright 1990 by Gefen Publishing House Ltd.

From "Problems in the Assessment and Management of Munchausen Syndrome by Proxy Abuse" by B. Neale, C. Bools, and R. Meadow, 1991, *Children and Society, 5*(4), 324–333. Copyright 1991 by the National Children's Bureau.

From "The Perversion of Mothering: Munchausen Syndrome by Proxy" by H. A. Schreier, 1992, *Bulletin of the Menninger Clinic, 56*(4), 421–437. Copyright 1992 by The Menninger Foundation.

From "Munchausen Syndrome by Proxy: Diagnosis and Prevalence" by H. A. Schreier and J. A. Libow, 1993, *American Journal of Orthopsychiatry, 63*(2), 318–321. Copyright 1993 by the American Orthopsychiatric Association.

Contents

PART III
MANAGING THE PROBLEM

APPENDICES

PART I

DESCRIPTION OF
THE PROBLEM

Defining
the Syndrome

Christopher M.[1] was 8 years old when he first came to the oncology clinic at a hospital in the midwest for a general checkup. His mother, Margaret, reported that the child had had leukemia when he was 2 and had been treated with chemotherapy for 18 months at a hospital in another city. Christopher had been in remission for several years and had been brought to the hospital for a routine exam. He was given a bone marrow aspiration (a painful procedure involving inserting a needle in the base of his spine) and was scheduled for follow-up in 3 to 4 months.

Ten months later Christopher and Margaret returned. On this visit Margaret expressed concern that her son might be suffering a relapse. She reported that Christopher was experiencing low-grade nausea, fatigue, night sweats, fever, abdominal pain, easy bruising, and severe headaches in the past month. Concerned by these symptoms, the clinic's attending physician, Dr. L., admitted Christopher to the hospital for a series of tests.

By physical examination, Christopher appeared to be healthy and in no apparent distress. He nevertheless corroborated his mother's reports of his symptoms. A series of blood tests were ordered for

---

[1]The names and other identifying information have been changed to protect the identities of patients and physicians described in our case material, unless otherwise indicated.

him as well as chest and abdominal X-rays, and another bone marrow aspiration.

During this second visit the mother provided more details of the family history. She reported that Christopher's father was wheelchair-bound due to a shooting accident years earlier. In addition, she said she had a son with multiple sclerosis and had had a daughter who died at age 3 of a brain tumor. She reported that she herself was suffering from a degenerative nerve disease and was eventually going to lose her ability to walk.

Margaret went on to tell more about Christopher's medical history. Two years after his remission from cancer at age 2, he had had a recurrence of fevers, fatigue, and respiratory distress. Margaret took him for treatment to a Dr. Z. in Arizona. She reported that because Dr. Z. wanted to use some experimental drugs to treat her son, she took Christopher out of his care. She also reported that more recently Christopher had had some surgery for tumors in his abdomen.

Because this story was rather puzzling, Dr. L. called Dr. Z. in Arizona, who reported that he had indeed seen Christopher a few years earlier, but that everything else the mother had reported about him was untrue. He was unable to confirm Margaret's reports of previous treatment. Far from recommending experimental drugs, he had actually confronted Margaret about what he suspected was false information and mother and son never returned to his office.

Now quite suspicious of the entire medical picture, Dr. L. began calling all the hospitals and physicians on the mother's list. Many hospitals named by the mother had no record of Christopher's treatment. Margaret's own physician confirmed that she had some medical problems (but no serious neurological disorder). One of Christopher's oncologists said he had never diagnosed leukemia and had suspected that Margaret was fabricating her son's illness because of her ongoing reports of a series of "terrible diagnoses out of the blue" about other members of her family. But like all the other physicians before him, he had been unsure of how to proceed and was reluctant even to confront Margaret with his concerns.

At this point, the psychiatric consultant was called by Dr. L. and asked to consult on this unusual case. After reviewing the data, he decided to meet with Margaret and her son. Far from appearing strange or psychotic, Margaret seemed to be an intelligent, articulate, and caring parent. As the physicians outlined the investigative steps they had taken and the contradictions in her story, she grew righteously indignant and proceeded to offer an *almost* believable explanation for each item that was challenged. Through 4 hours of continuous meetings, which at times included a social worker, Christopher, Dr. L., Margaret, and/or the psychiatric consultant, the mother never acknowledged her fabrications. And Christopher, although withdrawn and sometimes tearful, always corroborated his mother's story, saying, "My mom wouldn't lie, why would she lie?"

After 22 months of unsuccessful diagnostic procedures in a hospital setting in England to determine the cause of a baby's breathing problem, staff concealed a video camera in the baby's hospital room, and a policewoman and a nurse jointly monitored the scene. The following events occurred:

> Sixteen hours after the onset of video monitoring, the child was asleep in his cubicle with only his mother in attendance. She moved the chair away from the cot and lowered the cot sides. She then placed a soft garment (a T-shirt) on the bedding close to the child's face. Five minutes later she placed the garment over his nose and mouth and forced his head onto the mattress. He awoke immediately and struggled violently. After 10 seconds the policewoman alerted the nurses who went into the cubicle. . . . In this first episode the woman police officer had intervened prematurely [by legal standards] because of her own distress at what she had seen. She decided to continue surveillance. Twenty minutes later when the child was asleep on his side and the mother was again alone in the cubicle, she placed him in a supine position with his face upright and tucked his arms under the bedding. Ten minutes later she again applied the garment to his nose and mouth and forced his head onto the mattress. The child struggled violently. Forty-two seconds later the nursing staff were alerted by the police and went into the cubicle. . . . The mother claimed that he had woken screaming and that she was comforting him. (Southall et al., 1987, p. 1638)

WHAT IS MUNCHAUSEN BY PROXY SYNDROME?

These two disparate cases are both examples of Munchausen by Proxy syndrome (MBPS). These patients, usually mothers, systematically fabricate information about their children's health or intentionally make their children gravely ill. The children usually require extensive medical attention, often entailing serious and dangerous invasive medical procedures, surgeries, intravenous medicines, or multiple X-rays. Well versed in medical conditions, MBPS parents will seemingly stop at nothing to gain access to doctors and the inner circle of care in hospitals. Often they seek more general recognition of or public adulation for their devoted caretaking of a sick child. Sometimes the MBPS parent's interventions or the medical responses prompted by her fabrications result in the death of the child.[2] We know, based on parents' own admissions as well as observations of some of these incidents taped by hidden cameras, that the mother's behavior is calculated, and performed calmly and carefully. These mothers are generally not psychotic and not in a dissociative state when they harm their children. When confronted by physicians who suspect they are inducing illness, or even when confronted by documented proof of their abuse, MBPS mothers tend to deny vigorously and persistently their role in harming the child. Some mothers even deny abuse years after conviction in court, and others only gradually come to acknowledge their role over the course of many years.

The name "Munchausen by Proxy Syndrome" was coined from the adult "Munchausen syndrome" because it seemed to mimic the adult disorder of illness fabrication but involved the use of a child as a type of proxy, or substitute, for the adult's own body. Unfortunately, the similarity in names of the two disorders has engendered considerable confusion about the relationship between the adult factitious disorder and the "by-proxy" syndrome. The name "Munchausen Syndrome by Proxy," still widely in use, makes the unwarranted assumption that the proxy syndrome is simply a variant of the adult disorder. We have chosen to use the term "Munchausen by Proxy syndrome" throughout this book to clearly distinguish it as a separate entity from Munchausen syndrome. While some patients share symptoms of both disorders, in fact there seem to be distinct differences in behavior for the two syndromes. What they share most clearly is the "Munchausen" name.

Origins of the Syndrome Name

The 18th-century baron Hieronymus Karl Friedrich Freiherr von Munchausen was a military mercenary known for his skills as a raconteur who told fantastical stories of his exploits.[3] While Baron

---

[2]In our own survey of pediatric neurologists and gastroenterologists (discussed in Chapter 3), we found that approximately 10% of the MBPS patients seen by these specialists actually died and 5% of the total had siblings who died of mysterious causes.

[3]The baron himself was an oral storyteller. Rudolph Eric Raspe, having escaped to England to avoid prosecution for criminal activities, published tales he had heard from the baron. These stories became quite popular and were widely distributed.

von Munchausen's own daughter (for whom he disavowed paternity) died in infancy, there is no evidence of foul play or of any real harm from the baron's tales of his adventures. There are documented cases of fabricated illness in the medical literature as early as the 1800s, but the term "Munchausen syndrome"[4] was first used to describe self-induced or fabricated illness by an adult in order to gain medical attention by Dr. Richard Asher in 1951, and was first used as "Munchausen by Proxy" for a case of psychosocial dwarfism by Money and Werlwas in 1976.

The first clinical description of "Munchausen by Proxy" behavior as we know it today was published in 1977 by the British pediatrician Roy Meadow. He described several cases of children who were repeatedly and unnecessarily examined, hospitalized, tested, and treated for a variety of medical problems ultimately found to be fabricated by their mothers. Since 1977, approximately 200 professional papers have been published describing several hundred of the more unusual and life-threatening manifestations of this syndrome, running the gamut from the fabrication of fevers and seizures to the poisoning and asphyxiation of children.[5] And it is clear that for every published case, there are many more that are dealt with less publicly in doctors' offices, hospitals, and courtrooms around the world.[6] This phenomenon is strikingly more common in mothers than fathers,[7] though fathers often play a role of passive collusion in this form of abuse of their children. We will explore, in later chapters, the powerful societal, family, and individual developmental factors that contribute to the dramatic gender imbalance of parents with this disorder. Untold additional cases proceed, unrecognized, for long periods or until the child grows up, dies, or acquires some bona fide or iatrogenic illness.

[4]There is some controversy over the spelling of the baron's name. The real baron spelled his name "Münchhausen." We are told that Asher took the name "Munchausen" from the fictionalized accounts published in England by Rudolph Raspe in 1785 (Dirckx, 1992).

[5]Only about 10% of the Munchausen by Proxy syndrome journal papers have appeared in the psychological or psychiatric literature; the vast majority are found in general and specialty pediatric journals.

[6]While most of the literature is American or British, papers on the subject have also appeared in other countries, including Israel, Germany, Spain, France, Australia, The Netherlands, Belgium, Canada, Bolivia, Czechoslovakia, India, Italy, and Poland (see Rosenberg, 1992), New Zealand (Single & Henry, 1991), and Singapore (Lim, Yap, & Lim, 1991).

[7]Because 95% of the parents *directly* involved are mothers, we will generally use the female pronoun.

The Range of Cases

The range of MBPS cases that have been described in the pediatric literature is quite remarkable. The youngest presentation we know of involved a fetus, described by Goodlin (1985). The pregnant mother-to-be apparently fabricated fetal distress by learning to suppress the fetal heart rate in certain positions. The oldest victims of the proxy form of Munchausen syndrome were adults described by Sigal, Carmel, Altmark, and Silfen (1988) and Smith and Ardern (1989).[8] In Sigal and colleagues' unusual case, a man used several adults, including his wife and a girlfriend, as proxy victims. After being caught, he began using a prison cellmate as proxy victim by making him ill with medication or injection of gasoline. Smith and Ardern's Munchausen by Proxy victim was an elderly patient.

The youngest case of a MBPS mother that we know of involved a teenager who had her first child when she was 13 and a second baby by age 16.[9] Each was seen repeatedly for "apnea" though no episode was ever witnessed by anybody but the mother. Both died of unexplained respiratory arrests between the ages of 3 months and 20 months.

While the majority of MBPS perpetrators are mothers using their natural children, there have been dramatic cases involving adoptive mothers, foster mothers, nurses,[10] grandmothers, and even a few fathers. One of the more unusual cases of suspected MBPS involved a woman who ran a daycare facility. She was involved in at least 15 medical emergencies involving small children (including one in which a child died) over a 5-year span. "The medical emergencies include serious and repeated incidents of choking, seizures, and breath-holding spells in which children turned blue and passed out" (*Austin [Texas] American-Statesman*, 9 February 1988). Doctors testi-

---

[8]Meadow (1984b) has described child MBPS victims treated for epilepsy. The mothers had also falsified histories of nocturnal seizures (witnessed only by them) in their husbands who were likewise being treated for epilepsy.

[9]In a search of the English-language reports on adult Munchausen syndrome, Raymond (1987) reports that 41% of 186 patients for whom data was available had developed the disorder by age 18.

[10]We reviewed a case involving a nurse who appeared to show all the dynamics found in MBPS parents and foster parents: compulsive harming behavior, leaving obvious clues, a propensity for risk taking, and a need to be in the spotlight and be seen as powerful. She is believed to have injected some 60 patients with deadly medicines, killing many in one 10-month period while working in a pediatric intensive care unit. Most died on her shift and most were her patients. (See Moore & Reed, 1988; Elkind, 1989.)

fied that they believed all the children had been suffocated, though the parents whose child died were totally supportive of the daycare owner.

There are also cases of fabricated illness in children in which it is unclear whether the child is the victim or the actual perpetrator of the fabrication. In one case a 10-year old girl underwent extensive gastrointestinal tests and investigations, including endoscopy and colonoscopy, for a 2-month history of diarrhea and abdominal pain. When she was eventually caught diluting her own stool specimens with water, she and her family were confronted and the family demanded her immediate discharge from the hospital. The family failed to follow up with psychiatric outpatient treatment. This child may represent an extremely young case of adult Munchausen syndrome. Or it may be that some children eventually cross over the line into active medical fabrication themselves. Older children who have been involved as longtime by-proxy victims may also fabricate illness. Collusion between parent perpetrators and child victims is not uncommon; one of the youngest children we know of involved in such an alliance was a child who was "ill" as an infant and by age 8 was actively aiding his mother's efforts to overdose him by helping mother sneak the medications into a locked hospital unit.

Though most of the cases we have read about or been personally acquainted with involve a chronic form that becomes a compulsive way of life for the parent, we believe that MBPS may appear in an episodic form with varying intervals between episodes.[11] There is clearly a range of severity for the syndrome. A more severe type involves active and life-threatening action such as suffocation, inducing vomiting, poisoning, or removing the blood from a child. The milder forms can involve such behavior as amplifying the reported symptoms of a child with an allergic disorder or totally falsifying symptoms to gain tests and procedures. These latter forms may also include a different mode of simulation, in which the parent withholds treatment from a mildly sick child to make the illness appear worse. These children can develop *severe* medical problems from this behavior over time (Godding & Kruth, 1991).

Subtypes

It is difficult to know just how to categorize the "different" forms of MBPS. In a 1986 paper (Libow & Schreier, 1986) we talked about

---

[11]In a suspected case on the Gulf Coast, there was apparently a 4-year interval between the mother's reports of frequent sleep apnea episodes.

three forms of factitious behavior, *excluding* one category of fabrications from the MBPS spectrum, "Helpseekers," because the express purpose in such cases was to obtain help for an overburdened parent. The two primary categories of MBPS we termed "doctor addicts" and "active inducers" (the latter we described as prototypical).

Active inducers, we said, "are characterized by active and direct efforts of the parent to induce dramatic symptoms of illness in the young child. . . . These cases are noteworthy for a maternal style in the hospital which appears above suspicion; almost all the mothers have been described as cooperative, concerned, loving, devoted, and trustworthy; . . . their . . . victims are usually infants or preschool children." Doctor addicts we described as "obsessed with the goal of obtaining medical treatment for nonexistent illnesses in their children" (p. 606). Descriptions of cases by Woolcott, Aceto, Rutt, Bloom, and Glick (1982) and our own observations led us to note that the falsifications of the "doctor addicts" fell more into the category of reporting false histories and symptoms than of actually causing illness. In their 1982 article Woolcott and colleagues described in detail behavior they labeled "doctor shopping." In this description of four cases (involving children aged 6 to 17), the parents voiced the persistent belief that their children were ill in a variety of ways, and had seen a total of 99 physicians in eight states. The cases demonstrated a rather symbiotic mother–child relationship in which the children colluded with the parents' belief in their illnesses. The fathers were also noted to support their wives' concerns about the childrens' health. These families differed from previously described "more classic" cases of MBPS in that the children tend to be older and the mothers tend to be more suspicious, antagonistic, and paranoid (Libow & Schreier, 1986, p. 607).

We now recognize that these distinctions need refinement. We do find a difference between mothers of infants and mothers of older children in terms of personal style and presentation to the health care system. But the distinction we originally drew between inducers and noninducers[12] is not so clear-cut. So-called doctor addicts, who do not induce illness in the children, often use infants as well as older

___

[12]In Rosenberg's (1987) review of the literature to 1986, she found that 72 of the cases could be distinguished as either simulated or induced illnesses. Twenty-five percent involved simulation only. (Seventy-two percent of these cases took place while the child was in the hospital.) Fifty percent of the group involved induced illness only. (In 95% of these cases, the production of the illness took place while the child was in the hospital.) In 25% of the cases both simulation and production of illness were involved.

children. And some parents engage in both types of fabrication. Meadow's (1977, 1982a) earliest papers described cases in which parents used false reports along with some active efforts at creating sick children—leading, in some cases, to deaths.

We have also found that among the "inducer" mothers of young infants and children, the maternal style is not always compliant, cooperative, and above suspicion. One pediatrician described to us a MBPS mother this way: "She was too intense to work with. She had very clear ideas of what she wanted to do with this child [who was essentially starving] and she wasn't very interested in listening to what I said." While critical of the hospital, the mother also spoke in adulatory terms of this physician. The doctor found such extravagant praise "hard to take." Thus, while attempting to present herself as the devoted, medically knowledgeable mother, she did engender suspicion by her alternately ingratiating and demanding style. (This suspicion, unfortunately, was never acted upon.)

One would expect to find major differences in the severity of psychological disturbance in "inducer" mothers who slowly poison their infants, repeatedly suffocate them, or withhold medications to make their children sick, when compared with the mothers who bring in well children with simulated or fabricated symptoms (doctor addicts). Yet our experience suggests that this is not the case. We expected such differences based on a belief that the intense degree of caring these mothers often exhibit for their children is *"real,"* and thus the amount of actual harm done should be indicative of the degree of psychopathology. But, as we will attempt to demonstrate in Chapters 5 and 7 on psychodynamics, the child, *as person,* means less to these parents than the child as an *object* to be used to manipulate an intensively ambivalent relationship with the physician.

Distinctions such as aggressive versus compliant, or inducer versus fabricator, while useful for purposes of description and recognition, may not have heuristic value beyond these functions. Although it has been found that mothers who employ older children as their by-proxy victims seem dramatically more disturbed, this finding probably reflects the desperation required to involve a verbally active youngster in such a charade. As we suggest in the case of Danny H. (see Chapter 2), when the behavior begins with an infant or toddler but goes undetected for many years, these mothers of "older children" can appear quite caring, compliant, and trustworthy even over many years. Further, in these latter cases the child may be cooperating with the mother or may even be independently involved in causing his or her own symptoms.

We feel that a distinction between "mild" a[ ] " forms of MBPS certainly has significance for the child's ph[ ]ll-being and likely defines the child's psychological risk as well. [ ] *may* also be indicative of the degree of psychopathology of the mother, our data thus far do not support this hypothesis. Also, if the literature on adult Munchausen syndrome has direct parallels in the by-proxy forms, there should be mothers who resort to this behavior only infrequently during periods of stress along with mothers who pursue this course of life compulsively. The latter, as we will show, often take serious risks of being caught in the process. Difficult as it is to detect the more serious, compulsive, and blatant cases, we have little information on the infrequent ones, if indeed a substantial group does exist.

THE PUBLIC PRESENTATION VERSUS THE PRIVATE REALITY

Almost everyone who initially comes into contact with MBPS experiences some resistance to believing that mothers could intentionally harm their children in this horrifying way. The disbelief is in part engendered by the very dramatic discrepancies between the public presentations and private realities of these families. For example, one woman we will call Carla S. cared for seriously handicapped foster children and thrived on the praise she received for her activities from both the community and the media. Three children are alleged to have died in her custody before one of the myriad of specialists Ms. S. was involved with called the police after he found a suspicious hole in an intravenous feeding line ostensibly needed for nourishment.[13] The sterling reputation of this mother, who had been honored by Nancy Reagan at the White House, made it that much more difficult for her medical caregivers to question her involvement in the illnesses of her children.

While MBPS mothers appear very caring in front of others, they may show little interest when alone with their children. Covert videotaping has demonstrated that long periods can pass in which the mother scarcely communicates with her infant (Samuels, McClaughlin, Jacobson, Poets, & Southall, 1992). We know of several cases where there was emotional and physical neglect severe enough to produce growth retardation and developmental delay (see Lyall, Stirling, Crofton, & Kelnar, 1992).

---

[13]It was later determined that the feeding line itself had been unnecessary for this child, as were the feeding lines for two other children in her care.

Adding to the disbelief are the extraordinary lengths to which some parents will go in order to establish a medical problem in their children. Orenstein and Wasserman (1986) describe a mother who gathered names of patients from the Cystic Fibrosis Foundation under false pretenses and then called patients by phone in order to collect sputum for "research." She tried to use one of these samples to convince doctors that her child was ill with this serious disease. These vignettes seem too bizarre to believe, yet the existence of countless cases like these eventually help us to see this as an integral part of this disorder.

DEFINING MBPS

While this disorder can manifest itself in hundreds of different medical symptoms, modes of abuse, and victim and parent characteristics, the critical dynamic for comprehending this clinical picture is the mother's intense need to be in a relationship with doctors and/or hospitals. The child is used to gain and maintain this contact. Our definition specifically *excludes* malingering for secondary gain such as monetary compensation for injuries or attaining welfare payments as the *primary* motivation, although these may be present. The "absence of external incentives for the behavior, such as economic gain" was also one of the two defining conditions of the proposed diagnostic category "Factitious Disorders by Proxy" in the American Psychiatric Association's DSM-IV work in progress (1991).[14] For these reasons we would exclude from the MBPS definition those cases of fabricated illnesses that are primarily motivated by the parent's wish to prove herself a better parent for the sake of winning a custody battle. Thus we disagree with Rand's (1990) conception of fabricated child abuse allegations as a "contemporary" form of MBPS because the context and motives for such cases generally and quite clearly involve discrediting the other parent and gaining custody of the child or children. The dynamics and the motives involved in MBPS behavior are considerably more complex than this. But fabricated allegations of sexual abuse can certainly constitute MBPS when the primary motivation involves the maintenance of a relationship with the medical system, as opposed to winning a custody battle. We described one such case in our original paper on MBPS (Libow & Schreier, 1986).

[14]The committee of the American Psychiatric Association decided to place the Factitious Disorders by Proxy category in the Appendix, indicating a need for further study.

In fact, MBPS behavior can be defined by its perplexing absence of any apparent concrete or tangible benefit to the perpetrator of these dangerous fabrications. Therefore, our definition of MBPS likewise excludes parents seeking help because they are overwhelmed by the demands of caring for their children. These mothers will rapidly cease their generally obvious and noninvasive fabrications as soon as assistance is available.[15]

In the milder cases of symptom exaggeration, where the parent does not actually appear to be inducing illness in the child, the question often arises as to how a MBPS mother can be distinguished from a simply overanxious parent. This is often a difficult decision for the physician. It is not at all uncommon for physicians to encounter concerned and vigilant mothers (often first-time parents of infants) who make frequent calls and doctor's office visits, overreacting to minor symptoms and expressing persistent concerns that their child is seriously ill.

MBPS is a qualitatively different phenomenon. The overanxious parent does *not* want her child to be ill and shows relief (even if only temporarily) when reassured that her child is well. She does not push for invasive tests and procedures and is pleased when laboratory results are negative. In general, the overanxious parent responds well to a social services or psychiatric referral, taking advantage of the opportunity to express her fears, explore the reasons for her concerns, and admit to her high anxiety level. The MBPS parent, on the other hand, has great difficulty acknowledging any personal problems contributing to her frequent medical visits and instead focuses relentlessly on the child's "medical problems." MBPS mothers, unlike overanxious parents, often tell outright falsehoods about their backgrounds, medical histories, and life experiences. Their affect often reflects a surprising (and inappropriate) level of satisfaction with their child's medical problems. The overanxious mother does not evidence the strong attachment to the medical world one sees frequently in the MBPS parent, who often aspires to a nursing/paramedic career. While the overanxious parent may become annoying to a physician, she is rarely experienced by the physician as controlling, manipulative, or peculiar. Some sympathetic attention and extra reassurance from the physician are often very effective in reducing her inappropriate use of medical services. But the MBPS mother is often

---

[15]After being confronted, some MBPS mothers will try to present themselves not as intending to harm their children, but only "seeking to draw attention to intolerable pressures at home" (Southall et al., 1987, p. 1639). We believe this is belied by the often violent and compulsive nature of the means used to prove "illness" in the child.

experienced as insatiably needy. It may take many visits before the busy physician is able to sort out and distinguish the two; mental health consultation can be very helpful in clarifying this decision process. In Chapter 7 we will explore in depth the complex processes that create some of the difficulties in the doctor–patient relationship.

THE MEDICAL PRESENTATION

The illnesses that have been presented in MBPS cover a remarkable range of organ systems and physical complaints. Appendix A lists some 100 different factitious or induced symptoms for which children have been brought to the attention of physicians, including abdominal pain, apnea, bleeding, diabetes, diarrhea, eczema, fevers, infections, lethargy, rashes, renal failure, seizures, shock, tachycardia, vomiting, and weight loss. And the list is expanding all the time, as new cases are seen and described in medical journals. Unfortunately, since these "illnesses" are nonexistent or induced by other substances or manipulations, they generally fail to respond to the physician's usual treatments, or show an unusual and unexpected course of recurrence or intensification. The medical picture tends to get progressively more complicated by the addition of new medications and invasive interventions as the physicians search for ever-more powerful treatments for these persistent "illnesses."

The unusual patterns of illness behavior are often the earliest signs that tampering or deception are involved, as physicians grow increasingly puzzled by the child's unusual course of response to treatment. For example, symptoms at times will seem consistent with a condition such as mild stomach reflux[16] (found by X-ray study), but will persist even after surgical repair of the "problem."

Sometimes a pattern of unexpected symptoms in an illness can give clues that something is amiss in a puzzling medical picture. For example, frequent bouts of apparent apnea prior to a sudden infant death syndrome (SIDS) death occur less than 10% of the time in true SIDS but up to 90% of the time in active suffocation (Meadow, 1990b). In our experience a dramatic example of a MBPS symptom that raised suspicion because it did not fit the usual pattern of a known disorder was physiologically impossible amounts of outflow from a mild stomach condition being monitored by a gastric drainage tube.

---

[16]In our experience gastroesophageal reflux is commonly found and often seized upon as the cause of a child's bewildering clinical presentation.

In that case a mother was surreptitiously adding fluids to the collection bag. Another symptom sometimes seen in these cases is enteric pathogens causing a sepsis (blood infection), unusual without bowel disease. This symptom is usually caused by contamination of an IV line, which can be done in a variety of ways by an enterprising parent determined to convince the caregiver that her child is ill.

The fabrication of psychiatric symptomatology (psychoses) by adults on an inpatient unit has been reported (Pope, Jonas, & Jones, 1982). Factitious psychosis accounted for 6.4% of admissions to a unit at a Harvard teaching hospital. There are no reports in the literature of psychiatric symptoms fabricated in children, though we have had cases in our clinic where the mother appeared to exaggerate wildly her child's behavior problems both to her pediatrician and to our staff. A number of colleagues around the country have told us they have been highly suspicious of MBPS in cases where a child's psychiatric symptoms are the presenting complaints.

Unfortunately, one of the hallmarks of MBPS cases is that, for a variety of complex reasons, suspicion by the physician usually takes a long time to develop.

THE ACTORS AND THEIR ROLES

Mothers

A number of typical behaviors are often associated with MBPS cases. While these behaviors do not by themselves define the syndrome, they help alert us to the possibility of the diagnosis and also give important clues in our attempts at understanding the dynamics of the phenomenon.

By almost all accounts, these mothers appear totally devoted to their child. They appear intensely interested in their child's medical problems, persistently pursue tests and procedures, are actively involved in caring for the child, and usually are reluctant to leave the child or the hospital for any reason. They often develop first-name relationships with nurses, physicians, and ward staff. Yet a closer examination often reveals that these mothers are not devoting themselves solely to their child during the hospital stay. They can often be found far from their children having coffee with or offering solace and emotional caretaking to other mothers. Mothers with the syndrome appear to enjoy belonging to a social circle whose common bond is caring for sick children. Only rarely do they have outside visitors, including, most notably, their husbands. And they appear to have few friends outside of hospital personnel and other parents.

These mothers often are very knowledgeable about medical issues and questions, offering highly elaborated, technically proficient medical histories that reveal a medical sophistication beyond their general fund of knowledge. Indeed, many parents involved are connected to the field of medicine, working as nurses, orderlies, medical transcriptionists, and nurse's aides.

Their knowledge of medical matters would suggest an intellectually sophisticated and generally well-educated person. And yet paradoxically they often appear shallow in other interactions, have limited interpersonal skills outside of medical issues or general knowledge, and exhibit poor judgment. For example, we know of two MBPS mothers who were very convincing in their interactions with pediatricians and who could name several types of human blood vessels, yet one did not know what a U.S. senator is and the other did not know the number of weeks in a year.

Initially, at least, these mothers are very supportive of doctors and staff, despite the fact that their child's health is deteriorating under these professionals' care. Often aggressive about demanding new procedures and interventions for their child, they can get very angry when they do not get their way. We know of one mother who is believed to have convinced physicians to unnecessarily implant Broviac catheters (surgically placed intravenous tubing through which food and medicines are injected) or nasogastric feeding tubes in children who had no need for them. When thwarted, she searched for a doctor who would listen to her.

In our experience, when a mother's claims are disbelieved by her physician, this disbelief can lead to disastrous consequences for her infant, even to death. She may act rashly in a desperate attempt to convince the physician. We also suspect that she lashes out at the physician through her child, injuring the child as a way of taking revenge on the doctor for having doubted her.

When giving a family history to the doctor evaluating a child for hospital admission, the mother often volunteers elaborate medical histories consistent with "somatization disorder"[17] or adult Munchausen syndrome. She also may relate fantastical personal histories about herself or other family members. Typical is a mother of a 5-year-old who brought him to his pediatrician with symptoms of

---

[17]Patients with a history of multiple physical symptoms over many years. These may be vague and are usually confusing and unrelated.

seizures, vomiting, nasal congestion, wheezing, croup, pneumonia, ear infections, and knee dislocation. She claimed that her father suffered from epilepsy, and that her older brother had been killed in an equestrian accident. She reported that he took Dilantin even though he had not been known to have epilepsy (Guandolo, 1985).

Some of the parents have suffered from an illness similar to their children's medical problem. Godding and Kruth (1991), reporting from a Belgian asthma clinic, stated that of the 17 families that appeared with factitious asthma in the child, 16 mothers, 2 fathers, and 2 grandmothers had also reported suffering from asthma at some point in their lives. Two mothers we knew who induced vomiting in their children had had serious nausea and vomiting during pregnancy, and we also know of diabetic mothers who induced very high blood sugars in their children. Meadow (1982a, p. 94) reports in one of his studies that "five of 10 [mothers] . . . had a history within the previous 3 years of symptoms . . . similar to those which she fabricated for the child."

When their child is in the throes of a serious crisis, these parents often behave dramatically and draw attention to themselves; alternately they may be calm. While in general these mothers do not seem unusual to doctors, staff, or neighbors, sometimes they claim that bizarre and unverified incidents have happened (Meadow, 1990b; Egginton, 1990) to their families when they are in the hospital, including reports of fires and burglaries. Sometimes anonymous phone calls that suggest that these mothers are hurting their children or having affairs with doctors are received by the police or the hospital. It seems apparent that they themselves are making these phone calls. Their need to have the spotlight trained on them is seen in their use of the media[18] and is sometimes manifested at their children's elaborate funerals, during which they often appear more concerned about relating to the hospital staff than mourning their dead child.

At times the mothers may be inappropriate in their expression of affect: either calm and seemingly disinterested or elated or excited at calamitous moments.[19] This peculiar calm may continue even when they are confronted by the police. The mother may also be more

---

[18]One mother who had her healthy 12-year-old child confined to a wheelchair with a neuromuscular disease would often enter her in parades as a poster child (respondent's report in our survey of pediatric subspecialties, presented in Chapter 3).

[19]Two physicians have remarked to us that they have noticed constant or situationally inappropriate smiling in several of their MBPS cases.

cooperative than the evidence against her would immediately require. A child protective services worker investigating a MBPS case described it to us this way:

> "These Munchausen parents act differently from any other individual who is accused of child abuse. Well, at least the ones I have seen seem to have no semblance of guilt. They seem to be very, very normal. 'Normal' in the sense of being so sure of themselves. And also what gets me is that they are very, very cooperative. Now usually in our cases of 'normal' child abuse, we figure that if a person is extremely cooperative, it means they have nothing to hide. If they invite you in the door, that's always a more positive sign. If they become very defensive, then it makes us suspicious. We'd say 'What are they hiding?' But this kind of person is so very, very nice and so very, very cooperative, that it throws you off.
>
> "For example, we were with the alleged perpetrator in the hospital. We were insinuating that she could have hurt her child, deliberately, for some sort of pathological reason, like almost being a crazy person. And she didn't protest, she didn't fly off the handle, she didn't threaten that she was going to sue us! I mean, she just sort of smiled at us. . . . I asked her to sign this piece of paper saying our agency could be involved in her case. And most people would not have signed it, because they'd say 'Why should I?' She signed it, even after I told her all the legal consequences. She signed releases of information, she signed all kinds of things that most people wouldn't."

In other cases MBPS mothers, when confronted, may become frantic and angry and enlist support from other parents in the hospital. Occasionally they will vehemently deny evidence even when they are literally caught in the act, such as when a videotape shows them choking their child. In one report from England concerning 14 parents confronted with videotaped evidence of themselves suffocating their children (Samuels, McClaughlin, Jacobson, Poets, & Southall, 1992), most of the parents admitted their participation but "all continued to deny or minimise, however, the seriousness of their behaviour, any intent of harm, and any part in inducing previous episodes" (p. 165).

The compulsion of these mothers to repeat their harming behavior and prove their child ill both poses the greatest risks to the child and offers the greatest hope for discovery. In situations where the child is being closely observed by medical staff and the usual fabrications are being prevented, some mothers may be driven to up the ante in a desperate effort to prove that their child is seriously ill. Samuels, McClaughlin, Jacobson, Poets, and Southall (1992, p. 168) reported that the parents they studied were *more* likely to obstruct their child's breathing "when due to close nursing observation, they had been unable to demonstrate their child's 'symptoms' for a period of time. The median duration of surveillance required before diagnosis was 24 hours—fortunately short in view of the staff and equipment required to perform covert video surveillance." Thus a mother unable to maintain her child's "symptoms" may resort to fairly drastic measures to keep the medical system engaged with her child.

MBPS mothers of infants do not usually appear on the surface to be very disturbed, often presenting themselves as convincingly knowledgeable and concerned. Despite their normal appearance, however, some of these mothers have a history of psychiatric problems and some have been in jail. Psychological testing reveals evidence of nonspecific personality disorders with hysterical, narcissistic, antisocial, and at times borderline traits (Bools, Neale, & Meadow, 1992). While some of the mothers engaged in MBPS behavior have histories of being physically or sexually abused as children or victimized as adults, this is *not* frequently reported in their past histories, and when it is reported may be fabricated (Samuels et al., 1992). In her literature review of 117 cases of MBPS, Rosenberg (1987) noted that a history of physical or emotional abuse of the mother as a child was noted "infrequently" but that "the themes of loneliness and isolation, seemed to course through these women's lives with unusual prominence" (p. 556). It is our experience that early neglect and loss, resulting in feeling unimportant and ignored, seem to be more common themes than active abuse in these mothers' lives. (See Chapter 5 and Appendix B.) At times it appears difficult to understand the early family difficulties that have led to problems in the mother. Our interviews with the families of MBPS mothers have revealed that many MBPS mothers seem to have a "normal" family in their past. Therefore, constitutional difficulties as well as social environment may contribute to this personality disorder.

Fathers

Fathers can play one of several different roles in MBPS cases. An extremely small number of fathers have been identified as the actual perpetrators of fabricated illness in their children, but most fathers do play some ancillary part. In general they are observed to take a very passive role in their families, either through physical absence or emotional distance from wife and children.

In most cases of MBPS known to the authors from their work or reported in the literature, fathers appear to be completely removed from the medical arena and the mother and child's intense involvement in this world. The mothers dominate the decisions involving their child's illness and the fathers are absent, inconspicuous, or "less intelligent or capable" (Meadow, 1984b, p. 27). Fathers are generally minimally involved in the family, and it is not uncommon for husbands to be described as overly involved in their work. Many are absent from the home for long periods of time due to military duty, long-distance truckdriving, or other kinds of specialized work. Meadow (1984b) reports that 5 out of 23 husbands in his study were described as invalids (or at least reported to be so by their wives) and Light and Sheridan (1990) found that 3 of the 23 husbands they studied ostensibly had health problems—another form of "absence."[20]

Fathers often seem to be unaware of their children's problems. In the case described by Guandolo (1985), the staff felt the father had to have been aware of the large number of medical visits, for he paid bills of substantial sums (for a healthy-appearing child), yet chose not to question them. "Yet, once the suspected situation was presented to [him] he was anxious to resolve it." He cooperated with the staff's approach to the problem "though his attitude remained indifferent and aloof" (p. 529).[21] To some degree medical caregivers tend to collude with the "absent father." Rarely is the father's absence from the hospital questioned actively, as it would be for a mother. To our knowledge, moreover, fathers are rarely called for medical history verification, even when suspicions surface and they may help clarify details of contradictory information.[22]

When the mothers are discovered and confronted, these fathers are seemingly shocked into recognizing the severity of the problem

[20]In another family, a mother who had raised several healthy children of her own began taking in foster children whom she was suspected of abusing, after her financially successful husband came down with a chronic debilitating illness.

[21]Guandolo (1985) suggests that this passivity on the part of one parent, as in cases of paternal sexual abuse, actually encourages the other parent in her actions.

[22]Repeatedly in the psychiatric literature fathers are described as less affected by their children's chronic illnesses than are mothers. This may reflect a general lack of involvement on the part of fathers (see Engstrom, 1991).

and then they sometimes take action. But only occasionally do they leave their wives even when the evidence is overwhelming that the mother is harming their child.[23] More frequently, the father's reaction is the one described by Atoynaten, O'Reilly, and Loin (1988; also see Chan, Salado, Atkins, & Ruley, 1986): initial skepticism about the allegations followed by concern. If the mother threatens suicide, his attitude may change. He may then become very supportive of his wife and join with her to present a united front against the doctors. We have seen this dynamic even when the mother openly admits having hurt her child.

The father often plays a very different role in cases involving MBPS with older children. These fathers collude more openly in their wives' campaign for medical attention. Such women appear to be more disturbed than the mothers of infant victims, and the family dynamics are also more complexly related to the child's illnesses (which are usually fabricated rather than induced). In these families, fathers and the children themselves seem to play more of an active role in the disturbed family system, and at times the actual illness fabrication. In such cases we have witnessed the capacity of one or both parents to recruit the child for the purpose of helping that parent with some emotionally charged inner conflict. (Chapter 8 describes the dynamics of MBPS involving older children.)

In general, fathers have not been investigated in any depth by researchers. They are often unavailable to the physicians involved in the cases, except when the mother is confronted, and even then they are usually less than forthcoming. The effect of viewing the fathers simply as bystanders has led to a lack of any in-depth understanding of their contributions to the syndrome, however passive. There is said to be marital discord in between 10% and 80% of MBPS families, a range too large to be meaningful.

Only 11 published papers known to us (Boros & Brubaker, 1992; Dine & McGovern, 1982; Godding & Kruth, 1991; Makar & Squier, 1990; Meadow, 1990b; Morris, 1985; Mortimer, 1980; Orenstein & Wasserman, 1986; Samuels, McClaughlin, Jacobson, Poets, & Southall, 1992; Single & Henry, 1991; Zohar, Avidan, Schvili, & Laurian, 1987) have reported fathers as the primary MBPS parent. The behavior of a father with MBPS differs from that of the MBPS mother in that he does not fit the profile of a seemingly devoted, concerned

---

[23]Two fathers asked quite seriously if a child's dermatologic condition (caused directly by the mother) couldn't be due to their child's being "allergic to their mothers"! (Berger, 1979).

parent. He often seems more overtly disturbed.[24] For example, one case involved a father who appeared in an emergency room with a healthy baby. His agitated behavior immediately aroused suspicions. The father demanded that his child's hair be checked for mercury, for he claimed to fear that his son was being poisoned by the mother's breast milk. His family reported that he had had psychotic episodes in the past and he appeared frankly paranoid during the interview.

The only case of a MBPS father reported in a group of 14 parents found suffocating their children (Samuels, McClaughlin, Jacobson, Poets, & Southall, 1992) was described as verbally and physically abusive to the infant prior to the suffocation incident. He manifested other bizarre symptoms such as ingesting nails and pieces of razor blades. Interestingly, in this report on 14 patients (which included 12 mothers, 1 grandmother, and 1 father), only the father was given a life sentence while the 12 mothers all received probation. Whether he received a harsher sentence due to his guilt for the actual murder of a previous infant (in addition to the later attempted murder), or whether this represents a harsher treatment of male child abusers in the United Kingdom (since at least two other infant siblings in the sample had also died unexpectedly, presumably at the hands of their mothers) is unclear.

Colluding Parents

We have heard of a few cases in which both parents have been actively involved in MBPS. One case in New Mexico involved a mother *and* her boyfriend in fabrication and illness production. A 5-year-old Hispanic boy, Julio C., was referred for psychological evaluation after a 2-year history of failure to thrive. When admitted to the hospital Julio had a weight equivalent to a 3-year-old and the height of a 2-year-old. He gained well in the hospital. His mother, Patricia, presented as a cheerful, overweight woman who was strongly convinced that her son suffered from some as-yet undiagnosed medical problem (as she said she herself had, in childhood). Patricia gave an elaborate and improbable past medical history for herself and her boyfriend. She mentioned being angry at a neurologist who had refused to do sleep studies on her four other children despite her

---

[24]Meadow's experience (personal communication, August 1992) has been different: he found that male perpetrators "as persons and personalities, have seemed extremely similar to the female perpetrators."

insistence. During outpatient visits, Julio ate voraciously any food in sight in the therapist's office.

It took over 4 months to get the local child protective services to act, despite ketones found in Julio's urine—a sign of starvation. During a medical visit serious dental caries led to questioning about his vomiting. He revealed that mother's boyfriend often put a finger down his throat to induce vomiting; he said this was done in his mother's presence. It is of interest to note that shortly after this child's removal from the home, Patricia's own medical "problems" intensified, something often noted in other families.

In another case both mother and father were thought to be actively engaged in the failure to thrive of their 8-year-old son (through the constant use of ipecac). The child was the size of a 4-year-old. The father's mother was present during the confrontation with the alleged MBPS parents and told the interviewer that her grandson suffered from a genetic condition found in 1 in 100,000 births, which she called "curly nail syndrome," which turned out to be totally responsive to a nail clipping. The physician felt that the behavior could best be characterized as a *folie à trois*.

In summary, although little detailed demographic or psychological information is available on the fathers of MBPS child victims, it is clear that they too play an important role in the dynamics of families who become engaged with the medical system in this destructive way. On the surface they are very much absent and ignorant about the health problems of their children. Yet their behavior when their wives are confronted and the apparent collusion by some in the fabrications involving older children suggest that theirs is a complex role beyond being simply "uninvolved" in the abuse of their children. And for those very few fathers who play the primary role in fabricating their child's illness, the presentation and the dynamics appear to be very different than what is known about MBPS mothers.

The Child Victims

Children whose mothers engage in MBPS behavior can be of any age, and are as likely to be male as female. There is no known pattern related to birth order. In general, infants and preverbal children are most likely to be subjected to intrusive, active induction of illness. In the cases reported in the literature serious psychological damage to the children has been reported (McGuire & Feldman, 1989; Roth, 1990) and physical harm is frequently found. For example, in 75% of the cases reviewed by Rosenberg (1987), the symptoms were caused by actual induction and not just fabrication of symptoms.[25] In our survey of two pediatric subspecialties, 9.7% of the children treated, and 4.8% of their siblings, actually died. Rosenberg found a similar 9% mortality rate. Undoubtedly these mortality rates are inflated (see Meadow, 1990a, and Chapter 3), reflecting the more serious end of the spectrum that is identified as MBPS and finds its way into the literature. Godding and Kruth (1991) reported some "good" outcomes but gave no details by which to evaluate their impressions. In a long-term (1–14 years) follow-up by Meadow and colleagues of 43 victimized children and their 26 siblings, half of the victims studied and 65% of their siblings had unacceptable outcomes (R. Meadow, personal communication, August 1992). They expressed dismay, especially since the studied children had returned to their parents, and therefore were not even the most serious cases. These are sobering findings.

Infants

Very young children and infants used by their parents in MBPS generally do not show obvious signs of behavioral or emotional disorder. One does not often see the kinds of problems in attachment and relatedness that one sees in physically abused or depressed children. This does not necessarily mean that these children are un-affected by their mother's psychopathology and abusive behavior,[26] but it certainly indicates that we do not yet know what to look for and how to study the effects of what would seem to be a very disturbed relationship between parent and child.[27]

Long-term follow-up data on very young children subjected to active induction of illness do not exist. Even in cases in which some data are available, the information is biased by the fact that the abuse was discovered and subjected to various interventions. We know little about child victims of this form of abuse whose parents were *not*

---

[25]Morbidity was caused by the medical staff as well as the perpetrators through their ministrations and investigative procedures.

[26]As might be expected, children who were suffocated when older than 6 months did exhibit trauma-specific fears, for example, of baths, small cubicles, or having a cloth put on their faces (Meadow, 1990b). However some, such as one 2-month-old who was repeatedly suffocated by his mother (Southall et al., 1987), appear to have a normal relationship with their mothers.

[27]It is also not always apparent why a particular child is selected. We know of one case in which the mother abused her favorite child and left her difficult child unharmed.

detected, and how these children are affected psychologically, *if* they survive and grow up.

The gaps in our knowledge about what will happen when these babies grow up is understandable. Much about this disorder conspires against obtaining such information—not the least of which is the newness of its discovery. The study of outcome certainly deserves our detailed attention not just for what it can tell us about the process, but also because of the uniqueness of the disordered parent–child relationship and what this can teach us about development.

Older Children

Children who are first brought to physicians with fabricated illness when they are beyond toddlerhood appear with falsified reports or simulated symptoms more typically than induced illness. There are many cases in the literature of toddlers who are aware that their mothers are doing something wrong. One 3-year-old child spontaneously awoke from a stupor and said he wished his mother would stop feeding him honey. Another, when asked, told of his mother's playing with his "wee wee bag." In the case of Edith's child (discussed in Chapter 5), he appeared to adore his mother despite her withholding food enough to drive his blood sugar down to 40 and "feeding" him ipecac. It is doubtful that he made the connection between his mother's behavior and how he was feeling. In a case reported by Croft and Jervis (1989), a 4-year-old was trained by his mother to feign seizures and limb paralysis. In Danny H.'s case (discussed in Chapter 2) the child actually did have asthma and allergies to food from an early age, though he soon must have realized that "forbidden" foods caused him no harm, as he ate these at will on his own. When a mother appears caring, and understanding her harming behavior is beyond the sophistication of the child, the child need not be threatened by the mother to remain silent.[28]

In the cases of older children whose MBPS victim status *started early* in childhood, the children themselves eventually may be involved with validating their mother's fabrications or even in directly

---

[28]In cases of child abuse we have noted that children often appear close if not securely attached to their abusing parents. We consulted on a child abuse case involving a group of some 40 children from a nursery school (aged 6 months to 4 years) who suffered through not being allowed to talk, eat, play, or go to the bathroom all day. They were also subjected to periodic beatings, and for *over a year* gave only rare hints of their abuse. Many of these children later suffered from serious post-traumatic stress disorder symptoms.

harming themselves. In these cases we have found that the mothers more closely resemble those women who involve infants as proxy victims (rather than women who are aggressive, overtly disturbed, or frankly paranoid like many MBPS mothers of toddler-age victims). These older children, who become involved in colluding with or adopting some of their parents' illness fabrication behavior, do not tend to become psychotic but often do have significant emotional disturbance, even into adulthood. Frequently, the children appear psychologically damaged (Roth, 1990; McGuire & Feldman, 1989). Depression, withdrawal, poor sociability, and pseudosophistication have all been identified (Roth, 1990; Hughes, 1984; Herzberg & Wolff, 1972; Woolcott, Aceto, Rutt, Bloom, & Glick, 1982; McGuire & Feldman, 1989). That some children can escape these ills fits with our current understanding of invincibility: some children have the remarkable capacity to withstand significant mistreatment with little apparent damage.

A 13-year-old reported by McGuire and Feldman (1989) was said to have continued her symptom-producing behavior when grown. However, although many child victims carry the effects of their victim status into adulthood, McGuire's and Feldman's conclusion that it is common that "the child victims of Munchausen syndrome by proxy become adult Munchausen patients" (p. 291) is not substantiated. They cite evidence from "other cases" without giving details, and their examples only include children still living with their mothers while they are involved in doctor-seeking behavior.

We have also been impressed with how *in*frequently the family histories of adult Munchausen and MBPS patients involve an over-concern with illness or doctors on the part of *their* own parents. Given Roth's (1990) reported cases showing psychological disturbance but not independent doctor-seeking behavior in older children subjected to MBPS, it appears premature to suggest that adult Munchausen or MBPS is in any way a common outcome for children subjected to MBPS abuse. Psychological morbidity in various forms, however, is found with alarming consistency (see Sneed & Bell, 1976; Woolcott et al., 1982; McGuire & Feldman, 1989).

We are still left with the question of how or why children get drawn into this illness-fabricating behavior. Perhaps children involved in MBPS collude with their mother's activities to maintain the only kind of life they know. Given the fact that these mothers appear caring and spend enormous amounts of time with their children, they may seem to be perfect "moms" even to the victimized children themselves. No doubt much that we observe in the way of successful outcome for the child victims depends on the overall degree of disturbance in the rest of their family life. We have seen children, when taken away from a home environment in which illness was the focus, thrive physically, cognitively, and emotionally. But our data are only anecdotal. Experience tells us it is difficult to predict what will happen to these children when they grow up and generalizations are difficult given the individual constitutional differences and each child's circumstances.

Siblings of by-proxy victims are often involved in MBPS behavior also, generally serially rather than simultaneously. From a diagnostic perspective, the history of medical problems in siblings may be very useful information.[29]

Physicians

Little demographic data is available on the physicians who are involved in MBPS cases, but we do know that the doctor can be male or female. Tabulating our own cases and culling through articles in which the gender of the physician could be determined, we found that approximately 75% of the physicians in MBPS cases were male. This is not decidedly different from the overall gender distribution in pediatric medicine. We believe that gender issues are important in the relationship of MBPS mothers to the medical system (see discussion in Chapter 6), but we have found that female physicians can represent powerful parental and authority symbols to MBPS mothers no less than male physicians.

SOCIOECONOMIC BACKGROUNDS

The literature on social class distribution in MBPS is sparse and there are no population-based studies. Cases have been reported in all social classes from the very wealthy to the very poor. In Light and Sheridan's (1990) survey, the majority of suspected parents were receiving some form of welfare payments from the state. MBPS mothers include those with advanced or professional degrees and those described as intellectually slow (Kravitz & Wilmott, 1990). There is a

---

[29]For example, Meadow points out that in the cases of suffocation by mothers 48% of the child victims had a sibling who died of supposed "SIDS" (sudden infant death syndrome or crib death), which compares with 2% sibling death rate in what are felt to be true SIDS deaths. (See Appendix B.)

report in the literature (Alexander, Smith, & Stevensen, 1990) of a mother who was a member of a fundamentalist church, and we heard of a case involving a deacon in the Episcopal Church (which had *all* the earmarks of MBPS though the case was dismissed in court). We have seen highly religious mothers and several with excellent reputations in their professional lives or involved in community work with children. Some, as we have mentioned, are highly regarded nurses, childcare providers, or foster-care mothers.[30]

The statistics on MBPS mothers at the time of the abuse match those of average young mothers. The majority (Light & Sheridan, 1990) were married at the time of the abuse and most had more than one child. Divorce and remarriage were also not uncommon (Bools, Neale, & Meadow, 1992). The age of most mothers of infants ranged between 22 and 35. Most of the mothers in Meadow's various studies were still living with their husbands at the time the abuse was uncovered. In one Meadow study (1990b), for example, 26 of the 27 mothers were still with the fathers who were "unaware (and disbelieving) of the possibility of suffocation" (p. 353). Meadow's report on illness fabrication (1982a) included 17 mothers, 15 of whom were living with their husbands. Meadow (1982a, p. 94) found in this group a greater than usual discrepancy in the "social or intellectual grade of the parents," the wife appearing more intelligent or from a higher social class background. A single case report (Sugar, Belfer, Israel, & Herzog, 1991) from Massachusetts General Hospital noted a similar discrepancy between the spouses.

ADULT MUNCHAUSEN SYNDROME: ITS RELATIONSHIP TO MBPS

The fact that the adult Munchausen syndrome and the by-proxy syndrome share the Munchausen name has resulted in considerable confusion about the relationship between these two disorders. Further adding to this puzzle is the fact that a significant minority of mothers engaged in by-proxy behavior themselves manifest the adult Munchausen syndrome, either simultaneously, or following revelation of their child's factitious illness. Somewhere between one-tenth

---

[30]One respondent to our survey (discussed in Chapter 3) even suggested that the act of attending to the special needs of medically fragile children "cured" one foster mother of her own doctor-shopping tendencies.

and one-quarter of MBPS mothers are believed to also suffer from Munchausen syndrome (Rosenberg, 1987). This overlap between syndromes suggests that a similar dynamic in at least some subset of these mothers can manifest itself in both forms of illness fabrication.

Another common feature shared by the two disorders is that both seem to span a wide range of behaviors. There is a spectrum of frequency of the adult patient presentation, from the so-called hospital hobo who compulsively roams from institution to institution, to those for whom it may be an infrequent occurrence. The patients who are not as driven in their need to relate to doctors may simply be labeled as "crocks," humored, or go undetected over an otherwise productive lifetime. We believe that MBPS may express itself in a similar spectrum of frequency as well as intensity, with some mothers only engaging sporadically in fabrication or exaggeration of their child's medical problems. Given that even the most blatant and dramatic examples of maternally induced illness take a long time to discover, it seems probable that these less frequent, less obvious forms of MBPS often escape detection entirely or get "humored" in a manner similar to the occasional adult Munchausen patient.

Adult Munchausen syndrome differs from MBPS in that it has been known and studied for a much longer period of time. Although it was first named by Asher in 1951, it was discussed by Karl Menninger, who called it "an addiction to polysurgery," in the 1930s. Indeed, cases were described as early as the 19th century, when it generally appeared as factitious fever. Fevers up to 150–170° F. were reported! One unusual case was described as follows:

> The patient was a married woman, 26 years of age, who is said to have had repeated attacks of peritonitis during the period of observation of the high temperature, and to have passed per vaginam over 1000 pieces of bone which were believed to have come from a dead foetus of extra-uterine pregnancy. . . . Suspecting some deception, he [the doctor in the case] says the following test was made: "The patient was placed in a chair, all clothing removed, and a careful examination was made of her mouth and axillary region, every possible precaution taken in order to prevent any deception, and holding the end of the thermometer so that it could not be tipped in any way, we again proceeded to take her temperature; but gentleman, the result was the same; the thermometer under the axilla registered 137°F., while that under the tongue registered 131°F."
>
> There was nothing in the pulse or the general condition of the patient to indicate any elevation of temperature. Especially constructed and carefully tested thermometers were used. (Jacobi, 1895, p. 189)

This despite the fact that temperatures above even 107° F. cause destruction of animal cells!

A refutation was provided by an intern who saw this woman in another hospital, where she was labeled "an undoubted hysterical fake."

> The patient's temperature had continued to oscillate from several degrees below normal to any point below 150°F., with symptoms interpreted as those of peritonitis. On May 19, 1891, Dr. Summers performed abdominal section, and, save the presence of old adhesions about the uterine adnexa, found no evidences of peritonitis or of the previous existence of an extra-uterine pregnancy. Several pieces of bones which had been removed from the vagina, and had been attributed to a macerate foetus, were sent to Dr. Billings, at the Army Medical Museum, where they were pronounced to be "portions of the sternum of some bird, probably a chicken; also one of the long bones nearly complete, and a portion of the skull of a chicken or some bird about the same size." (Jacobi, 1895, p. 190)

In any case, there are now more than 360 papers in the medical/psychiatric literature on adult Munchausen syndrome. While women predominate, the significant proportion of male adult Munchausen patients (about a third of published cases) differs greatly from the overwhelming gender imbalance of women to men seen in MBPS. There are also a number of features of adult Munchausen cases, particularly in the dynamic relationships that unfold in these cases, that distinguish them from by-proxy cases. Cramer, Gershberg, and Stern summarized the adult Munchausen patient succinctly in a 1971 paper:

> The patient has an extensive knowledge of medical jargon which helps him to capitalize on whatever real organic disturbance he has, often presenting the picture of an interesting and challenging diagnostic problem (such as porphyria or a myopathy). He is very demanding (of attention and drugs) and beneath his helplessness one detects a bitterness and a resentment against physicians. The patient's ambivalence becomes manifest, he complains that he is being mishandled, and accuses former physicians of having misdiagnosed him or of having contributed to an aggravation of his state. Indeed, he often succeeds in seducing surgeons to operate on him, in spite of very poor indications: then, it is easy for him to accuse physicians of selfish, sadistic behavior. . . .
>   The patient usually arranges to foul up his own plot and to have the hoax uncovered. At this point, the staff responds with an angry condemnation of the patient, and with total loss of interest in his fate. The

patient signs out—accusing the physicians of incompetence or malpractice—or he is discharged. At this point, it is difficult for the physician to recognize the psychological suffering of the patient and to refer him to a psychiatrist, and the patient is off until his next hospitalization. (p. 575)[31]

This rapid, stormy course, characteristic of the frequent adult Munchausen patient, is quite different from the longer period of admiration and appreciation enjoyed by the typical by-proxy mother in her extended relationship with her child's physicians. The use of the infant or child patient clearly allows for a very different course in the unfolding of the relationship of the MBPS mothers and the medical staff. It seems likely to be meeting different needs in these women than the sturm und drang, the brief and angry confrontations instigated by the adult syndrome patients. Our data lead us to tantalizing hypotheses about the different dynamics at play, but such understanding awaits our ability to identify cases earlier and to gather more data through long-term psychotherapeutic work with these challenging patients.

THE TRAGIC COSTS OF MBPS

MBPS can take a dramatic toll on its victims: deaths of innocent children, long-term psychological morbidity, severe family dysfunction, and turmoil for physicians, attorneys, therapists, and protective services workers who become involved. These cases also take a serious toll in medical costs to society, given the repeated medical visits, costly laboratory tests, extended hospitalizations, surgical procedures, specialist consultations, and equipment costs that these induced and fabricated illnesses extract from our health care system. One case we consulted on cost a local hospital close to $1 million in unnecessary procedures involving multiple long admissions, surgeries, and so on. While many pediatricians are aware of individual Munchausen by Proxy cases that went undiscovered for years and generated many hundreds of thousands of dollars in unnecessary costs, few have studied the cost factor in any systematic way. The only report known to the authors comes from Columbus Children's Hospital (Kaufman et al., 1987) and examined the costs associated

---

[31]Cramer, Gershberg, and Stern (1971) reported sexual infatuation with the doctor in all four of their cases.

with 14 known or suspected MBPS cases seen in a 2-year period. With hospitalizations *averaging* 32 days per child, and an average of 10 X-ray or nuclear exposures and 7 invasive procedures for each child, Kaufman and colleagues estimated the average hospital cost per child at approximately $21,000 and the total cost of the 14 children as a group at approximately $300,000. These costs included standard hospital costs, physician fees, procedural costs, radiology interpretations, and laboratory fees. They did *not* reflect separate billings for some medical specialists such as anesthesiologists and surgeons. If we consider the inflation factor in medical costs since 1987 and consider that these data were collected in a medical center relatively sophisticated (and probably fairly quick) in identifying MBPS, it is sobering to consider the present-day medical costs to society of even a single MBPS case, particularly one that remains unrecognized for months or years while the child *and* our ailing health care system continue to be abused.[32] Meadow (1989a) reported that some children have been hospitalized for more than 18 months for fabricated illnesses.

Similar disturbing findings are reported from a Michigan community hospital. Over a 2½-year period, six inpatient MBPS cases accounted for 1.1% of all medical admissions. The mean length of stay was nearly twice the average pediatric medical stay and accounted for 2% of total hospital days accrued by pediatric patients (Sturm & Roberts, 1990)! This "rare" disorder can be a substantial drain on limited community medical resources, not only *before* discovery but for years afterward. Long after a case is first reported and handled by the courts, there is extensive (and expensive) involvement and collaboration between primary care physicians, subspecialists, public school personnel, attorneys, child and parents' psychotherapists, child protective services workers, foster care personnel, foster parents, child's guardians ad litem, and a host of other involved parties. Depending on how vigorously a case is prosecuted and how long the children are kept in foster care, a case of MBPS can include many costly years of professional involvement in the legal, mental health, law enforcement, and social service realms.

In summary, MBPS is a disorder that can cause enormous physical and emotional suffering to the children involved, result in deaths, abuse of our health care system, and turmoil for our physicians and other guardians of childrens' well-being. Even when these cases are detected and proven, they pose major difficulties in manage-

---

[32]One mother in our area ran up a bill of more than $750,000 on just one of several children for whom she sought unnecessary procedures.

ment for the staff of hospitals and the courts. Though the physician is generally the one to raise suspicions,[33] it is usually only after a long period of exasperating and exhausting medical detective work. Complex psychological and societal forces are at play in the very challenging task of unmasking each unique case, even before the issue of treatment is confronted.

[33]However, we know of cases where physicians resisted "seeing," and it was nurses or social workers who campaigned for psychological consultation after which a MBPS diagnosis was confirmed.

CHAPTER 2

The Challenge of Discovery and the Reluctance to Act

"As a physician one of the things you learn early on is to listen to the parents. And what makes Munchausen by Proxy syndrome so difficult to deal with is that your ally in the child's health care is really not your ally. I don't want to use the word 'adversary,' but in fact I guess it is an adversarial relationship, because they are playing a game with you, except you don't know you're playing a game.

"And frankly, I'm not a detective. I'm not Perry Mason and I don't want to be. It's difficult enough to accuse somebody, but for me to have to start snooping around and becoming a detective, and looking through drawers—I don't want to do that. That's not my role. . . . And I think that that makes it even more difficult because when you finally accuse the person, it's a question of, 'Well can you prove it?' Well no, I can't prove it. . . . If they are looking for hard evidence, it's not going to be there. I'm not going to find a bottle of Milk of Magnesia in the mother's purse with her fingerprints on it, and I'm not going to put a hidden camera or a hidden microphone in a room to try to catch the person. . . . And the thought of putting cameras in rooms and trying to catch people is repugnant to me. We seek alliances with parents, not adversarial relationships."

—Thoughts of a pediatric gastroenterologist
on experiences with Munchausen by Proxy cases

"No, I didn't have a whole lot of doubt about being wrong. I just didn't know how to accuse the mother or confront the needs of the child given that she was sort of between me and the kid. I should have, in retrospect. I should have called the social worker and said 'You know, something weird is going on.' Because we were all convinced of it. We had these hallway, stairwell, and elevator conversations. I remember vividly how we all decided that she was crazy."

—Retrospective thoughts of a physician about a
mother with several children who died in
suspicious circumstances

Munchausen by Proxy syndrome cases frequently go on for months or years before they are revealed, if they are uncovered at all. Yet the diagnosis is often greeted with amazement that the deception could have continued for so long. A host of complex reasons interfere with our ability to suspect, much less confirm and confront, a MBPS case. Even with rather simple forms of fabrication or illness induction, such as poisoning with a single agent, the cases tend to unfold slowly like intricate medical puzzles. As we will see, this is due to the interaction of many factors, but especially to the ability of these mothers to make very compelling clinical presentations of illness in their children, which are taken to be true by physicians and other guardians of children's welfare because of particular clinical and psychological mind-sets. Other factors such as the complex nature of modern medical diagnosis and treatment, and fears of malpractice lawsuits, also play a role.

This disorder is relatively new, and it does not fit very neatly into other categories of child abuse. Nor does it tend to fit the customary presentations of common physical or psychiatric disorders, which further complicates the process of discovery. In fact, if it were not for the peculiar compulsion of these mothers to repeat or to escalate their behavior or sometimes to present trivial or obvious fabrications, many would never be discovered. As one child protective services worker put it in discussing a case, "It's certainly made me more aware. Now there's another category that we have to watch out for. Everything before was so neatly organized. You had physical abuse, you had molest, you had neglect. And now, to me, this is like a whole different category. It does really involve a lot of medical knowledge too, and it can take so many forms."

SYMPTOMS GALORE

Anna was 14 months old when we were first told about her case by a pediatrician who had cared for her during his residency at an east coast hospital. We learned the details of her case during her sixth admission, this time for apnea (nonbreathing episodes). Her mother, Sandra W., had also expressed her concern about bright red blood as well as diarrhea in her diaper the previous week. When the staff failed to find any signs of these symptoms, they began to suspect that the mother was fabricating the illness.

After a telephone consultation with the child's doctor we raised the possibility of MBPS. She assured us that she was aware of the disorder and was herself concerned. But, she added, Ms. W. seemed to be a very caring parent, and Anna did have genuine medical problems. One pediatrician who had looked in on the family seemed incredulous that we could express strong suspicions that this mother was hurting her child.

Anna was born at full term in Canada to a very young mother of two. The medical history stated that she had apnea spells at birth and was on oxygen for approximately 4 months in the hospital after which time she had been sent home on an apnea monitor; thereafter her spells were known only by report. She was found to have mild gastroesophageal reflux (a slight tendency for food to move back up and out of the stomach and into the esophagus or to cause vomiting). Her apnea, according to Ms. W., had ceased when she was 6 months old, though she soon after developed pneumonia and was rehospitalized. She also had diarrhea and continued vomiting and was felt to have what is called a "dumping syndrome" (too rapid movement of food through the gut) which led to a surgical procedure to tighten the sphincter in the lower part of her stomach. When, after discharge, she continued to vomit and failed to gain weight, a Broviac catheter was surgically placed to enable her to be fed intravenously.

Anna's family eventually moved to the northeastern United States and began treatment in the outpatient department of a local hospital. Two months after arriving she had a repeat apneic episode and was hospitalized after her mother reported that she also continued to have diarrhea. She quickly improved in the hospital, where no apnea episodes were observed. Her older brother was being treated for persistent skin rashes and was also being followed in the neurology department to monitor seizure medications, prescribed for him in Canada. (Since the mother possessed medical summaries, the Canadian doctors had not been contacted.)

A month after this first hospitalization Anna was again hospitalized for diarrhea and failure to grow. Two weeks after her discharge (again having had no problems while she was in the hospital), she appeared at the emergency room. Her mother reported continued diarrhea and an apnea episode requiring her to do CPR (cardiopulmonary resuscitation) at home. This hospitalization lasted 3 weeks. Anna was again discharged after her stay proceeded without incident. When Ms. W. reported that she continued vomiting after discharge, she was readmitted once again. This time a previously placed central venous feeding catheter was found to be clotted, so during this hospitalization a feeding tube was surgically placed directly into her stomach. She soon began to tolerate oral feedings and was returned home, only to be readmitted one month later with her first reported seizure.

A neurological workup found her EEG to exhibit mild slowing (a nonspecific finding sometimes seen after a seizure) and she was placed on antiseizure medication, in part because of the family history. A month later she was admitted to hospital once again when Ms. W. reported Anna was having episodes of cyanosis (turning blue). Although this problem was not seen on admission, Anna was found to have serious and documented gastrointestinal bleeding accompanied by lethargy severe enough to require several transfusions, though no cause could be found.

Anna again improved rapidly in the hospital. It was a month after discharge that Ms. W. reported blood in the diaper which could not be traced to any physical problem in the child. It was this episode that aroused both our suspicions (when we were told about the case) and those of the attending doctors, and led us to ask about the possibility of MBPS—something the attending physician herself suspected. The physician told the mother that she suspected that someone was deliberately hurting Anna. Ms. W. responded by acting totally baffled about who could possibly want to do such a thing. Child Protective Services felt there was inadequate evidence to file charges, so no other action was taken at this time.

Another month went by before Ms. W. brought Anna to the emergency room again, this time in a semistuporous state. She was admitted and toxicological screens were drawn for the first time. We were officially called to consult and immediately recommended a consultation meeting of all the physicians involved. It became clear that no one had ever witnessed a seizure by Anna's brother nor did either of the children have a documented abnormal EEG. It was during this meeting that a resident rushed in with the results of the toxicological screening which showed a blood level of isopropyl (rubbing) alcohol of 0.24, more than two times the adult intoxication limit for ethyl (drinking) alcohol. It was concluded that the observed slowing on the admission EEG and the stupor that had at first been diagnosed as postseizure phenomena were probably related to rubbing alcohol poisoning. In retrospect the staff realized that the rapid blood loss of the previous admission was probably secondary to a gastritis caused by alcohol injected through the feeding tube into the stomach.

Anna was placed on police hold, which temporarily restricted anyone from removing her from the hospital. When Ms. W. was accused of deliberately harming Anna she responded with anger and denial. Despite all the evidence we now possessed, she seemed almost believable. She promised to go home and "search for which household product the baby could have gotten into." A neighbor who was a nurse was present and swore that Anna's illness could not be caused by her mother. She loudly and tearfully denounced the medical staff for even suspecting her. Since we now had hard evidence—the high level of blood alcohol could not have been ingested by mouth without causing a gastritis (she now had another central venous feeding catheter which bypassed the stomach)—we convinced child protective services to place Anna outside of the home. Within 3 days she was free of symptoms, eating by mouth. Within 1 month she was growing normally.

A year later we are told that she continues to do well. The other child (initially on asthma and antiseizure medications) was placed out of home and is being followed medically. He does not require medicine for "seizures" and his skin rashes are gone. We later learned that this family had lost a child to a SIDS death at age 4 months. Sandra W. continued to deny any involvement in her children's illnesses through the time of our last contact, after which she left town; her children continue to thrive in the care of others.

It was the last test, the toxic screen that showed a blood level of isopropyl alcohol, that confirmed our growing suspicions—we knew that such a thing could not have happened except by means of injection into the central venous catheter. Although the child protective services attorney was convinced of Ms. W.'s guilt, we would have had a difficult time convincing a court of maternal abuse without this evidence. Anna had clearly received toxins to make her ill, and her brother was also in danger because he had unnecessarily received medication that carried a certain risk for morbidity. This family is of particular interest in that two children were involved simultaneously—one child suffered an induced illness, the other had fabricated symptoms, and the death of another child remains an unsolved mystery.

Anna W.'s medical problems illustrate many of the challenges in uncovering a MBPS case. She arrived at the hospital with a believable medical history (parts of which seemed to be confirmed by records from another hospital) of apneic spells that required oxygen in early infancy and apnea monitoring. Furthermore, her extensive medical workups revealed some mild but "bona fide" findings of mild GE reflux and mild EEG slowing. So in order to even begin to suspect a

Munchausen dynamic, Anna's physicians had to be willing to question the most basic "established facts" and entertain the possibility that their hypotheses were built on inaccurate or extraneous medical information about their patient. The coexistence of some "real" medical problems along with symptoms fabricated by the mother is a common occurrence that tends to add to the physician's reluctance to question the genuineness of *any* of the symptoms. Dogged parents, or persistent illnesses that do not respond to treatment or that respond and recur also lead to complicated feelings (see Chapter 7) in the physician that can start a process that obfuscates rather than clarifies the medical picture.

Even if the physician can overcome this narrowed focus on medical causes and begin to perceive the larger picture, in which the possibility of fabrication by the parent can be entertained, he or she is then faced with the even greater problem of collecting adequate evidence in order to protect the child. This is not an easy process: an accused mother can respond with righteous indignation, the decision to remove her child from the physician's care, a lawsuit, or—worst of all—a deliberate effort to make the child very seriously ill in order to prove to everyone involved that she was "right." In the case of Anna, a lucky break late in the process, afforded by the isopropyl alcohol laboratory results, clinched the diagnosis and permitted action to save the child. Most other MBPS cases are not resolved medically or legally by such concrete and conclusive evidence.

Our retrospective discussion of the case of Anna was, thankfully, not a postmortem, but it easily could have been. It became clear that there had been many lost opportunities to confirm a diagnosis along the way. The initial gastritis which appeared to "come out of the blue" was probably related to ingested alcohol but toxic screens were not ordered at that time. The stuporous state that cleared up and the slowing on the EEG were all consistent (as were other nonspecific lab tests) with alcohol ingestion. The reported hematuria (blood in the diaper) combined with a normal urine test was the beginning of the end of the medical imposture, although, as we mentioned, there was a long denouement and we could easily have lost the child at any point. This latter possibility led to a discussion of how her physicians could have been more observant and whether they could have instituted some procedures involving closer surveillance. But in fact it was clear that for a long period the doctors involved in the case were not ready to believe that this seemingly concerned and very caring mother was poisoning her child. Nor was it just the doctors or this woman's neighbors who were fooled. Though experienced with MBPS, even the mental health consultants found this mother a very convincing, devoted parent.

Interestingly, it was the ward clerks who pointed out that they had always felt that something was wrong with this woman. In a case review and support conference later held with the nursing and ward staff, they said they had noticed that Ms. W. stayed around the hospital long after Anna was asleep for the night, despite the fact that she had another child at home. The ward clerks reported that she "loitered" by the nurse's station, seemed engrossed in the "medical gossip," and appeared unusually dependent, if inoffensive. It is not surprising that the health care workers with the highest level of suspicion about the mother were those who had prolonged informal contact with her of a nonmedical nature. Their opportunity for observation of her social behavior stood in sharp contrast to the medical focus of most nurse and physician interactions with Ms. W. As Anna W.'s case makes clear, a team or *group* discussion of a puzzling case can often generate useful observations and validate suspicions more rapidly, overcoming some of the individual obstacles to entertaining an MBPS diagnosis faced by the lone physician. But many factors mitigate against such useful meetings, not the least of which is the busyness of frontline hospital caretakers.

Anna's mother was certainly convincing both in her apparent concern for her children, and in her medical knowledge which appeared well beyond the capabilities of someone with little formal education. The problems created—bleeding, vomiting, diarrhea, stuporous states (with a sibling said to have a seizure disorder), and apnea spells—are among the most serious in clinical medicine. Medical diagnostic procedures of the kind and number called for by these symptoms, as in any statistical study, are likely to occasionally produce a misleading finding. In this case it was a rather common one: gastroesophageal reflux. The physician can also be ensnared by the belief that colleagues have in the past or even now are treating "bona fide" conditions in this child or other family members. The tendency in busy medical practices to uncritically accept medical chart statements concerning the existence of previous illnesses contributes greatly to this belief. Often these bogus illnesses are unquestioningly passed on from chart reading to chart reading. In our litigious society physicians faced with complex medical problems are reluctant to leave any stone unturned; when the symptoms are as serious as Anna's, few practitioners of the art of medicine have much patience for passive observation. Nor would most MBPS mothers tolerate much waiting.[1]

As we will discuss below and in Chapter 7 on the physician and the impostor mother, the orientation of doctors is to exhaustively test and "rule out" every imaginable physical cause of a presented symptom. Hewn in medical school and honed in overwhelmingly busy hospital-based internships, this approach can easily lead to endless dark alleys of nondiscovery. As Yudkin (1961, p. 563), a pediatric consultant, said 30 years ago in a paper paraphrased by Waring (1992), "When a child is brought to a doctor two different diagnoses can often be made. These diagnoses are the answers to two questions: (1) What is the matter with the patient? and (2) Why is this child being brought for care at this moment? The answer to the first question is taught in medical schools . . . whereas the ability to answer *both* questions . . . is 'the beginning of real medicine' " (Waring, 1992, p. 753).

MY EYES ARE DIM . . .

The case of Joan V. illustrates how the mind-set of the physician can interfere with understanding even nonsensical symptoms when they appear in the context of a serious and unexplained medical picture.

Joan was a 16-month-old who was admitted to a major medical center in the South for the first time at age 9 months, having been transferred from a small community hospital after 10 days of vomiting. Joan lived with her mother; her father had left the family years earlier. Andrea V., Joan's mother, said Joan had had a fever and was sleeping 18 hours a day and that the vomiting first noted in the community hospital was thought to be related to a viral illness. On her admission of three months duration, the following procedures were completed: an X-ray of the abdomen, an upper gastrointestinal (GI) with small bowel follow-through, a computerized axial tomography (CAT) scan of the brain, a magnetic resonance imaging (MRI) scan of the brain, a neurological consult, endoscopy with

---

[1]In a case sent to the hospital of a colleague in New England for a "second opinion," a girl with chronic pain was found on X-ray examination to have a swelling. An experienced pediatrician strongly felt that the evidence still pointed to this being a MBPS case, and told the mother that he and other consultants believed the swelling to be enlarged lymph nodes from chronic infection and not a tumor. He advised against surgery and recommended waiting. But before nightfall the mother had convinced her insurance company to fly the healthy-appearing child home in a private helicopter, with a nurse in attendance, to be operated on.

biopsies, and a gastric emptying study. This last test was the only positive test to that point, and showed very mildly delayed gastric emptying. Stool cultures were also done. Though Jean continued to vomit during her hospital stay, nurses noted that she always looked normal, cheerful, and completely healthy. An outside consultant recommended that a gastrostomy be performed with a tube to bypass the stomach until the mildly delayed gastric emptying had improved.

Joan did well for over a week and was very close to being discharged. But then one evening she had two separate "seizures" associated with cardiorespiratory arrest and developed a right-sided hemiparesis (weakness) and bilateral pneumonia. She was placed on nasogastric suction. Over a week's time, she had no active seizures, but increasing amounts of drainage in physiologically impossible quantities began to appear in her drainage receptacle. Though these reached gigantic proportions (five to six times what is physiologically possible), a diagnosis of MBPS was still not made.

Another consultant in a distant city was called, and he suggested that Joan was clearly the child of a MBPS parent. When confronted, Andrea became tearful and turned the accusation around by repeatedly suggesting that someone in the hospital was causing her child's problems. After the conference in which she was apprised that people felt that she was the person responsible, she began to engage other parents in conversations, suggesting that the hospital was tampering with her child's care. She actually succeeded for a time in lining up other parents against her pediatricians. After Andrea was separated from Joan by a Family Court order, most of the child's medical symptoms began to disappear and she remained healthy. (After the mother was in mandated therapy for a year, the baby was returned to her and she left the state.)

Pediatricians are trained to listen to mothers as a source of knowledge and understanding about their child's illnesses. When a patient presents with the serious symptoms that Joan V. exhibited, pediatricians often narrow their focus in their relentless pursuit of the medical causes. This singular mind-set, understandable in cases where symptoms are dramatic and life threatening, is exactly what makes MPBS such a difficult disorder to identify.

To demonstrate how profound this mind-set can be, we should mention that this same pediatrician had had an altogether different experience in a previous case. In the case we next describe, of Danny H., this pediatrician had fought tirelessly to try to protect Danny from his mother's efforts to keep him an invalid with overdoses of harmful medication. Following his involvement in that case, the pediatrician spent much time giving lectures to educate other physicians about the difficulties that MBPS cases present. Yet only several months later he failed to recognize the problem in Joan V.'s mother. While this may seem inconceivable, it is *far* from uncommon in cases of MBPS.

WHEN JUSTICE IS BLIND

The case of Danny H. and his family demonstrates that even when physicians *are* suspicious of fabrication, the road to discovery and prevention can be full of obstacles.

Elizabeth H. described her family of origin as close-knit and religious. According to her, most of her parents' affections were focused on a younger sister, described as quite competent and talented. She felt her parents wanted to program her life and did not really care for her as an individual. She reported no abuse. She married at 21 and immediately became pregnant. Several years after the birth of a daughter she sought a physician to impregnate her with donor sperm provided by a medical student. Divorce followed soon after the birth of a daughter, Amelia.

When reviewing Danny's case, we learned that Amelia was hospitalized on at least 10 occasions between birth and age 25 months, for failure to thrive and intractable diarrhea. Metabolic clinic testing and multiple biopsies revealed an apparently normal female infant, paralleling the third percentile on standardized growth charts. Dissatisfied with the first hospital's evaluation, Elizabeth took the child for evaluation to a medical school hospital in another city where testing also revealed no cause for her failure to thrive. She returned with the child months later, complaining about her intractable diarrhea, but Elizabeth strenuously resisted her admission and instead requested medication.

When she was 15 months old, Amelia was admitted again with a 7-month history of intractable diarrhea and intolerance of foods other than mother's milk. An extremely invasive series of evaluations failed to account for the diarrhea. At one point she lost half of her blood volume but no source of bleeding could be found. A consulting dentist was called because Amelia was losing her teeth and hair, and he suggested the child be screened for mercury poisoning, but this was not done. Amelia died 7 months later. At Elizabeth's insistence, an autopsy was not performed.

Elizabeth was hospitalized for depression soon after. The hospital record at that time noted streaks and sores on her abdomen which were believed to be self-induced. Shortly thereafter she became pregnant with Danny.

Danny was born 15 months after his sister's death. He was in good health at discharge from the hospital but this may have been the only time in his life he enjoyed such health. He began having symptoms in the first weeks of life.

Danny's early history involved a reported inability to tolerate any foods other than breast milk. Elizabeth claimed that any attempts to feed the child cereal, vegetables, or meats caused diarrhea and rash. At the age of 14 months Danny was hospitalized at a university hospital with pneumonia and wheezing. According to the mother, Danny was able to tolerate nothing but breast milk until the age of 5 and would take the milk either directly from his mother's breast or frozen in the form of popsicles.

A physician in the clinic remembered the mother from the time he had taken care of Amelia. He set up an 8-hour-per-day outpatient observation of Danny's condition during which the 5-year-old Danny was able to tolerate a feeding of nonallergenic formula despite Elizabeth's insistence that he could not do so at home. He was sent home and finally started kindergarten, reportedly taking a thermos of breast milk to school with him each day. Inexplicably, however, Danny appeared to be normal in body weight and height, notwithstanding his reported inability to tolerate other foods. Soon after the clinic food trial, mother and child disappeared from contact with the clinic for 3 years.

After seeing several pediatricians in the community, Danny again suddenly appeared at the hospital. His mother reported that he had been unable to attend school since kindergarten and instead had been tutored at home. His diet reportedly consisted entirely of breast milk expressed from the mother and a neighbor, sourdough bread, and a liquid diet supplement. He was on a regimen of 11 different medications and exhibited complications associated with prolonged administration of huge toxic doses of corticosteroids, ostensibly prescribed by someone for asthma. He was noted to have high blood pressure, obesity, a cushingoid (moon-faced) appearance, and osteoporosis (bone thinning) with six spinal compression fractures. Virtually all of his medications were prescribed based on a falsified history, though he was often brought in for physical examinations or observation by physicians.

The various physicians caring for Danny at the medical center met to discuss the case. The medical staff questioned the need for such an intensive medication regimen. It was felt that the diagnosis of MBPS had to be considered and that Danny needed to be hospitalized.

About this time an article about Danny appeared in a local newspaper. The article described how a local charitable foundation for terminally ill children had mobilized community support to provide a trip to Disney World for him. The article quoted the mother as saying that her son was the "oldest living person with his disease" and that "no one knows how much longer he will live." Reading this article alarmed and helped mobilize Danny's physicians, who knew the whole story to be false.

After an intense lobbying effort by the medical staff, Danny was taken by police from his home and hospitalized. During the hospitalization a series of controlled food challenges resulted in no adverse reactions of any kind to any solid food, although Danny and his mother continued to maintain that the only diet he could tolerate was breast milk, sourdough bread, and a liquid supplement. At times during the food challenges, Danny or Elizabeth would insist that there had been an allergic reaction to a specific food although there would be no objective evidence of such a reaction.

Danny later admitted to having "sneaked" a wide variety of foods at home over the years. Elizabeth claimed to be unaware of these actions. Danny was weaned from his complex medication regimen including all steroids, with control of symptoms being achieved with theophylline, a standard medication for asthma. When blood levels of this medication proved impossible to stabilize in the hospital, a review was performed that indicated that he was intermittently receiving nonprescribed doses of the drug. The family was confronted and angrily denied administering extra medication, although Danny's blood level stabilized immediately following the confrontation. Danny experienced several mild asthma attacks related to emotional stress and two somewhat more severe attacks, each occurring prior to critical disposition hearings with the child protective services personnel concerning Danny's posthospital placement. About the time of one of these hearings the mother became acutely symptomatic with asthma for the first time and was hospitalized.

In the hospital milieu Danny showed little ability to interact with peers. Instead, he sought out adults or older adolescents to whom he related in an artificially cheerful, doll-like fashion. He often fabricated reports of mistreatment or unfairness by staff and he typically maintained these fictions even after confrontation.

Although it was agreed by all the medical staff involved in the case that Danny had suffered irreparable psychological and physical damage as a result of his mother's misrepresentation of his medical condition, the attorney representing the child protective agency concluded that it would not be feasible to pursue placement of the child out of Elizabeth's home, given the general track record of the court regarding out-of-home placement and lack of judicial familiarity with MBPS. Despite vociferous objections from his doctors, Danny was instead named a dependent of the court and was placed in his mother's home under conditions of a return to regular school, continued psychotherapy for him and his mother, coordination and approval of all medical treatment by a designated team of physicians, and visits by a public health nurse.

After Danny's discharge his condition deteriorated dramatically. He was seen several times in the emergency clinic with reports of asthma attacks, on two occasions requiring admissions. A pattern ensued in which he would appear quite healthy at a clinic visit with a normal level of the antiasthma drug theophylline, but would arrive the next day in the midst of an attack. The theophylline levels at the return visit were sometimes found to be subtherapeutic. Soon after discussions were started about sending him to another hospital, he arrived at the hospital and had a respiratory arrest. He was difficult to revive, which resulted in substantial and permanent neurocognitive deficits. (Two days prior to this arrest Danny, who had been generally quite resistive to psychotherapy and symbolic play, suddenly began anxiously and animatedly playing out the story of "The Boy Who Cried Wolf" in one of his sessions.)

The day of the arrest Elizabeth dropped Danny off at a park, where he came into contact with Danny's three known asthma-inducing conditions: pollen and grass, dogs, and exercise. When brought to the emergency room that night, he at first appeared moderately distressed. A nurse overheard his mother sitting on his bed saying "You can't breathe" several times, and soon after Danny suffered a respiratory arrest. Intubation (insertion of a breathing tube) was difficult, possibly because of a tightening of the vocal cords that line the passageway to the lungs.[2] During the arrest Elizabeth appeared completely calm. The respiratory arrest resulted in moderate to severe brain damage for Danny and a profound memory loss.

[2]While there was no evidence here for voluntary vocal cord adduction (closing), it has been described as part of a syndrome called Munchausen Stridor, which causes breath sounds very similar to asthma (Christopher, Wood, & Eckert, 1983). During a previous hospital visit this child was found to have laryngospasm (see Freedman, Rosenberg, & Schmalling, 1991; see also Stephenson, 1990, on syncope and anoxic seizures).

At this point the court agreed to send him to a national center in Washington, DC, for evaluation of his condition. Elizabeth reluctantly accompanied her son to the next hospital. There the staff notes make reference to a "pathologically close" relationship, describing Elizabeth as "manipulative, less than honest, hovering, and unable to allow [Danny] the independence or autonomous functioning of a child [his] age." Elizabeth became anxious during any separations. Interestingly, during therapy sessions when Elizabeth would be emotionally withholding, Danny would adopt a sickly, helpless position. He also threw himself from his hospital bed and caused a self-induced fracture during his time in the hospital. Despite all the known history and despite recognizing Elizabeth as a possible threat to her son's life, the clinical staff notes indicate that they declined to diagnose MBPS because they "saw no evidence to indicate that mother willfully . . . created physical illness . . . in her child to procure medical care."

When MBPS starts early and continues through childhood, especially when there is an enmeshed relationship between parent and child, the continuance of the behavior may be ego-syntonic (comfortable and nonconflictual) to both parent and child.[3] Because of his participation (self-injury, taking extra pills), it was suggested by some observers that Danny had developed a Munchausen syndrome himself. We would not agree. The dynamics of his self-medicating would be very different from the usual Munchausen's patient's need to be in a relationship with a doctor. In this case it appears to have served to please Elizabeth and continue the enmeshed family system.

Danny H.'s case represents a blatant and serious example of a MBPS case having been identified yet not acted upon adequately by the appropriate child protective agencies. For reasons we will discuss, many people other than doctors have trouble believing that a mother would deliberately do harm to her child. This is a not uncommon situation which is likely to be only somewhat ameliorated as this syndrome becomes better known and understood. Management of Danny's medical needs was also complicated by the coexistence of a "real" medical problem (asthma), which introduced a level of doubt and uncertainty into each new episode of "illness."

---

[3]Enmeshment is not a necessary part of the syndrome. We have known of quite independent children who went along with their mothers' ministrations until they were asked about what was going on, at which point they expressed a wish that mom would stop what she was doing.

THE DIFFICULTY WHEN ABUSE
IS PSYCHOLOGICAL

Not all cases involve serious harm to a child or sophisticated deception on the part of a parent. In the following case a pediatrician tells us in her own words how a milder case of MBPS unfolded and suspicions were aroused. In this case, ironically, the physician diagnosed the disorder relatively easily. Yet she faced even greater obstacles in finding a meaningful way to manage the case and prevent future episodes for the very reason that direct and life-endangering harm was not being done to the child.

"I encountered my first MBPS case when I was a pediatric resident. Maureen really wanted to have a son. She had had two girls before her last child, Kevin, was born, and he was clearly her favorite. He was about 4 years old, and according to his mother, he had a chronic seizure disorder for which he was on anticonvulsants. He was admitted to the hospital because she said he was having repeated seizures and was vomiting incessantly. Yet there was nothing in his physical exam to suggest that he had either of these conditions. He had been treated by many physicians, and had a history of care in a number of different medical centers. Kevin didn't look dehydrated, and his laboratory studies were incredibly normal, despite her report that he was vomiting many times a day.

"We weren't immediately suspicious. I think we were trying to figure it out. We had his record, the nurses would try to keep track of how many times he vomited, but it didn't quite make sense because nobody had ever seen him vomit. And we figured that out after a number of days in the hospital. The mother also told us that she was a nurse and that she had had a number of surgeries. Only later did we discover that she had also had a number of admissions for suicidal gestures.

"In the hospital we started to be suspicious that the vomiting wasn't real. We asked the nursing staff to try to keep an eye on what was going on from a distance. In those days the rooms had glass running from midwall to the ceiling, but often the curtains were drawn. I don't remember the exact sequence when we finally caught her, but somebody was suspicious because she came running to say that he'd vomited again. The nurse went in and found that the floor was covered with a mixture of cold chocolate milk and 7-Up that was still bubbling. Supposedly the last time he had drunk anything was 3 hours earlier. So the nurses watched very carefully and eventually they caught her putting a blue Chux on him like a bib, and then she poured some milk over him, poured it on the floor, and then came yelling that he had thrown up again.

"His anticonvulsant levels were also questioned. I don't remember whether they were high or low, but they were inconsistent. And he never had a seizure that anyone witnessed. The mother would come and sometimes say, 'He just had a seizure' and yet he looked perfectly fine! He hadn't been incontinent, and there was nothing unusual about his appearance.

"Well, we investigated and eventually found out that the mother's hospitalizations had been for phenobarbital overdoses. The child had at some point had an EEG that was abnormal, which justified people giving him anticonvulsants even though he had never had a clinical seizure. We also found that the mother had been hospitalized twice for surgery for a "mole" at two different hospitals. The surgeons in the operating room had discovered that her mole was fake when they scrubbed her thigh to do the surgery and the painted mole washed off. We put all of the pieces together while the son was still in the hospital.

"We knew Maureen was strange, but we couldn't quite figure out why. She used medical lingo but not always completely appropriately. I was a resident involved with his care, and I was pretty naive to the fact that this kind of thing could happen. It was just amazing to watch the pieces fit together. We anticipated that we would have a lot of problems confronting her. What I remember about this case from so many years ago is that the mother decompensated when we told her. As the child was being taken away from her, she went screaming after him. She ran down the hallway after him and fainted in the hallway outside the administrator's offices. And she was out. I felt sorry for her and I knew that there was something terribly wrong with her. I anticipated that she might completely fall apart when we confronted her, but I really felt for the child's sake that we needed to do it. I was hoping that the child's older sisters might fess up that they were aware of all this, but they really were very protective of their mother, and completely denied that she could be crazy. And yet they had heard and seen everything that was going on. I was very upset when I found out later that the boy went back to his mother."

Kevin was lost to follow-up, so we know nothing about his ultimate fate. As we will see again and again, this is a common outcome when a child's psychological health, rather than his life, is at stake because our child protective and legal systems are reluctant to intervene unless grave physical danger to the child can be proven.

Other examples of "milder cases" that caused psychological harm to the children yet could not be managed easily by our child protective systems can be gleaned from Warner and Hathaway's (1984) report of 301 children seen at a clinic designed to treat food allergies. The authors noted that "where no food intolerance or allergy could be shown, most parents readily accepted the diagnosis and reintroduced normal diets without problems." But they also pointed to 16 cases of what they called "pseudointolerance," in which "food intolerance could not be established, [but] the mothers refused to accept the opinion and maintained the diets against advice. The parental obsession with diagnosis was very abnormal and was adversely affecting their child's life" (p. 152). The authors gave several detailed examples. For example,

> Case #12 was a tall and extremely healthy looking girl with a single mother. She had mild perennial allergic rhinitis due to house dust mite sensitivity. The half-hearted recommendations on house mite avoidance measures made by one of us resulted in the girl's life being made a misery. The family moved house twice and she changed schools three times within a very short period. The mother was convinced that her daughter was extremely ill and debarred her repeatedly from school. Her exchange of correspondence with the Allergy Clinic and the local housing and education authorities was unprecedented. (p. 152)

In most of these "allergy" cases, parents rejected the physician's recommendations and the children were lost to follow-up. Unfortunately, we have reason to believe that our child protection system will be slow to develop a more active role in protecting victims of this "milder" form of abuse. This is particularly distressing because we have so little data available on the long-term outcome for these children and their families.

MBPS, CHILD ABUSE, AND PSYCHOPATHOLOGY

MBPS versus Child Abuse

As clinical and research data has shown, many parents abuse their children emotionally, physically, or sexually, or abandon them (Study of National Incidence and Prevalence of Child Abuse and

Neglect, 1988). Children of divorcing parents, especially those involved in serious disputes over custody, often suffer emotional and physical abuse (Johnston, Campbell, & Mayes, 1985). Other children in our society are traumatized by catastrophic events such as crime, natural disasters, wars, accidents, or the daily violence around them (Terr, 1990; Garbarino, Dubrow, Kostelny, & Pardo, 1992). Sexual abuse of children is a much greater problem than we have been willing to admit (Finkelhor, 1984). We are now much better equipped to notice the telltale signs of abuse in children: anxiety, withdrawal, sleep problems, irritability, aggressive behavior, or bruises.

What differentiates MBPS abuse from other forms of child abuse is the false perception on the part of others that the abusive parents are deeply caring and concerned about their children. Apparent good or even exemplary parenting, when combined with none of the usual signs of child abuse and no obvious indications of a disturbed parent–child relationship, make it quite difficult to even entertain the *possibility* of MBPS.

Children of MBPS parents rarely show the typical physical or psychological signs of abuse. While some parents in a jealous rage may attack their children and cause great harm (Meadow, 1990b) pounding assaults are highly unusual.[4] We do not see infant victims of MBPS who suffer retinal hemorrhages from brutal shaking attacks, broken blood capillaries on the face from choking assaults,[5] or multiple fractures caused by direct blows. Yet the effects may be catastrophically worse, as when a mother cannot resuscitate the child whose breathing she has halted. An infant or young child who is repeatedly given a dangerous substance by his or her mother, where the effects such as vomiting or diarrhea are delayed, has little capacity to associate these effects with the hand of his or her mother. In fact, what the child sees—much like what the world at large sees—is the mother's concern, constant presence, and caring behavior. The power of this apparent reality can be appreciated and attested to by adults who have interacted with these parents.

Typically, the physical harm inflicted on children in MBPS cases is the result of elaborately calculated, long-term maltreatment. As often as not, the harm is compounded by the agency of a well-intentioned physician seeking to discover the cause of a symptom. MBPS mothers are frequently so knowledgeable about medicine and

---

[4]Bools, Neale, and Meadow (1992) have reported a fairly high nonaccidental injury rate in the past medical histories of these children.

[5]See Samuels, McClaughlin, Jacobson, Poets, and Southall (1992) on the lack of outward physical manifestations when a child is suffocated.

physiology that they can stimulate serious concerns about their children's health by medical caretakers without (initially at least) arousing their physicians' suspicions.[6]

MBPS versus the Psychopathic Personality

The only other syndrome known to psychiatry in which such dramatic differences between social presentation and private behavior exists involves the psychopath. Serial murderers, for example, can compartmentalize rather normal lives in one area of their existence while stalking and brutally murdering their innocent victims in another "life." Meloy (1989, p. 88), for example, notes that after serial killer Allen De Salvo strangled his 12th victim, a 23-year-old woman, and then raped the corpse, "he . . . had supper, washed up, played with the kids until about 8 o'clock, put them to bed—sat down to dinner [watched TV] and didn't think about it at all."

But the psychopath's relationship with his victim takes place from afar until the final moments in which a "real" encounter destroys the fantasy and leads to horrific brutalization as well as display of the body in a clear attempt to humiliate those who discover the crime. MBPS parents have ongoing relationships with their infants and children that may continue for years while they are inflicting harm on them. With the exception perhaps of incest, this simultaneously long-term, close-yet-destructive relationship between perpetrator and victim has no parallel in human psychology.

MBPS may be a gender-related form of psychopathy. While MBPS can be linked to early childhood trauma, in truth such trauma is almost universal in the histories of psychopaths (Meloy, 1988) but found less reliably in the histories of MBPS mothers. Psychopaths and MBPS mothers do share an uncanny ability to convince others of their sincerity and goodness through carefully planned deceptions and lies. In both cases their friends and neighbors are shocked to learn of their misdeeds.

THE MOTHER–DOCTOR DYNAMIC

The Mother's Relationship with the Pediatrician

In order to see similarities with other forms of mental disturbances, we need to look beyond the mother's relationship to her child, even

---

[6]Often (but unfortunately often only in retrospect) these same careful plans exhibit serious flaws and inconsistencies, or at times simply demonstrate an inability of the parent to stop her behavior when staff become suspicious.

though the child's presence is necessary for this pathology. But the mother's relationship with "it," the child, is not at the center of the syndrome: the true center is her relationship and involvement with the *physician* (see Chapter 7).

These mothers are often very skillful at "organizing" their caregivers to respond in predictable ways to their presentation of the child with certain symptoms or histories. Their effectiveness in convincing others that they are ideal mothers can be gleaned from the contrast between the assurance of a MBPS diagnosis we as consultants feel after a review of the victimized child's medical chart versus the intense sense of doubt we often experience after a face-to-face encounter with the child's "devoted" and "concerned" mother.

Pediatricians are trained to listen to mothers because they are often the primary source of information about the problems of their child patients. This attitude, bolstered by their medical mind-set, causes them to get caught up in the relentless pursuit of the medical causes of a child's reported or induced suffering.

This difficulty in looking beyond the medical symptoms and the mother's presentation is fostered by the fact that most parents who induce serious illness use preverbal infants in their elaborate deceptions. The usual signs of derailment described by those who do psychotherapeutic work with mother–infant pairs are generally not seen.[7] It is of interest that even verbal toddlers often show little spontaneous fear or upset in the presence of these parents. They will at times, however, report their mother's actions when asked! It attests to the forcefulness of these mothers and the intensity of the dynamic between the mother and the physician that these somewhat older children *are* able to talk about what is happening to them, yet are almost never asked.

The physician plays a key role in this process. One doctor involved in a case where a child died after years in his care described it this way: "Pediatricians are very busy and tend to minimize the reports from what appears to them as an overly concerned mother. This minimalization leads to an escalation of reported symptoms or actually producing symptoms in MBPS mothers whose goal is really

---

[7]Whether they are there but missed will only be determined by careful and close observation, using some of the newest tools of infant psychiatry (for example, videotape recordings and attachment evaluations). Of interest in this regard is the report by Samuels, McClaughlin, Jacobson, Poets, and Southall (1992, p. 164) on the videotaped surveillance of 14 patients caught smothering their children: "During CVS [covert video surveillance] the nursing staff and police officers commented on how little the parent handled, played, and talked to the child when alone in the cubicle."

more contact with the pediatrician. This 'pursuit' causes the pediatrician to want to withdraw—to pull back.[8] Even the hint of withdrawal, which might not be conscious on the pediatrician's part, causes the process of illness-making to escalate. And this is like walking into quicksand."

Nurses, who generally spend more time developing relationships with the parents of ill children than physicians do, face a more intense and complicated situation. As Blix and Brack (1988) point out:

> The dilemma causes more of an interpersonal crisis and intrapersonal crisis [for nurses]. The majority of the staff seem to have formed a positive perception of the parent. The physician's presumptive diagnosis, and subsequent evidence, suggests that these primary perceptions were blatantly wrong. Seemingly, the nurse was then left with discounting her perceptions, or the physician's diagnosis. Both choices go against the staff's basic motivations. . . . The result . . . is a vague distrust of their basic perceptions. It is little wonder that their immediate reactions were so severe—nausea, shock, anger. (p. 407)

The Role of the Pediatrician

In Chapters 5 and 7 we will examine particular dynamics of the doctor–mother relationship. Needless to say, all of us are prone to expect more from people to whom we entrust our lives than they can actually deliver, and physicians have not made strenuous efforts to dissuade us of their power.

Aspects of medical education also cause the physician to appear to fit the role many of us would have him or her play. Pediatricians, while they value qualities of parent–child relationships that are less important to other medical subspecialists, are nevertheless subjected to a training that places great value on the quality of certitude. Surgeons, for example, the physicians most often involved with adult Munchausen syndrome patients, appear to value their coolness in life-and-death situations; anything less is thought to make them more vulnerable to mistakes. Cassell (1987, p. 232) in an "anthropological" study of surgeons, found similarities between "the macho, death-defying, almost exclusively masculine world of the general surgeon, and that of test pilots and astronauts." While she was sympathetic to

---

[8]This withdrawal happens for complicated reasons, not the least of which are the parent's insatiable needs for contact with him.

the requirements of this particularly difficult field of medicine, the statements of her surgeon "subjects" are telling:

> "A guy who becomes a surgeon rather than an internist is a guy who needs a lot of positive ongoing feedback; every day the moment of truth occurs in the operating room and that confirms he is right." (p. 233)

> "Surgeons have tremendous egos . . . they attribute every challenge to their judgment as a personal assault." (p. 237)

> "A surgeon can't stand a chronic patient." (p. 233)

While these positions are somewhat exaggerated, there is no doubt that there is a need for control and certitude in the day-to-day existence of a surgeon who holds life or dealth *literally* in his (or her) hands.

Certitude, unfortunately, is a highly regarded quality in all doctors, and is encouraged by medical school instructors, who are wont to "criticize their students when they display too much unsuredness [because] doubt will impair their effectiveness with patients" (Fox, 1957, p. 208). Katz (1984, p. 188) warns us that this approach to training doctors creates "a mask of infallibility" and a "traditional authoritarian relationship . . . between physicians and their patients, that few in medical fields escape." Though the training of mental health workers is quite different, since they are taught to expect and therefore to deal with ambiguity and uncertainty, it is often a career-long goal to feel comfortable with these issues, especially among those frequently faced with life-and-death decisions.[9] Though "certitude" can be highly problematic, it is, of course, not at all clear that patients would permit physicians too much latitude in relinquishing its comfortable hold.

Pediatricians, who are also intent upon solving problems of a medical diagnostic nature, find some relief from this intense focus on problem solving and the need to cure illness because they regularly see healthy clients: "well baby visits" are very much a part of standard practice. These allow the pediatrician to bask in the special excitement and warmth of the early relationship between mother and child when it occurs. Physicians whose practice includes time spent with de-

---

[9]As one hospital-based psychiatric consultant put it, "The child and adolescent psychiatry fellow, after consulting . . . [on a suspected MBPS case in which the child died unexpectedly] either becomes a consultation/liaison psychiatrist or never wants to see another consult in a pediatric setting" (Sugar, Belfer, Israel, & Herzog, 1991, p. 1020).

veloping, healthy children have a chance to enjoy their child patients and interact with their parents, activities that are a valuable and valued part of their professional lives. Some pediatricians now make a well baby home visit just after the mother and newborn arrive from the hospital. One often hears them talking, as we psychotherapists do in our clinic, of valuing a family's warmth, caring, courage, and togetherness and their own relationship to the family. This significant difference between pediatricians and, for example, surgeons, unfortunately does not make them better at detecting MBPS mothers; in fact the opposite may be true. Pediatricians get closer to mothers *because* they are not their patients. This closeness can raise expectations for the emotionally needy MBPS mother. Presumably, many pediatricians are particularly vulnerable to a "good mother," a woman who seems to embody our society's ideals concerning motherhood.

In our view, the major difficulty arises from the fact that this often elaborate charade by the mother, in the service of forging an intensely *pathological* relationship with the physician, is finely tuned to these and other aspects of medical practice. While some time in medical school (too little in our opinion) is devoted to learning how to interview and best relate to patients and parents, little or no time is devoted to teaching future doctors how to recognize transference and countertransference issues—the complex feelings aroused in patient and caregiver by both the relationship itself and the personal issues of each individual—or how to identify another agenda in a mother's presentation of her child's problem. Precious little time is available for practicing and honing such skills for the usually overburdened resident on the wards of busy hospitals, where the training of most doctors continues after medical school.[10] These difficulties make it unlikely that the physician faced with ostensibly good mothers will easily be able to tease out the dynamics of mothers who fabricate illness or be able to understand the feelings they arouse.

Nor are mental health professionals immune to this problem. We were told of a possible case of psychological MBPS in which a mother convinced psychiatrists that her child had a thought disorder and had her admitted several times to a psychiatric hospital and heavily medicated, despite serious side effects.

And it is not only physicians who are susceptible to the protestations and countertransference issues stirred up by "good moth-

---

[10]There is even a trend in *psychiatric* training programs away from focusing on such dynamic skills (Wallerstein, 1988).

ers." In a MBPS case a few years ago, a mother believed to be repeatedly inducing seizures in her 2-year-old daughter and then calling the paramedics for resuscitation efforts was finally confronted with the evidence. Her threats to commit suicide resulted in a brief psychiatric hospitalization. During her hospitalization, we learned, she received several letters from a group of nurses who could not believe she had harmed little Amy and wanted to offer their support. Their lack of faith in the MBPS diagnosis was particularly surprising given the rough handling of the child by this mother while she was in the emergency room and the mother's very blatant lies about so many details of her life (claims that her teen-age sister was a neurosurgeon, stories that she herself was a TV talk show host and the like).

The Good Mother

As we will demonstrate when we examine the dynamics of mothers and physicians in greater depth, this deadly "dance" cannot be viewed as if it took place in a vacuum. Society's firmly held but distorted images of mothers and medical practitioners help to obfuscate the intense interactions between the sick and their healers. The last 2 decades have seen great upheavals in the definitions of family, motherhood, and childhood in Western society.

Our social agendas in the last 2 decades led to the "romanticization" of motherhood, particularly in the 1980s, by both the left and the right, and by feminist, nonfeminist, and antifeminist factions in our society. This romanticization has in turn led to various distortions in child endangerment cases. Lowenhaupt-Tsing (1990) appropriately cautions us to consider the powerful societal biases that can overpower the "facts" of particular cases where mothers are found to be harming their newborn infants. She argues that mothers who harmed their babies (the cases involved women who delivered and then abandoned their newborns) but who appeared controlled, unemotional, and acting "rationally" in terms of their own framework, were seen as *unnatural* and treated more severely than women who acted in fits of passion. The former were seen as selfish people who "flourished in the dangerous climate created by career women and feminists" (p. 297), though, as she points out, the women involved often were neither. The "flip side" of those cases, the reaction to MBPS subjects described in this book, supports her position. Social distortions cause us to idealize motherhood, to take the appearance of "good motherhood" for its reality, and therefore to often ignore evidence that points to the mother as the cause of harm to her child. (see also Korbin, 1989).

We have seen child protective services workers, D.A.'s, and judges refuse to believe clear-cut evidence put before them by concerned physicians. For example, we recently heard of a MBPS case in which two experts convinced a judge that the mother suffered from MBPS, the child was removed from his mother's care, and his health subsequently improved. However, when visitation rights were being removed, her psychologist, admitting that he was unfamiliar with the disorder and that it was not being discussed in therapy, testified that he did not think she had the syndrome. The judge, amazingly, was convinced and returned the child home. We later heard that the mother's attorney was organizing a group to institute lawsuits against the hospital, the pediatricians, and both expert witnesses. While often this disbelieving response is due to unfamiliarity with what seems so fantastical, we feel it is also related to a broader, barely conscious defense against a perceived "attack" on the traditional family as much as a concern for the best interests of the child. (See Vaughn and Brazelton, 1976, for the medical profession's early responses to feminism.)

The Good Doctor

Nor are our needs to see mothers as good and caring the only distortions that play a role in making this disorder particularly difficult to detect. Our idealized images of doctors are reflected in the media portrayal of a certain kind of fantasy based on traditional sexual politics. It seems we can't get enough: there were 7 medical dramas on TV in the 1950s, and *28* in the 1970s! As J. Turow (1989) notes:

> Ben Casey (Vince Edwards) and Dr. Kildare (Richard Chamberlain) found themselves besieged with letters and people asking for advice: According to *McCalls*, "Chamberlain received 3500 letters a week . . . women opened their hearts to him." The two actors found that everywhere they went they were subjected to mobs of screaming fans. (pp. 69–70)

It appears that the matinee idol of the "soaps" found a particularly intense vehicle when he was endowed with the ability to cure what ailed us, through the laying on of hands. The importance of fatherly images coupled with female passivity was particularly strong in these shows. While there were a few female doctors, the male doctors were the heroes. In Casey, for example, Ben and Dr. Zorba were the forces of healing. "With the exception of the operating room sequences (where she was shown to be quietly competent), Maggie (an anesthesiologist on the show) stood around the nursing station waiting for Ben to say something" (Turow, 1989, p. 176). Both reflecting and shaping a social message, these programs mirrored the lessons of female upbringing and communicated to women that their problems could be solved not by becoming the active healer or problem solver themselves, but by being the passive recipient of a male physician's wisdom and authority.

It was not just the isolated women in the rapidly expanding suburbs who were susceptible: doctors themselves began to believe in their superhuman powers. Newly endowed with the appurtenances of modern scientific medicine, they became enamored with their own power and goodness. TV drama was not just reflecting life: it was helping create it.

We are not suggesting that MBPS was created by expectations raised by TV soap operas or in popular culture. Rather, these shows and their popularity reflect the playing out of fantasies fueled by social forces of unequal power between men and women. The images portrayed in the media help illuminate the complexity of the syndrome and the difficulty of its detection. Any attempts to understand this problem must grapple with forces that run deep in our culture, both socially and psychologically.

CHAPTER 3

The Extent of the Problem

*"Over a period of about 13 years I've seen about 15
Munchausen by Proxy patients. In fact I* know *we miss some,
because these people tend to shop physicians and emergency
rooms. And with our health care system now as fragmented as it
is, it's really easy to go to different hospitals in different areas.
. . . There are patients whom we've discharged who don't come
back for follow-up visits and the addresses change, and you don't
have any idea what happened to them. Well, they could be down
in Florida doing the same thing all over again to somebody else."*
—From a pediatric subspecialist

*"I think that Munchausen by Proxy is becoming more prevalent.
I think a lot more goes on than we know. I just don't think
we've identified it. I think perhaps a lot of kids have been killed
and buried and we were not aware that maybe there was a person
instrumental in it. I think that literature should be dispensed to
every child protection unit and I think it should be required
reading for every emergency response worker working daytime or
night. There should be a workshop that they have to attend.
Because I think this is going to become more prevalent once it's
identified. We're going to find out there's a lot more cases than
we ever dreamed of."*
—From a protective services worker who has
seen several MBPS cases

*The possibility of Munchausen syndrome by proxy behavior by
mother seems as preposterous to most people today as child sexual
abuse seemed 20 years ago.*
—McGuire & Feldman (1989, p. 292)

EPIDEMIOLOGY

Our review of the literature and a survey of pediatric subspecialists undertaken for this book suggested that MBPS is not an uncommon disorder, although even many people who have written about the syndrome portray it as rare.[1] The literature suggests a lack of involvement by mental health professionals in the majority of reported cases. Of the 187 papers that we have been able to locate, only 14 were published in psychiatric and psychological journals.[2]

We conducted a survey by questionnaire mailed in the spring of 1991 to all 880 pediatric neurologists and 388 gastroenterologists in the United States included in the official membership lists of these two subspecialties (North American Society for Pediatric Gastroenterology and Nutrition, 1990–1991; International Directory of Child Neurologists, 1989), with a 21.8% and a 32.4% return rate, respectively. These groups probably see the most common presentations of MBPS, given the preponderance of GI symptoms and seizures reported in the MBPS literature. Though our survey cannot in any way be used as a valid estimate of incidence or prevalence, it nevertheless indicates that there are more than nontrivial numbers of such cases, *and* that we likely have been missing and continue to miss diagnosing many of them[3] (see Tables 3.1, 3.2).

Rosenberg (1987) reviewed the literature and summarized approximately the first decade of experience with the disorder. Where there was doubt in some of the authors' report concerning the accuracy of the diagnoses, she omitted such questionable cases; she also made an effort to eliminate overlap of reporting. She identified 117

---

[1]Adult Munchausen syndrome may be more common than most physicians think as well. In a study conducted at Montefiore Hospital in New York, physicians in a busy consultation service found approximately 0.8% of 414 consultation requests were for factitious disorders (F. P. McKegney, personal communication, January 24, 1992).

Pope, Jonas, and Jones (1982) found that of 219 patients admitted to a research unit at a Harvard psychiatric teaching hospital, 9 patients (or 4%) were felt to be factitious psychotic disorders.

[2]There are approximately 361 papers on the adult form first described in 1951 (Asher, 1951). One-hundred-ten of these were published in psychiatric or psychological journals.

[3]We are currently involved in a computer survey of a large HMO to see if we can identify cases by blind chart review. We already knew of six MBPS cases among members of this group. All six were identified—along with 46 other patients—when we asked the computer to list all children aged 0–12 with over six hospitalizations. We are reviewing the remaining charts to try and develop an algorithm to differentiate MBPS cases from other sick children.

TABLE 3.1. Munchausen by Proxy Syndrome Survey of Pediatric Neurologists

No. of questionnaires	870
Responses	190
Response rate	21.8%
No. who reported case contact	107
No. of cases confirmed	109
No. of cases suspected	89
TOTAL	198

cases and presented 68 of the most common symptoms (many children had more than one symptom), which included abdominal pain, diarrhea, feculent vomiting, hematemesis, bacteremia, and seizures, derived from the 72 cases for which this information was discernible from the articles. (See Appendix A for an updated version of her chart.) Despite her review, a study by Light and Sheridan (1989), another study by Rahilly (1991), and our own data collection, we still do not have enough data to generate statistically meaningful statements about prevalence. We can safely say that the disorder is far from rare, and that it is frequently missed. Our uncertainty about prevalence can be traced to a number of factors besides inadequate data. First, case definitions are still imprecise and not sensitive, especially for the milder forms of the disorder and those in which older children are involved. Second, it is likely that legal and monetary disincentives hinder reporting. (Direct evidence for MBPS behavior is usually lacking, and we know of at least three incidents where the reporting physicians and hospitals were sued for malpractice—none successfully.) Third, none of the studies has a defined population base and all suffer from low physician response rates, making generalization difficult.

TABLE 3.2. Munchausen by Proxy Syndrome Survey of Gastroenterologists

No. of questionnaires	388
Responses	126
Response rate	32.4%
No. who reported case contact	103
No. of cases confirmed	164
No. of cases seriously suspected	103
TOTAL	267

Our conclusion that this disorder is more common than previously suspected is based on: (1) sibling data; (2) length of time to diagnosis; and (3) enormous variability in the number of cases seen by individuals in the same subspecialty.

Sibling Data

Meadow (1990b) reported on 27 young children who over some 13 years were reliably found to have been suffocated by their mothers. Nine children had died and one had suffered severe brain damage. These 27 children "had 15 live older siblings and *18* who had died suddenly and unexpectedly in early life" (p. 351). In another study describing 32 children who presented with factitious epilepsy, Meadow found that 7 SIDS deaths had occurred among 33 siblings (Meadow, 1984a). In a recent summary of a follow-up study of 56 victims of MBPS, Bools, Neale, and Meadow (1992) reported that 39% of the siblings were subjected to illness fabrication. In a study conducted by Samuels, McClaughlin, Jacobson, Poets, and Southall (1992) of 14 suffocation cases, 3 out of 14 siblings of the child victims had died suddenly and unexpectedly. Meadow (1990c) correctly cautioned against any generalization about the degree of morbidity and mortality from these individual reports or collective reviews of the literature; that caveat holds for our survey as well.

Alexander, Smith, and Stevenson (1990) reported on a phenomenon they called "serial Munchausen-syndrome-by-proxy" in which more than one child in the family was involved. An early report (DiMaio & Bernstein, 1974) appearing in a forensic journal reported on the harming of nine children (seven of whom died) in one family over a 23-year period in the years prior to the naming of Munchausen by Proxy syndrome. Mary Beth Tinning was imprisoned for the death of her last child after several of her children died under suspicious circumstances over a 12-year period (Egginton, 1990). In our own survey of pediatric gastroenterologists and pediatric neurologists, 25.8% (n = 120) of the known MBPS cases had siblings believed to be involved as MBPS victims. The high percentage of likely involved older siblings, who probably represent missed cases from the past, supports the likelihood that MBPS diagnoses are often missed (see Table 3.3). Rosenberg's (1987) literature review of 117 victims included reports of the deaths of 10 siblings "*which occurred in unusual circumstances*" (p. 555, our emphasis).

TABLE 3.3. Outcome from Surveys of Pediatric Neurologists and Gastroenterologists

Total within groups	
Confirmed	273
Suspected	192
Total	465
No. removed from home	120
No. not removed	163
Children who died	45 (9.7%)
Sibs who died of mysterious causes	23 (4.8%)
Father as agent	3
Mother and father as joint agents	3

The Length of Time to Diagnosis

In our survey (see Table 3.4), the average length of time to diagnosis was greater than 6 months in 33% of the cases, and more than a year in 19% of cases. In Meadow's report (1990b), "repetitive suffocation (11 children had ten or more such episodes) usually began between the ages of 1 and 3 months and continued until it was discovered or [until] the child died six to twelve months later" (p. 351). Rosenberg (1987) was able to gather data on length of time to diagnosis in 67 cases and reports a mean of 14.9 months (± 14 months) from the onset of symptoms. (The range for all 117 cases she reviewed varied from just days to 240 months.) In the Samuels et al. (1992) study, two patients suffered more than 20 episodes and nine experienced 4 or more apneic episodes requiring resuscitation before video surveillance was initiated. These data add to our belief that such behavior may frequently go undetected.

Table 3.4. Length of Time to Diagnosis ($N = 362$)

Months	n
0–1	60
1–3	67
3–6	83
6–12	63
> 12	89

Varying Sensitivity among Practitioners?

It is clearly difficult to determine if our respondents accurately identified and diagnosed cases of MBPS in their practices. Our respondent rate was small (21% of 888 pediatric neurologists and 32% of 388 gastroenterologists), and those individuals who did respond reported a range of cases. Some reported no cases and others had as many as 15. This large variability between physicians raises the possibility that at least some of the variance may be due to individual physician differences in ability to identify this disorder. Some physicians may not be diagnosing cases in their care.

WIDE CONTINUUM OF CASES:
LESS DRAMATIC PRESENTATIONS

Early in our investigation of this disorder we became aware that MBPS was more common than had previously been suspected (Libow & Schreier, 1986). As we have already noted, parents do not need to administer drugs or induce illness to be classified as MBPS cases: they can manifest the syndrome less dramatically through all manner of clever misrepresentation of a child's medical history, his or her symptoms, or of lab specimens. In reporting on five cases we saw at our hospital in a fairly short period of time, we reevaluated a paper (Hughes, 1984) written by a psychiatry consultant at a large children's teaching hospital affiliated with Harvard Medical School. In a 6-month period Hughes evaluated 47 children with abdominal pain, concluding that 23 of them had no definitive organic pathology. These children had been repeatedly investigated and hospitalized, and some had been subjected to multiple abdominal surgeries, without findings. Hughes concluded that these children, ranging in age from 5 to 16, were suffering from depressive illness based on their affect, anhedonia, and morbid preoccupation with illness. While he acknowledged that the children's depression "may be a reflection of maternal issues of depression and loss" (p. 153), he also suggested that the strikingly parallel mother–child depression "may also represent hereditary or genetic vulnerability (p. 147). Citing Sperling (1959), he suggested that depression in childhood often "manifests itself predominantly in a somatic form, most frequently involving disturbances of the digestive system" (Hughes, 1984, p. 147). We felt, however, that there were indications that several of these mother–child dyads could better be explained as a form of "doctor addiction" rather than the result of depressive illness. The mothers were described as "watchful, hovering, critical and needy." In fact, Hughes (1984, p. 152) observed that "mothers were neither significantly reassured nor encouraged by the absence of biological abnormalities but continued their efforts to help their children through an anxious, pessimistic pursuit of medical solutions." We concluded that it "is possible that at least some of these child patients were depressed because . . . they were colluding with 'Doctor Addict' mothers who needed their child to be sick as a means of enacting a particular relationship with doctors and the hospital system" (p. 609). This conclusion was eventually validated in one case from Hughes's study in which the mother was reported by a respondent to our questionnaire to be a confirmed MBPS patient.

Light and Sheridan (1989) reported on a national survey of infant apnea monitoring programs. Fifty-four centers out of 127 responded to the survey questions about whether the childrens' condition may have been fabricated or induced by a parent. A possible 54 cases of MBPS out of 20,090 were reported (0.27%). These were apparently serious in that two-thirds of the children received cardiopulmonary resuscitation at home, one-half had ambulance calls, and one-tenth were known to have died.

Rahilly (1991) investigated 340 babies who suffered from "apparent life-threatening episodes" using pneumographic and other medical methods (gastroesophageal reflux was common and was found in 211 patients). He felt that five (1.5%) were possible MPBS cases. In our own survey 316 respondents in the two pediatric subspecialties reported a total of 273 confirmed cases and another 192 suspected cases (see Table 3.3).[4] Given that some percentage of this latter figure may represent false positives (that is, parents of chronically ill children with other dynamics, whose demeanor might have falsely raised suspicion of MBPS), we are still left with a substantial number of cases from just two pediatric subspecialties.

As in the adult form (Nadelson, 1979), there are indications that there may be less dramatic, less compulsive, and less serious forms of the by-proxy form (see, for example, Warner and Hathaway [1984], who reported on 16 cases out of 301 children attending an allergy clinic). Less-serious forms of this disorder may make detection more difficult, which would lead to underestimating its prevalence. While physical harm *may* be less likely in these cases, serious

---

[4]Our cases were screened for overlap in order to avoid multiple tabulation of any patients seen by more than one physician.

psychological damage may be as great. Godding and Kruth (1991, p. 956), reporting from Belgium, diagnosed "noncompliant" families of asthmatic children as having MBPS "because the parents lied or concealed information" when describing the symptoms or treatment. They found 17 such families (involving 15 mothers, 1 grandmother, and 1 set of parents) in a caseload of 1648—1% of the patients in that clinic. They also identified 10 "undertreaters" who caused true asthma to become much more serious and 7 "doctor shoppers" (p. 957) who sought out treatment and engineered repeated procedures frequently for fabricated symptoms with little follow-through on the part of the parents. (The authors point out that even where illness is not actually caused, the consequences for the child may be grave.)

The possibilities raised in this chapter, while speculative, are disconcerting. MBPS cases take a major toll on all involved. Infants are damaged for life, if they survive. Enormous energies are required by child protective workers, the police, laywers, and the courts. Doctors are often scarred and increasingly scarce medical resources are wasted. For those who have not experienced this problem, McGuire and Feldman's (1989) words that this disorder "seems preposterous" must seem apt (p. 292). Those of us who have witnessed this phenomenon as commonplace feel that to continue to see MBPS as rare poses a grave risk. We are too close to the syndrome to be entirely objective. Our hope is that works such as this increase public awareness so that accurate estimates leading to improved detection of this disorder will be possible.

C H A P T E R   4

The Risk of Misdiagnosis

"I can also tell you that there have been cases where people have been accused and it hasn't been Munchausen by Proxy syndrome—it's turned out to be a slow-growing brain tumor, or something else causing the vomiting. Then you really have egg all over your face. I haven't personally, but I can tell you that I know people who have done that. That's why we are a little hesitant to make the accusation. Still in our society, that's a heinous accusation to make. To tell somebody that 'I think you're doing this to your child,' that's not an accusation you make lightly, especially if you happen to like the person or you've gone through this in the past. Maybe a month later you found out you were wrong, it was a brain tumor. So the thing is, you have to work these kids up the wazoo."

—From a pediatrician

CHRONICALLY ILL CHILDREN: PROCEED WITH CAUTION

One of our main purposes in this book is to encourage professionals who treat children to be suspicious when signs of MBPS appear. Nonetheless, a strong caveat needs to be registered: signs associated with the syndrome are not necessarily proof of the syndrome. Just as overzealousness and hypervigilence can lead to an identification of child abuse when no such abuse has occurred, MBPS can be misdiagnosed, causing increased stress to a chronically ill child and his or her overwhelmed family.

Krener and Adelman (1988) point out that there are situations associated with the care of chronically ill children and their parents' responses that can evoke misplaced suspicions of a MBPS picture. First, "the many medical consultations inflicted on the long-term patient may stimulate growth of parental obsessions on the details of the child's illness" (p. 949). Second, many families "fail to comply with medical prescriptions, but in . . . chronic illness the stakes are higher, the surveillance is better and . . . [failed compliance] becomes a contended issue" (p. 949), in which parents are thought to be purposely harming their children when they do not comply. Third, difficult families will often cause a pediatrician to ask for a psychiatric consultation, a suggestion that many parents will greet with hostility. Krener and Adelman suggest that the parents of chronically ill children "[have] been socialized to expressing their worries and fears in the language of medical terminology" (p. 949). Often they "deny that their own personal history is important" (p. 949). This is also a way they try "to keep up their emotional strength" (p. 949).

Fathers who take little or no part in the treatment of their ill children are not unique to MBPS families (Engstrom, 1991): such fathers are common enough in fairly normal families who must deal with chronic illness. Communicating with the parents of chronically ill children is often difficult, and their compliance with suggested medical regimens can be problematic. A child's condition may actually worsen while in the parents' care because of these factors. Parents may give confusing, complex medical histories. They may switch doctors frequently in a desperate effort to find the one doctor who will "cure" their child. They may be critical of previous doctors and of the entire medical establishment. They may appear very medically knowledgeable and often quite enmeshed in their childrens' physical and emotional lives. While families displaying many of these characteristics may be suspected of MBPS, suspicions will be groundless in many cases. Fortunately, some other characteristics can help to distinguish true MBPS.

MBPS parents differ in that they usually are very ingratiating and complimentary, even adulatory, toward their caregivers. While many parents will push for diagnostic procedures, MBPS parents appear compliant and rarely wary of medical procedures, even when they involve a good deal of risk or discomfort. MBPS parents are likely to actively encourage doctors and seem unperturbed when the latter seek out further invasive tests and procedures for their child. An exception to this attitude *may* occur if the MBPS parent fears that the procedures or tests could reveal her deceptions. MBPS parents do not withdraw from contact. The initial feeling medical staff has when working with MBPS parents is not dislike, but rather an internal sensibility that one is not doing enough for them.[1] As the medical situation begins to generate suspicion, however, MBPS parent cooperation begins to unravel and the usual signs of major difficulties begin to appear. Angry outbursts, denials, threats of lawsuits, and occasional threats of physical violence are not uncommon. But even here there are differences between MBPS parents and the disturbed parents of true chronically ill children. Some MBPS parents who have been openly hostile will, oddly enough, continue to seek care from the same physicians who are the object of their complaints and will continue their harming behavior if allowed to! Others, of course, will flee immediately if possible. They may also begin enlisting other families against the doctors and hospital.

Nevertheless, we are only at the beginning of understanding this rather complex disorder, and familiarity with the dynamics of families of chronically ill children such as those suggested by Krener and Adelman are necessary and useful to help differentiate the bona fide Munchausen parents. As we become more sophisticated in such matters, and with increasing utilization of consultation-liaison services in our hospitals, we will be better able to distinguish these very different phenomena.

OTHER CAUTIONS

Errors of misdiagnosis are more common than most of us in medicine would like to admit. The case of Patricia Stallings holds a lesson for us all. She was sent to jail for life without the possibility of parole at the age of 26 for the murder of her 3-month-old son (Chin & Breu, 1991, pp. 111–116). The child had been placed in foster care after an emergency room visit in which he vomited uncontrollably and was found to be barely breathing. Ethylene glycol, an ingredient found in antifreeze, was discovered in his blood. Four days later his mother visited him at the foster parent's home and was left alone with him briefly. He began vomiting, was rehospitalized, and soon died. Accused of murdering her child, Mrs. Stallings appeared to show "no remorse." She was then tried, convicted, and sentenced.

---

[1]Occasionally they will become "pushy" and overtly manipulative which can lead doctors to "wash their hands" of them. (See interview with the physician in Chapter 7.) This can lead to disastrous consequences for the child. (See also Chapter 8.)

She would still be in jail today except that she had another child after she was imprisoned. The baby was then placed in foster care. Two weeks later the child was admitted to a hospital because of vomiting and difficulty breathing. Eventually the child was diagnosed as having a rare genetic disorder, methylmaloric acidemia. Samples from his dead brother's frozen serum showed the original finding of ethylene glycol to be inaccurate. "Technically speaking," said an outside genetic evaluator called in to study the data, "I've never seen such lousy work" (Chin & Breu, 1991, p. 116).

While the point of this book is to raise awareness and sensitivity to MBPS in the very diverse communities likely to come in contact with these cases, the diagnosis is difficult enough to make without inaccurate laboratory data, or the problem of overzealousness. Medical staff can rely too much on their expectations of "normal" parental behavior in evaluating atypical situations. But we are actually aware of very few cases in which MBPS was misdiagnosed. Indeed, we have found that the syndrome tends to be the last option considered by a generally skeptical if not openly disbelieving (but frustrated) physician. Yet the horror of mislabeling a parent as a MBPS perpetrator and the terrible damage that could follow by forcibly separating a sick child from his or her parents unnecessarily and destroying a good parent–physician alliance in the process all speak to the urgent need for a cautious and systematic approach to identifying these cases.

At times we find ourselves quite confused despite our own extensive experience with this disorder. One of the most difficult aspects of dealing with this problem is the very nature of these mothers' presentation which robs us of one of our most important clinical tools. Simply put, we cannot rely on our intuitive reactions to the veracity and importance of what we are being told. Furthermore, the complexities of differentiating "real" versus induced conditions and emotionally disturbed from actively fabricating parents in individual cases is by no means an easy task, even when we follow careful guidelines.

MBPS IN THE MAKING?
THE CASE OF CINDY M.

We were recently called by a general pediatrician in southern Texas to consult on a puzzling case. Baby Cindy was admitted to the hospital after a seizure was witnessed in the emergency room. It was said to be her third spell. In the hospital she was quite fussy but had no further episodes. She did have an occasional slowing of her heart rate and her lips turned cyanotic at times. Her mother, Donna M, was noted to smile a lot while seeming stressed, even overwhelmed.

Donna gave the physician the following personal and family history. She said she had lost her mother recently to breast cancer and that cancer ran in the family, along with diabetes. In a later interview with the consultant she elaborated on her own medical and psychological history. She said she suffered from a rare kidney disorder. She said she had saved her younger brother's life in a fall from a second story window. In so doing, she said, she suffered a serious arm fracture and several spinal disc dislocations. Periodically she goes to emergency rooms because of severe neck pain.

Donna did not mention a psychiatric hospitalization to us, though she did mention it to the obstetrician and it was later confirmed. She also related that a man had kidnapped her daughter years earlier and had taken her to Japan. Relatives who worked for Interpol, she said, had advised her against charging him with kidnapping because he was politically influential.

She appeared appropriately anxious during Cindy's hospitalization. When asked about why she was smiling in light of Cindy's serious condition, she told about a very difficult childhood. She said the smiling was an adjustment she had made to ease her psychological pain.

Following our guidelines on assessing possible MBPS cases, we talked with Donna's husband. Some of the above history was elicited from Donna in her husband's presence and "confirmed." She seemed genuinely concerned about Cindy, who was a fretful baby by everybody's observation, but Donna was also very focused on her own problems. She was noted to follow the resident around the floor one evening, complaining of various aches and pains. Also, when one day she did not show for an appointment, the social worker called her and was told that she had been badly burned in a kitchen accident. However, when he called the emergency room where Donna said she had been treated, he discovered that she had never been registered there.

On paper the evidence seemed to fit the clinical picture of MBPS (even down to the detail that her mother had been a nurse and Donna had worked in a dermatologist's office). The problem, as usual, was that all her health care providers found Donna to be very believable. And Cindy truly seemed to have problems that seemed independent of her mother's influence. We suggested a conference and the group decided on the following course of action:

1. The physicians planned a thorough check of Donna's medical history. Though she seemed somewhat suspicious of the doctors' motives, she readily gave them permission to gather information and even to talk with the aunt who raised her.
2. They met with Cindy's father and confirmed parts of Donna's story.
3. They kept the baby a bit longer in the hospital than they normally would have for further assessment and observation.
4. All consultations were done in the hospital and were reviewed with the consultants directly.
5. More frequent outpatient visits were scheduled upon discharge and a psychologist was to attend these regularly to follow the family's progress.
6. As the psychologist could vouch for how irritable and difficult Cindy was and how anxious Donna was, she arranged for a visiting nurse.

The medical records from the delivering hospital came in slowly but confirmed only some of Donna's medical history. When Cindy's regular doctor went on vacation, the psychologist tried to call Donna at home unsuccessfully. After 2 weeks of trying she finally reached Donna's aunt in a nearby city who said that her niece and the baby had been with her for the past week. She also reported that Cindy had been taken to a local hospital because of repeated seizures and had been admitted for a week. The aunt confirmed that she was a fussy baby and had kept them up all night, but she also felt that Donna's anxiety was a contributing factor.

The aunt was willing to talk about the family's medical history when the psychologist identified herself as a mental health worker trying to help. She verified some of the medical history, though much of what Donna had reported seemed overstated or exaggerated and some of it totally false. The aunt knew of the accidental fall but denied it had produced severe injury. She said there were siblings with health problems but not a significant family history of cancer or diabetes. Donna's mother had indeed died of breast cancer, but the aunt herself had never had the diseases reported. Donna did have a serious kidney disorder which had indeed been treated. The aunt also confessed that she lived in a house where there were many family problems but her niece had been spared from the most serious ones. She reported that Donna did not have a child who had been kidnapped.

Even though Donna had been given lots of love and nurturing, she still strove mightily to attract attention, according to the aunt. And she could create or enhance a situation to get attention focused on her. Asked about Cindy, she confessed that she believed that Donna exaggerated her condition. In phone calls her niece would make it appear that Cindy would not live out the day, hoping to get her aunt to come to be with her.

Our description of Cindy's case takes place as we are putting the final touches on this book. Her physicians tell us they are wary but also confused. They feel that Donna is a person who needs a lot of attention and fabricates stories about her life and medical history. They felt they had covered all the medical bases and that Cindy was having a difficult time. They could not find her mother's agency in her medical problems, however, and were not sure that it existed. They did not feel sure that her seizures were caused by her mother. They felt that they had hard evidence only regarding a strange conflu-ence of a needy mother who exaggerated and fabricated history to gain sympathy, and who also had a difficult baby. They thought, however, that they could be witnessing the *development* of a MBPS process. Ironically, they thought, their intense support of this mother may have been fostering the process. They decided to redouble their efforts to see if there was any way of her causing the bradycardia or decreased respirations or seizures. They were gravely concerned be-cause the other hospital had given her two medications, both poten-tially quite dangerous, to treat this child's condition. As of now, they are still unsure whether Cindy is safe in her mother's hands or if a MBPS dynamic is indeed in the making. They can only try to watch carefully—and respectfully. Perhaps time will tell.

Ultimately, we believe that a multipronged approach involving an exhaustive medical workup of the child, interdisciplinary collaboration of all involved caregivers, scrupulous efforts to locate concrete confirma-tion of intentional harm to the child, in-depth medical history from at least one other person in the family, and psychosocial assessments of family members are all critical to a fair and meaningful diagnosis. Sometimes we feel like we walk a fine line indeed between protecting a child from a life-threatening assault by his or her mother and cruelly tearing a child away from a mother victimized and falsely maligned. This book is dedicated to expanding our collective knowledge in an effort to sharpen the line between these two dramatically different realities. We turn now in Part II to an attempt at a deeper understanding of the dynamic forces involved in this syndrome, not only in the mother but in the physicians, and the cultural context in which this system of disordered relationships is embedded.

UNDERSTANDING THE DYNAMICS OF MBPS

Introduction

In another film I saw recently, a supposedly beautiful, gentle, and loving mother, in order to regain her father's love and obtain a socially desirable marriage, coolly and slowly poisoned her four equally beautiful and loving children who more-or-less passively submitted to this. A perversion indeed of mother love! This is a cruel movie, strangely fascinating and exciting to the audience, who seemed to identify with excited horror with the sadistic grandmother, the sadomasochistic mother, and the masochistically submitting children.

   —Meyers (1991) (The movie Meyers refers to is
based on a popular pulp novel, *Flowers in the Attic,*
by V. C. Andrews.)

The response to *Flowers in the Attic* suggests that there is a receptive audience that can, in the darkness of a movie theater, be drawn into excited identification with sadomasochistic mothers. And our investigations too reveal the narrowness of viewing Munchausen by Proxy syndrome simply as a bizarre manifestation of the individual dynamics of these mothers. This part of our book will deal in turn with the individual psychodynamics of the disorder and their childhood roots, the social context that leads women to such profoundly disturbing behavior, and the role the physician plays both symbolically and practically in allowing this behavior to unfold.

  There are many aspects of this disorder that limit the development of a solid psychological or psychodynamic explanation. First, the relatively recent recognition of MBPS means few cases have been followed long term. Second, our belief is that it continues to be underidentified, limiting our ability to determine the breadth and depth of the disease. Third, the cases that dominate the reports tend to represent the most severe forms of abuse, such as chronic poisoning or suffocation, but it is likely that lesser expressions of the disorder are far more common.

There are only sporadic discussions of MBPS patients who have been in treatment, and few adults have been successfully treated. The very nature of the syndrome requires such a profound level of deception and denial that it may be extraordinarily difficult to engage patients psychologically, or to even help them understand the process of treatment.

While we currently have patients in long-term therapy and have therapeutic material on others, the literature and our own experience indicate that therapy can be a fairly futile encounter. Much has been learned from long-term therapies of people with severe personality disorders, even imposters and "as if" personalities, but these people, however ambivalently, *wanted* to be in therapy. For most MBPS mothers, the major reason for attending therapy appears to be a wish to get the "system" off their backs, and to win the return of their children. Since these therapies are not very intensive (usually once a week at most), and since most therapists are unfamiliar with the powerful dynamics these patients present, the patient often remains quite guarded and the therapy fairly superficial. The treatment usually tells us little about the character structure of these patients or ways of effecting significant change.

Our understanding of the psychology of the disorder is thus necessarily based on limited evidence. We have used descriptions found in the literature coupled with our own experiences with some 25 cases. Interviews and psychological test data gathered from colleagues around the country have also added enormously to our data base. Despite our efforts to gather as much information as possible— from patients, doctors, lawyers, and social service workers—we lack sufficient numbers of long-term psychotherapy patients to present conclusive evidence for our formulations.

Despite these limitations and the wide spectrum of pathology, there are enough consistencies in the data to take our hypotheses beyond the level of speculation. Yet we also feel that many of these patients challenge and push to new limits psychodynamic theories of developmental psychopathology and personality disorders. From the perspective of the individual mother, we have come to see the dynamics as a perversion, a form of mothering imposture. The term "perversion" is used here neither in its common pejorative sense, nor in its traditional psychoanalytic sense, relating it to particular sexual practices. It is rather used to describe a particular form of "unreal" relating and the mental processes that permit its continuance.[1] The object of this unreal relationship is to connect to a powerful and unattainable person, the doctor, who in fantasy can repair early experienced trauma. The sick child is not the object of this process but rather provides the means for the connection and allows these patients to live out their fantasies, much the way the fetishistic object allows for "sexual activity" for the person with a sexual perversion.

In the next chapter (Chapter 5) we focus on this "perverse" form of relating by women who appear to be imposters—in this case, imposter mothers. Because we have more data on their styles of relating than on their early development, this chapter has somewhat less to say about how this pathology develops. Just as the early histories of anorexics often do not seem to explain satisfactorily the depth and power of their pathology, so too the childhoods of these women, often much less traumatic than we expect to find, leave us more tentative about our dynamic hypotheses.

What appears to come up repeatedly for these women is a sense of feeling unwanted or uncared for, particularly by their fathers. This data is derived from their histories and lacks the contribution of information revealed in long-term therapies, as these are rare and unreliable for MBPS mothers.

This discrepancy has led us to explore the wider social context in which women are raised in our society. Our examination of the expectations and training for many women growing up helps explain their desperate need for recognition as well as the powerful rewards of the "perfect mother" role inherent in this disorder. Our exploration of the role of mothers within the medical world highlights the ways in which the "perfect caretaker" fabrication may temporarily provide these mothers some nurturance as well as the sense of control they so desperately seek (see Chapter 6). Although this analysis goes far to explain the role of the medical system in this disorder, it still leaves us wanting a deeper explanation of why only certain women actually manifest the disorder.

The idea that other forms of female perversions are also com-

---

[1] "Perversion," because of its usual connotations, may be an unfortunate choice of terms. Nonetheless, we chose it because in our reading of the current understanding of this form of relating, it fits the clinical material very well (Kaplan, 1991; Bach, 1991; Stoller, 1991).

monly overlooked because they, too, closely resemble ideal feminine behavior is a painful and sobering thought. This fact undoubtedly leads to the difficulties doctors have in understanding and discovering MBPS. This issue and the role the physician plays in this process are discussed in Chapter 7.

Chapter 8 focuses on the dynamics of the somewhat more disturbed families who involve older children in the Munchausen by Proxy process. If we have learned anything in the realm of personality development and disorder, it is that no individual form of psychopathology can exist or be understood outside of the social and social-psychological context in which it is found. We hope that our systemic and psychodynamic formulations will add to our growing fund of knowledge and understanding about the nature of early female development in our society, a subject neglected until very recently.

The Perversion of Mothering: The Danger of Being Ignored

[T]he enemy of attention [that which enables growth] is "fantasy," defined not as rich imaginative play which does have a central role in maternal thinking, but as the "proliferation of blinding self-centered aims and images." Fantasy . . . is intellectual and imaginative activity in the service of consolation, domination, anxiety, and aggrandizement. It is reverie designed to protect the psyche from pain, self-induced blindness designed to protect it from insight. Fantasy, so defined, works in the service of inauthenticity. . . . Attention to real children, children seen by the "patient eye of love," . . . teaches us how real things [real children] can be looked at and loved without being seized and used, without being appropriated into the greedy organism of the self.

—Ruddick (1980, p. 358), with reference to
Iris Murdoch's "Sovereignty of Good"

"I was just tired of dealing with sickness and hospitals and doctors . . . but on the other hand, that was my life. . . . It's just so hard to have two kinds of feelings inside at the same time: to hate something so much, and at the same time not feeling I could live without it. . . . Hating it, and at the same time feeling that you belong there [at the hospital]."

—A mother's report to her therapist (She was
in mandated psychotherapy following MBPS
abuse of her young child.)

Munchausen by Proxy syndrome presents us with a haunting paradox: in it two of society's most intensely heartfelt yet diametrically opposed states, "good mothering" and "callous child endangerment," occur *simultaneously*. The difficulties associated with detecting the syndrome cannot be seen as problems solely for physicians to handle, and are not due merely to the cunning of the perpetrator. In fact, symptoms at times are manifested in ways that would ordinarily seem quite amenable to detection. Nonetheless, an individual's MBPS can go on undiagnosed for years. In this chapter we will demonstrate why understanding the dynamics of the complex relationship between the doctor and the mother is necessary to understand this phenomenon.

When we were called to consult on our first cases of MBPS, we expected to find grossly disturbed mothers.[1] We were mistaken, and quickly learned to appreciate the problems pediatricians, judges, lawyers, and child protective workers face when confronted with the possibility of MBPS. We found ourselves simultaneously believing and resisting belief in the stories told by these mothers. Sensitive to the tendency in medicine, and especially in child psychiatry, to blame mothers for their children's problems, we wanted to believe that these mothers were innocent of their deeds. We could easily understand how a medical doctor, faced with a seriously ill child, might resist all hints that the child's own mother was responsible; and we could also understand how the need to prove one's competence could blind a doctor to the sophisticated medical traps these mothers devised.

That women with this disorder differ from mothers who are simply overwhelmed and need help (Libow & Schreier, 1986) or want some attention, and also from parents afflicted with the various syndromes of child abuse, can be gleaned from the peculiarities of the presentation: pathological lying, causing repeated serious harm to the child when simply by fabricating symptoms they could achieve most of the effects they desire, a compulsive need to repeat the behavior, unnecessary risk taking, and at times a kind of gleeful excitement at just those moments when their children's lives hang in the balance.

We believe that the mother's relationship with her pediatrician is paramount in the development and continuance of what is a process of mother *imposturing*. This clinical condition is a form of relating

---

[1]A police officer put the same feeling in these words: "I had been told a lot about this mother's actions. I found her by physical appearance to be more passive-looking, much less conniving-looking than I had expected."

(here, to a physician) in which lying is the essential mode of interaction and represents a particular form of "character perversion" as described by Arlow (1971). The mother becomes a "perfect" mother in a perverse *fantasized* relationship with a symbolically powerful physician,[2] and the harm that she does to her child is but a *by-product* of that relationship. Our use of the term "perversion" does not refer to particular sexual practices, but rather to a mode of mental functioning in which reality and fantasy coexist, though their distinction is blurred. It occurs in nonpsychotic people who have a poorly developed capacity for guilt and difficulty facing reality when faced with unpleasant affects. (Renik, 1993).

In the scenario enacted by a mother who brings her child for treatment and a physician who becomes implicated in the mother's fantasy, the infant serves as a fetishistic object. "It" (the dehumanized infant) becomes a material object to be kept close by the mother at all times, much like the fetishistic objects in other forms of perversions, and as such provides an intense degree of conviction about the reality of the relationship and the fantasy and protects against loneliness and despair. Her need for closeness to the infant–object furthers observers' false impression that the mother is truly caring.

It is difficult to discuss all the complexities involved in the relationship between two of society's most potent symbols, the mother and the physician/healer, as they unfold in this disorder. We will describe the adult Munchausen syndrome patient's dynamics first, for the "simple" syndrome casts light on the more complex MBPS. We will next offer a case history of a MBPS case that highlights the dynamic issues associated with these patients and illustrates the differences between MBPS and Munchausen syndrome. In this discussion we will elaborate our ideas about the use of the infant as a fetishistic object, explain how we came to see this activity as a perversion, and present our thoughts about how this disorder develops and why it is found almost exclusively in females.

---

[2]Meadow (personal communication, August 1992) reports that mothers he has questioned adamantly insist "that it has not been their fixation on a particular physician, nurse, or other person, but their need for escape from home or an unsupportive husband, or just their own general insecurity, that has caused them to make their child ill in order to escape into the hospital environment." There is much evidence that leads us to doubt this explanation (see Chapter 1). It may be the case on occasion, but we have been more impressed with the frequency of mothers with fixations on their child's physician, and wonder as well about the real nature of the "institutional transference" of these other mothers. In any case, our speculations from the more extreme forms provide us with a window on a fascinating dynamic.

ADULT MUNCHAUSEN SYNDROME PATIENTS

Adult Munchausen syndrome patients, judging from those who have been detected, appear with false symptoms or serious, if at times bizarre, lesions, and seek admission to a hospital. Their chief aim is to convince a surgeon to operate on them or, alternately, to get the surgeon to refuse to treat them. When the latter happens, according to Cramer, Gershberg, and Stern (1971, p. 576), "bitterness" and "resentment" spew forth. "The patient begins to attack and accuse physicians of not handling the case well and even demands operations and procedures in an attempt to get his case treated right. Often the patient then reveals the hoax and invites attack, dismissal and discharge."[3]

This process, which occurs rapidly, is repeated compulsively by some people with the syndrome and less frequently or only occasionally by others. Some of these patients are highly successful and continue to work in their fields, others are reduced to the status of "hospital hobos." Syndrome sufferers create a life in which they repeatedly set up a series of intense scenes. Unlike with MBPS, Munchausen hoaxes are usually discovered quickly, the patient is confronted, and the exposed patient reacts by raging at his or her physician–accuser.

Nadelson (1979), in reviewing a few cases from charts and interviews with relatives, has suggested that Munchausen syndrome patients are people with borderline personality organization. But the few cases in the literature where dynamic formulations have been attempted reveal mixed diagnoses and may not be representative of people who do not present this symptomatology compulsively.[4] Cramer, Gershberg, and Stern and other writers (Spiro, 1968; Sussman, Borod, Canselmo, & Braun, 1987; Wahl & Golden, 1966) point

---

[3]In the four cases described by Cramer, Gershberg, and Stern there was a strong sexual component to the relationship to the physician by both male and female patients. We have rarely found such a sexual component in the relationship between MBPS mothers and their children's physicians, but should it exist it would not at all detract from our interpretation of case histories.

[4]We heard of a highly successful professional whose life's work involved working with physicians. As a young man he took care of an ill mother after his father lost most of the family's money in the Great Depression. When stressed, he would check himself into a hospital and frequently obtain an operation. His wellness was not "discovered" over a 40-year period, and other than mild depressions he appeared not to suffer from any psychiatric disorder. After a convincing but fabricated Alzheimer "stay" he committed suicide using a pain medication prescribed after an operation for a nonexistent tumor.

to serious problems in identity, stemming from disordered families, abandonment themes, and the identification of the doctor as an idealized parent, either through actual contact or through fantasy.[5] They suggest that these patients often enter the fields of medicine and nursing in order to act as caretaking agents, which allows them to deny their intense dependency needs. Those not actually working in the health professions are nevertheless often quite knowledgeable about medical issues and often know as much about their conditions as the physician with whom they consult about a particular complaint.

According to Cramer, Gershberg, and Stern (1971, p. 577), rejection "brings up sadistic wishes towards the abandoning parent and the rage prevents them from working further in their professions, often nurturing ones, and they become patients." Menninger (1934) saw the process of submitting to multiple surgeries as an attempt to expiate guilt stemming from rage at a parent, by sacrificing part of the body to "prevent the threatened destruction of the whole." Munchausen syndrome patients find themselves in a perplexing and profound bind: Insofar as they project their own serious ego and superego deficits onto staff and doctors, they come to devalue the very people from whom they wish to receive nurturance. But in so far as they are successful in fooling staff, they cannot accept the care they receive as genuine. Thus they are trapped in a hopelessly unsolvable dilemma.

MBPS PATIENTS

As we have noted, there are major differences between adult Munchausen syndrome patients and the usual MBPS cases, even though a significant minority of the mothers with MBPS are adult Munchausen syndrome patients themselves. The quickly unfolding sturm und drang scene of the adult patient is often absent (or only appears when the MBPS mother is finally confronted), and the relationship with the doctor, the hospital, and the ward staff continues often for very long periods of time.[6]

An infant can be demanding, but cannot threaten to abandon or actually abandon his or her mother.[7] Although a very intense re-

---

[5]Rarely are these hypotheses derived from treatment interactions.

[6]An exception occurs in cases involving older children. These mothers (see Chapter 8) are more overtly disturbed and quickly arouse suspicion.

lationship is possible, it can be heavily weighted with fantasy on the mother's part without arousing suspicion on the doctor's part. The relationship with the child lacks the threat to the mother's self-concept that a truly intimate adult relationship invariably brings. When the infant becomes demanding, the outlet is not to turn to the spouse for support (most MBPS mothers are married, albeit to distant, unavailable men), but to turn up on the doorstep of the newly found idealized parent, the doctor. The pediatrician's concern, perhaps fostered by a need to be up to the challenge of a difficult problem, the desire to be admired for successfully solving the case, and the need to be seen as caring, keeps the game going. An intense relationship develops, albeit a narcissistic and sadomasochistic one, in which the mother needs to control the distance and intensity of interaction between herself and the caring doctor. The physician provides a safe theater and plays alongside her "reality" in a very convincing manner for reasons we will discuss in Chapter 7.

While one sees the defenses of splitting and denial in narcissistic pathology and these can abet the deadly sadism found in the psychopath (Meloy, 1988), neither of these conditions adequately captures the long-term intensely compulsive "career" pursued by ostensibly wonderful mothers who repeatedly offer their children's bodies to entice and simultaneously control their powerful, professional victims.

THE CASE OF CHRISTOPHER

In one not particularly unusual case on which we consulted, Christopher died at age 4, after 25 hospital admissions and over 300 pediatric office visits.

Christopher was born in June 1981 in the southeastern United States. He was first seen less than 1 month later at his pediatrician's office. Edith, his mother, reported projectile vomiting, runny stools, and crying during bowel movements. Despite normal workups at a major medical center that specialized in the treatment of children, he

[7]While Meadow (1990b) has reported infants being harmed in a jealous rage when an otherwise "absent" husband begins to pay more attention to the infant than to the mother, Samuels, McClaughlin, Jacobson, Poets, and Southall (1992) found no parent reporting a recent stress in her life. Surreptitious video recording revealed that these mothers (and one father) "did not appear to smother the child in anger or in an attempt to silence them; their actions appeared well thought out and were performed calmly and carefully" (p. 169).

eventually was fitted with a nasogastric feeding tube; this tube was later replaced by a percutaneous gastrostomy tube, surgically implanted through the stomach wall for feeding. He was diagnosed as a failure-to-thrive infant.

There were times when he was receiving as many as 14 medications for chronic infections, asthma, allergies, and feeding disorders. A purported "immunoglobulin deficiency" turned out to be a delayed maturation of immunoglobulin synthesis. Frequently Christopher would show up with a history of 105–107°F temperature the night before, but his temperature was found to be normal in the doctor's office. On more than one occasion he came in for a bruise secondary to a fall or running "into a concrete wall." On several occasions during his second year of life his blood sugars were found to be in the 40s (symptomatically distressing); the pediatricians discovered that the mother, though medically knowledgeable, was "using the wrong scoop for his glucose" and giving the child half the sugar he needed.

In his third year of life a conference was held at the medical center to discuss his recurrent vomiting. A child psychiatrist raised the possibility of a disorder based on a "learned behavior pattern." An inpatient psychological evaluation was recommended, but was refused by the mother. Several months later Christopher was brought to his pediatrician for serious dehydration and given intravenous fluids. The vomiting continued and the patient started to lose weight. Two months before his fourth birthday he again developed severe vomiting and diarrhea. His mother began taking Christopher to the doctor on an almost daily basis. Numerous attempts in and out of the hospital were made to stop the diarrhea through changes of medications, changes of food, and taking Christopher off food and allowing him to be fed only through his gastrostomy tube. Despite all these efforts, Christopher continued to fail. But it came as "a surprise and a shock" to Edith when he died, for he appeared to her to be doing much better physically.

Edith was later charger with murder when it was discovered that her son had died of chronic ipecac poisoning. The poisoning had to have gone on for 2 to 3 years to have caused the deterioration in the heart muscle that was found at autopsy.

Edith later admitted that because Christopher begged for food and because he was denied so many other activities of a normal childhood, she felt that she should give him something enjoyable to eat, followed by ipecac to cause him to vomit. She insisted that she did this only a few times in the last months of his life.

During her evaluation several people who knew the mother well were contacted. *Not one* believed that she had hurt her child. Her own mother, who broke off most contact with her after the charges were filed, said that when Christopher was born, "her [Edith's] whole personality changed. She was the happiest person alive with that child. She kept him spotless. Everyone loved him." Edith's godmother, who was in her 80s and seemed quite knowledgeable about many family dynamics, said, "He was her life. She was a wonderful mother. Christopher was not afraid of his mother. Nor was he intimidated by her. He loved her and he had nice manners." They lived in a one-bedroom apartment, she said, and mother slept on the couch so that Christopher could have his own bedroom.

Edith's history provides many clues to why she developed MBPS. Christopher's mother was the second of 4 children. She came from an upper-middle-class family that lived in a suburb where her father held a responsible executive position. The marriage broke up when Edith was in elementary school. She was apparently a mediocre student in comparison to her siblings. A sister stated that she "got away with a lot more" than the rest of the kids, and was always a "poor-me" person once she learned that she could get what she wanted that way. This sister also noted that from a very young age Edith lied a great deal as a way of gaining more attention. She reported that her sister had a history of broken bones and accidents when she was a kid. Edith's claim that her mother was upset when she found out she was pregnant with Edith was confirmed by her mother. She hastened to add that she, however, had been satisfied with the pregnancy, in that she wanted a girl.

Following a junior college education, Edith went to work in a hospital, where she met her first husband. After about 2 years the husband left her. She subsequently held a number of low-paying jobs and had, as she admitted, a problem with "lying." She checked herself into a psychiatric hospital 2 years after the breakup of her marriage; the immediate cause was her failure to fulfill a promise to some friends that she could get them a producer for a show. A hospital note from that admission stated that "she seems to have a 'social worker' inside of her, a drive to take care of the sick and needy."

She told a major lie to a young man whom she subsequently married. She told him that she had cancer and required chemotherapy, an admission that apparently hastened their marriage. She would occasionally leave the house, telling her husband that she was going out for kidney dialysis but actually spending 4 or 5 hours driving around aimlessly before returning home.

Edith could not recall the years prior to her father's leaving. She said that she always felt that her mother had not loved her, and indicated that there were no physical expressions of affection in the family.

Her father remarried. Edith visited him on occasion but he was "obviously not interested" in her. Even so, she wrote to him often and never missed his birthday or Father's Day.

Edith's medical history included many visits to emergency rooms, claims of numerous miscarriages, a history of peptic ulcer disease, some dysfunctional uterine bleeding, hypothyroidism, and chronic laxative abuse.

All the court evaluators noted that Edith revealed no signs of psychosis and had a fairly normal affective range in interviews, as well as some tenseness and tears when discussing her son. One observer from the hospital, however, noted that at the funeral she seemed quite garrulous and lively and more intent on interacting with staff than expressing grief over the loss of her son.

With one of her psychological examiners, Edith talked about her lying problem and noted that she had "fabricated a life for herself to such a degree that she began to believe her fabrications." Personality testing suggested dynamics of angry feelings, overt and covert, related to a sense of being hurt or unfairly treated. Tests pointed to an extrapunitive reaction she had when she felt rejected, a tendency to blame the environment and a wish to get even.

The patient was charged and tried, with the charge reduced from murder to manslaughter once the dynamics of MBPS were explained to the district attorney.

MOTHERING AS A MASQUERADE

MBPS raises many questions about normal developmental relationships and psychopathology, many of which we will not be able to answer until more patients, representing the full spectrum of the disorder, are recognized and treated in intensive psychotherapy. Furthermore, little in the recent and very rich field of infant psychiatry prepares us for the findings in this condition. Noncontingent interactions, serious depression in a caretaking parent, and other derailments in the interaction between mother and infant have been shown to be powerful tools in understanding symptomatic behavior in infants and toddlers, as well as understanding parental dynamic issues (Brazelton & Cramer, 1990; Zeanah, 1989). But the usual signs of derailment are *not* seen in MBPS. As the case of Edith suggests, the mothers involved in MBPS appear on the surface to be constant, caring, and concerned attendants to the needs of their infants. How can we explain this phenomenon?

Giving birth to a baby provides some women with the rare chance to assume a role in which they can enjoy constant attention and care. A fair percentage of these women have enjoyed something of a rehearsal for this role, having received extended treatment from a physician previously. Pregnancy, which brings the mother into close contact with her obstetrician, often serves to whet the appetite for more of the kind of attention that derives from being a patient, while at the same time it underscores the advantages of finding a condition that does not rely on fabricating symptoms in oneself. Instead of having to live with the threat of discovery, which can happen quickly when one's symptoms are fabricated, these women can enjoy their highly regarded status as new mothers.

Soon after the baby is born yet another physician appears at the bedside, spending time caring for infant and mother alike. The attention the pediatrician pays to the infant could easily cause jealous feelings in the mother, but the benefits of the doctor's relatively nurturant, warm acceptance of her, and the attention he must also devote to her, is a wholly new experience. It is an experience that echoes, more than any other she has had in the medical world, a throwback to the TV soap opera and medical show image of the powerful and/or kindly physician.[8] The role of patient/mother comes easily to her in the familiar environment of the pediatric hospital.

It is usually only in retrospect (after a case has been solved) that

---

[8]In an apt description of how intense the paternal representation of physicians in the mass media was in past decades, Ella Taylor, in *Prime Time Families: Television Culture in Post-War America,* described doctor television shows which were unlike many other professional situation programs such as the ones about law and journalism that focused on serious social issues:

> NBC's Dr. Kildare and ABC's Ben Casey, the first nighttime soaps, brought the medical profession to the television screen in a highly idealized and sentimental form. The drama came not from social issues but from florid story lines, in which patients died or were miraculously cured of rare diseases that did nothing to diminish their physical beauty, or in which the young doctor's progress, both personal and professional, was threatened by the errors of youthful inexperience. Common both to *Dr. Kildare* and *Ben Casey* was an essential relationship between an older and a younger professional in which the former played father and teacher to the latter, providing authority—moral and cultural as well as legal or medical—that firmly but gently molded his protegé to fit the requirements of his organizational surroundings. Dr. Gillespie and Zorba were as much psychological counselors and family therapists as they were physical healers. (Taylor, 1989, p. 36–37)

the hospital staff pieces together the oddly discontinuous elements of the woman's hospital sojourn: an intense interest in her child's medical procedures coexisting with a surprising absence of parental concern; a response of relief or even excitement when her infant goes under the scalpel for yet another procedure, or teeters near death from an illness she herself has caused; the long hours spent in the hospital during which less attention is paid to the child than to ward clerks and other parents; and finally behavior that puts her at risk of being caught, only to continue her "pursuit" compulsively as clues to her deceptions are overlooked.

Our historical investigations only *inconsistently* uncover physical and sexual abuse in the childhoods of these mothers (see also Rosenberg, 1987; Meadow, 1990b). More common are themes of psychological neglect and psychological abandonment.[9] Psychological test data point in the direction of narcissistic personality organization, not borderline pathology. Cognitive slippage, the ability to dissociate affect, and suppressed anger are common findings. Bursten (1973, p. 289) has described "craving" and "manipulative" types of narcissists, whose overarching life themes are "of having been disappointed and betrayed by someone who was not powerful enough or ready enough to give when they needed it," and this dynamic fits our patients well.

However useful the narcissistic category might be in explaining the ability of these patients to deny and split off the meaning of their everyday grotesquely disturbed behavior and yet function so well, it leaves us with a rather unsatisfying understanding of how this particular and peculiar set of relationships evolves. We believe the key is to be found in the mother's intensely ambivalent *fantasy* relationship with her child's physician which in astounding ways defines the use of her own infant.

MBPS AS A PERVERSION

Pregnancy and the neonatal period put the mother in a relationship with physicians that appears to her to be significantly different from

---

[9]In the Samuels, McClaughlin, Jacobson, Poets, and Southall (1992) study, there was significant reporting of sexual and physical abuse, but this was after the patients were charged, and in at least two cases a reported rape was found to be a fabrication. In one of our cases reported early childhood sexual abuse appeared as well to be a part of an exaggerated medical history. Another possibility is that a history of physical or sexual abuse may be more likely in cases of the most severe MBPS abuse, as in those discussed by Samuels et al.

all other relationships in her life. For the MBPS mother-to-be, a "powerful" figure, perhaps for the first time ever, is sharing *her* emotional space, listening to *her,* perhaps valuing *her* opinion and even admiring *her.* What develops in the individual who is susceptible is a sadomasochistic relationship that can best be characterized as a form of perversion akin to those found and described recently as being particularly though not exclusively female.

Kaplan (1991) in her book on female perversions describes the process in this way:

> A woman dissatisfied and disillusioned with everything the real world has offered to her, is possessed by the idea that a certain kind of person does have the power to fix her—a father, a priest, a husband . . . a movie star, a surgeon . . . a son or a daughter . . . and to bring her illusions to life and satisfy all her frustrated desires. He or she will compensate for the humiliations of her childhood and rectify the mortifications of her feminine condition. When that certain kind of person . . . is found, . . . created . . . invented . . . the . . . pursuit of this fictive phallic power assumes a force and intensity that eventually subsume and consume all a woman's strivings and ambitions. (p. 527)

Most writers on the subject would agree that a perversion is an elaborate strategy that produces intense anxiety, even fears of disintegration, if not compulsively carried out repeatedly. Its aim is to rectify and/or revenge, while keeping from consciousness a dreaded mortification at the hands of caretakers from the past. As Kaplan tells us, unlike neurotic symptoms, where the actor feels compelled to accomplish good acts to assuage a sense of guilt, the person involved in a perversion feels a sense of elation when brazenly defying the moral order. Until recently female perversions have been overlooked because analysts looked for them in the places where we find male forms. Perversions take on the appearance of exaggerated qualities of society's *assigned* gender roles: macho aggressive sexual behavior in the male, but self-denial, caretaking, and passivity in the female. In the anorectic "good little girl," the intense denial of her body, her self-effacement, accompanied by her good grades, constant exercising, and feeding of others, belie her extraordinary power over and revenge against her family. Anyone who has ever treated an anorectic knows that she can see none of this: she only sees places where her body bulges. The painful irony is that if it were not for the extreme physical state of these patients, they could easily be mistaken by most of us for high-functioning young women, their caricatured "femininity" seen in the most positive light. In this way they are reminiscent of the "too good to be true" MBPS mothers. The overly submissive woman is another example. In the adult form of Munchausen syndrome, it is easy to see masochism at work when the patient manipulates surgeons to cut into her repeatedly. What is easily missed by those unfamiliar with the disorder is that this most powerful masculine symbol, the surgeon, is humiliated in the process.

Stoller (1975), Kaplan (1991), and others have pointed out that the actions involved in perversion, however dangerous to the actor and seemingly unintelligible to the observers, are small prices to pay to prevent the terrors and mortifications of childhood trauma from being repeated, or even remembered.

The idea of viewing MBPS as a perversion became increasingly persuasive as we became familiar with the mother's relationship to the physician and to her infant, and began to gather data on the childhoods of these patients. These mothers have integrated their dynamics into characterologic traits of chronic lying (Arlow, 1971), even imposturing. They seize the opportunity afforded by the birth of a child to actively relate to and control physicians by amplifying a minor ailment in their children or inducing an illness in their infants. In so doing, they try to maintain an intense, yet distant, perverse, and ambivalent, relationship with a powerfully loved and powerfully feared paternal representative. As we will demonstrate, the physician comes to represent a second chance at a longed-for relationship with her father. But the fear of yet another abandonment is equally, if not more, powerful. That this is a much more complicated and fragile relationship than any other in the lives of both the mother and the doctor may not be discovered for months, even years, with the harming or death of one or more children the disastrous outcome.

While some authors insist on the underlying importance of sexual issues in the perversions, others (Bach, 1991; Welldon, 1988; Renik, 1993) do not. What our case studies suggest is that the "good MBPS mother" is a masquerade of mothering that springs from childhood roots that were *quietly* traumatic and include a profound absence of recognition of the child who will become a MBPS mother.[10] Our next chapter will explore in greater detail some of the profound social factors that leave so many young girls feeling neglected and desperate for approval and recognition.

[10]Welldon (1988) in her book *Mother, Madonna, Whore* talks about the "perversion of the maternal instinct" and its relationship to child battering, the production of transvestitism, and gender identity disorders and incest. (See also Kaplan, 1991, on child abuse.) She along with other writers on this topic see women who have developed perversions as attempting to turn "childhood trauma into adult triumph"

For Bach (1991, p. 76), "Sadomasochistic object relations arise as a defense against and an attempt to repair some traumatic loss which usually occurs in *childhood or adolescence*" (our emphasis). "This loss . . . may take the form of loss of a parent, loss of a parent's love through neglect or abusive treatment (which the child denies), or loss of the self through childhood illness, [or] traumatic disillusionment" (Bach, 1991, p. 76). The resulting relationships are "seen as a kind of denied or pathologic mourning, a repetitive attempt to disclaim the loss or to repair it in fantasy" (Bach, 1991, p. 76).

Applying Bach's formulation to MBPS mothers, the "masochism" appears in a message to the pediatrician: "Do anything to my infant, but don't *leave* me." But whenever the mother feels threatened by abandonment or conversely is allowed to get too close, with both possibilities containing the potential for releasing rage, she may gleefully "play" with the pediatrician, control his actions, and devalue him by confusing him. Rosenberg's (1987) review suggests that most of the harm done to infants occurs in the hospital, usually at the hands of the physician. As in adult Munchausen syndrome cases, the physician must be devalued for the mother to feel secure, but insofar as he is fooled he cannot provide the recognition, protection, and strength her bereft sense of self craves. This elaborate "game" is carried on in the service of confusing reality; in Bach's (1991, p, 78) pithy phrase, the game creates a life "forever frozen in a lifeless stereotypy." The ante staked on her child's increasingly fragile body can be raised, but it is a "no-win game." It continues until the need to be "discovered as powerful" or to seek revenge leads to risk taking and discovery *or* the child dies.

One need only attend the typically elaborate funerals of these children where their mothers try to regain "relationships" with their children's caretakers while ignoring their dead children, or "play" to the sympathy of the attendees through elaborate rituals, to see the aptness of this framework. Despite outward appearances to the contrary, preliminary psychological test data often point to a profound lack of remorse or depression in these mothers, even when their children die.

(Stoller, 1975, p. 4). According to her they wish not so much for their father's love, but rather for revenge against the humiliations of childhood. Her observation that the main aim of the act in the female perversion is "usually against their [own] bodies, or against objects which they see as their own creations: their babies" (p. 8), is apt for the conditions she describes. However, we feel the act in MBPS is not primarily directed against the baby—either as baby or as maternal representation. It is an act with and against the pediatrician. The clinical syndromes of child abuse, physical or psychological, are very different from the dynamics of MBPS.

As in the perversions, narcissism, and psychopathy, the harm that the mothers do to their infants, at times ghastly and even fatal, takes place as if it were not of their doing. This altered state is different from transient psychosis.[11] Rather, it is the very fabric from which their personalities are woven. The personality of these mothers is built by means of imitations and simulations rather than on the more typical identifications that lead to stable character formation in normal development. Glasser (1986), in a paper on identification in the perversions, calls this a process of pseudoidentification.

One is reminded here of Greenacre's (1958, cited in Meloy, 1988, p. 138) imposturing patients who exhibit "an intense and circumscribed disturbance in the sense of identity; an infarction in the sense of reality characterized by a sharp and quick perceptiveness, yet a failure to protect against detection; a strong sense of exhibitionism . . . and a compulsive urgency to perpetuate fraud!"

THE INFANT AS FETISH

The infant, we believe, is dehumanized by the mother and serves as a fetishistic object, which permits her to regulate her disastrously ambivalent relationship with the physician.[12] The fetish, like those so often found in male sexual perversions, be it an object (such as a piece of clothing or a talisman) or a fantasy, enhances feelings of powerfulness and wards off fear. In a perverse relationship involving a fetish fantasy can be maintained "alongside reality with equal conviction" (Renik, 1993). It produces "perpetual avoidance of clear thinking so that the distinction between reality and fantasy is blurred. . . . At times one holds sway, and at times the other, with equal power" (Renik, 1993). Objects used as fetishes may be anthropomorphized and given human powers, not unlike the transitional objects of infancy (Winnicott, 1953; Meloy, 1988; Greenacre, 1969). However, in the case of MBPS, the infant is first *de*humanized and then an-

---

[11]See Meloy (1988) for a useful distinction between perceptual and conceptual object relations in narcissistic psychopathology. These patients can distinguish the former because there is adequate reality testing, but the latter is a fusion of self-representations and object representations as *only* an *extension* of the self.

[12]While some mothers are aware of hateful and jealous feelings toward their children, most are not. Years later they would agree that the degree of unnecessary suffering they put their infants through (they could have simply fabricated symptoms rather than harming their child), probably indicated a greater degree of hostility than they themselves had believed (Meadow, 1990b).

thropomorphized, that is, turned into a fetishlike object to sustain the relationship the mother compulsively seeks with the child's doctor. The evidence provided in the covert video recordings made by Samuels, McClaughlin, Jacobson, Poets, and Southall (1992) where the mothers rarely played with their children when alone in a room with them, in marked contrast to their behavior in front of others, supports this contention. Not only does the infant serve to keep the relationship alive by holding the physician's interest, but "it" also serves to keep the mother's fear of and rage at the powerful/accepting doctor under cover, in ways that could not occur if the mother herself was being cut into and mutilated.

THE ROLE OF THE MOTHER'S OWN FATHER

We have been impressed with how often a longed-for but absent father appears in our clinical data. In Chapter 6 we will examine the social roots of absent fathers and the commonalities of women's experience in general in our society. Edith pined after her father for years after he left the family. Despite his near-total disregard, she continued to have a fantasy that he would one day recognize and care for her. Another mother who subjected her son to several un-necessary operations denied in therapy having felt a lack of nurturance from her own mother. She described her father, however, in quite different terms, as a disciplinarian who set high standards. In treatment, she remembered working very hard to please him as a child and had memories of how her brothers got away with things she could not. As the therapy progressed, her resentment toward him and the brothers became more obvious, as did her envy about the closeness they shared.

Further exploration revealed her painful sense of being left out because of being female. She told her therapist that she pushed hard to conjure up positive images of her relationship with her father to neutralize the negative feelings and the pain associated with them. There was an escalation of her illness-inducing behavior toward her children (involving hospitalizations) when her husband became jealous of the attention she paid to the children, and began to withdraw from her.

For these mothers, childhood relationships with doctors, whether in fantasy or in reality, may have included the idea that the parents would certainly be sympathetic to an ill child, or may have represented the first time they have ever felt listened to. Perhaps these relationships helped to deny rage felt at their abandoning parents. Later, a nurturant or paternalistic pediatrician provides an intensely tempting but ambivalently regarded ideal parental substitute choice. He offers a second chance at "ideal love." One mother told us of a growing infatuation with her child's pediatrician, but could not explain the intensity of her wish to be near him. When he took his first vacation, she began subjecting her son to infection by injecting his intravenous lines with pathogens.

For Benjamin (1990) in her discussion of normal female development, the father assumes for the child the crucial role of standing for freedom, separation, and desire, not the supplier of need, but the other who *gives recognition*. In Benjamin's view (p. 465), "it appears that what is crucial to masculinity is not the phallus *or* the father, but the internal relationship towards the mother that cancels the primary identification with her (as her helpless baby). . . . Separateness appears to be the essence of male identity." According to Benjamin, the little girl is more vulnerable in her development because her transition is more difficult because she has a more intense narcissistic attachment to the mother. Benjamin goes on to say, "too often little girls cannot or may not use their connection with the father, in both its defensive and its constructive aspects, to deny helplessness and to forge a genuine sense of separate self-hood" (p. 465). Benjamin sees females as drawn into relationships of submission because they seek a second chance for "ideal love." Such a relationship gives a female "a chance to reconstitute father–daughter identification in which their own desire and subjectivity can finally be recognized. Even in those relationships that involve annihilation of the self, one can often discern the fantasy of resolving the conflict between activity and passivity." (p. 465).

Overly submissive women, women prone to develop perversions, turn to a defense against *real human qualities* in order to protect themselves against the vulnerability of loving. They marry cold and/or distant men (a consistent finding in most MBPS cases) who are often actually absent or play little role in their lives. The birth of a child and the ensuing relationship with a caring doctor rekindles a hope for a second chance. Their early relationships with their uninterested mothers and unavailable fathers, however, leave these little girls, Munchausen's syndrome and Munchausen by Proxy syndrome mothers-to-be, forever hungry and doomed to pursue at a distance a bizarrely controlling relationship with a powerful physician. If the physician becomes suspicious and abandonment is threatened, no risk to the infant or even the risk of being caught is too great in order to try to keep control. (One mother twice tried to suffocate her baby even though she knew she was being watched on a video monitor.) As Stoller (1975, p. 115) has pointed out, "The risk that one will again fully experience the early childhood trauma is the primary one that energizes perversion formation, and for some people that is more awful than risking one's life or being arrested."[13]

The moments of greatest medical threat to the infant are the moments when the mother feels most powerful. Indeed, this truth may explain her excited behavior. If the infant dies, there is no immediate panic, as when a child loses his transitional object, because the doctors and staff continue to be attentive, perhaps more so. But frequently the charade, with the infant always close by, goes on for months or years (one case was not discovered for 20 years! [Rosenberg, 1987]), sometimes in a waxing and waning course as in the perversions, with the infant's death usually an *unintended* result. Should that happen, there may be a hiatus until the next child is born, but if there are other children at home to manipulate, they may soon be involved. For example, in one case from 1972 reported prior to the syndrome being named, it was only after the death of the seventh child that the mother's actions were uncovered! (DeMaio & Bernstein, 1974). Another mother was not suspected of killing her children, which she allegedly started to do in 1972, until the last of seven died some 13 years later (Egginton, 1990).

CONCLUSION

It is not unusual in the history of psychiatry for a common disorder to go underdetected or unnoticed for decades. This is true of the spec-

---

[13]For example, the exhibitionist is attempting at all costs to avoid present humiliation (that recalls past humiliation). Any hint of inadequacy in his current life can lead to his going out and displaying his penis—and it must be to someone who will be shocked and upset. This is necessary as a symbol of his "powerfulness" but it is often not enough. Exhibitionists do not try to get away too eagerly and have the highest rate of arrest found in of any of the perversions. To be arrested is to be *recognized*. "They aspire, not to safety from the police, but to safety from the inner dread of being an inadequate man" (Stoller, 1975, p. 115).

Another glaring example of this occurred in the case of a mother whose child was removed due to serious concerns about MBPS. Unknown to the psychological consultants, the mother was granted supervised visits with the child. On one such visit, the aide turned away for the briefest of moments, and when she looked back the mother was cradling the child, who had suddenly gone to sleep in her arms. It was not until the youngster did not wake for several hours that the *new* caretaker became alarmed and took her to the hospital. (It was too late to test for toxins.)

trum of dissociative disorders (Putnam, 1991), the more organic forms of obsessive-compulsive disorder (Rappoport, 1989), child sexual and physical abuse (Herman, 1981), and children's psychological susceptibility to trauma (Pynoos & Eth, 1985; Benedek, 1985; Terr, 1990). The "discovery" of such disorders often teaches us much about clinical theory and practice, our own psychological functioning, and the societies in which we live. Happening upon such a group of "nonpatients" and beginning to piece together a pathology not examined before is akin to the anthropological "discoveries" of hitherto undocumented aboriginal societies, which may tell us as much about the anthropologists themselves as the natives. (See Rosaldo, 1990). Law enforcement groups, social agencies, and judges, for example, have had difficulty believing physicians, no matter how convincingly they report their findings in such cases.

MBPS must be seen as an aspect of a complex historical era during which an intense contest over the definition of "motherhood" has been waged. Another of our society's most powerful symbols, that of the father/healer, which has itself been subjected to a definitional battle, has provided the complementary ingredient necessary for the establishment and maintenance of this extraordinary disorder. We will argue in the next chapter that this particular syndrome is more common in women *not simply* because women mother, but because of the social and familial relationships extant in our culture, in particular the way in which young girls are generally reared. The appropriately strong outcry that has been heard against "mother blaming" in the psychological literature is only beginning to erode the tendency to place responsibility for all of the ills that befall a child at his or her mother's feet. Our reading of the reactions stirred up by these MBPS cases has, on the other hand, uncovered an intense longing for the kind of stay-at-home "nonworking" mothers who have not been a reality in this country for a very long time (Stacey, 1990). This vision along with essentialist thinking about motherhood has produced in some an inability to "see" mothers who directly harm their children. Such thinking, we feel, actually reinforces our biased childrearing practices which leave susceptible little girls no choice but to develop two-dimensionally, for example, as very thin anorexics[14] who are "models" of good little girls, slavishly submissive women, or in MBPS cases, mothers who are caricatures of

---

[14]Interestingly, Samuels, McClaughlin, Jacobson, Poets, and Southall (1992) reported for the first time a high degree of eating disorders in the 12 mothers found to be suffocating their infants.

mothers. That *we* have so much difficulty seeing these mothers as charades says as much about our wishes and needs as it does about the women themselves. The problem cannot be overstated. "Not seeing" or resistance in sociocultural contexts is no less necessary (and likely as valuable) to explore than it is in individual psychotherapy. Perhaps the groundbreaking work that led to the recognition of the extent of child sexual abuse, incest, and the long-term effects of trauma on the psyches of children (often females) will also translate into more openness that will allow us to better "see" these MBPS mothers as women with grave needs, who use their infants in an almost totally parasitic way. These are complicated and painful issues. But our willingness to grapple with them may provide us with knowledge not only of this particular syndrome, but may add to recent work underway attempting to understand the prerequisites of normal female development.

CHAPTER 6

Why Women? Why Medicine?

In the previous chapter we proposed that MBPS involves the mother's need to maintain an intense, if perverse, relationship with the powerful authority figure of her child's physician. We also postulated a relationship between this need and the experience of traumatic loss or more subtle forms of abandonment in the mother's earlier life. However, it is clear that MBPS is a complex and multidetermined problem. A dynamic, individual conceptualization of the disorder does not explain both the striking fact that 95% of the parents who engage in this form of abuse are women, and why the pediatric health care system is the chosen arena for this deception.

The very act of seeking relationships with physicians by means of a pattern of behavior that endangers one's child suggests a desperate need for recognition and a problematic relationship to the act of caretaking. This is where our inquiry into gender issues will begin. A focus on the *context* in which women grow up and care for their families will help us to understand why it happens that some women come to feel desperately hungry for recognition yet unable to directly obtain it. We will examine the ways in which mothers, in particular, are socialized by our familial gender arrangements and expectations to put their own needs secondary to the caretaking of others. MBPS can be seen as an extreme distortion of this highly valued caretaking role for women, but one that exacts a high personal cost. We will look at the sometimes unreasonable expectations we as a society impose on mothers of chronically ill children and the ways in which

MBPS is a predictable outcome, for certain vulnerable women, of a health care system that is dependent to a large degree on the skills and sacrifices of a class of devoted caregivers.

The role of fathers is another important component of the social context of these families. Therefore we will explore the impact of paternal neglect both on the developing daughter and on the over-functioning wife, to understand the father's contribution to a family system that can generate this degree of neediness and endangerment. Our examination of the medical establishment will highlight the ways in which women have played an essential collaborative role in the health fields yet have been granted little status by medical caregivers. Ironically, the unusual and damaging role that some women eventually embrace for themselves by means of medical fabrication offers them an opportunity to obtain "power" over physicians and gain entry into an exciting social world without threat to their "perfect mother" status. The complex and sometimes conflictual relationship of mothers, caregiving, and medicine creates some impossible binds that can eventually lead a susceptible woman to a tragic perversion, or caricature, of the "devoted mother" role vis-à-vis the physician, even at the expense of her child.

WOMEN AND CAREGIVING

The role of "devoted caretaker" may paradoxically offer some women one of the few avenues they can find to try to meet some of their own pressing needs while remaining socially acceptable in the eyes of others. The seeds of this tragically limited behavioral repertoire are sown early in their lives, in familial arrangements and societal expectations based on gender. Differences between men and women in their relationships to others and to their own individual needs begin developing very early in life.

Our society's primary caregiver for children from birth onwards is almost always a woman, who plays the most important, intimate, and influential role in their early lives. As the infant gradually matures into early childhood and beyond, he or she gradually moves from a state of total dependence on this powerful object to a position of increased separateness, with the emergence of his or her own desires, feelings, and strivings. Because the young girl shares the same gender as her mother, her earliest experience of the relationship with her mother is that of intense closeness, connectedness, and identification, emotional experiences that facilitate the development of many positive "feminine" qualities. As Bograd (1990, p. 75) notes, "The female self develops and is validated through reciprocal processes of understanding and empathy, in which mutual connectedness and empowering the other lead to further articulation of the self. Within this context, women develop complex interpersonal skills, such as highly developed cognitive and emotional capacities that facilitate their sensitivity to the emotional nuances and needs of others."

Feminist writers have addressed the fact that this intense experience of connectedness has many positive aspects, and that developing girls are likely to experience a different process from boys of separating emotionally from their mothers. There is some disagreement about the relative importance to the growing child of establishing a separate identity in order to achieve "psychologically healthy" functioning and the degree to which this notion is rooted in a male-biased model of psychological health. But the development of a sense of self is clearly a developmental task facing all children, as is the ability to identify and assert one's needs. Many young women grow up better equipped to empathize with and care for others than to articulate their own individual needs. This expectation is strongly reinforced on a societal level as they mature.

Most young women become mothers when they reach adulthood. For many, pregnancy is not a matter of choice, for a variety of reasons including familial and societal pressure for maternity, limited access to contraception, and restrictions on abortion rights.[1] But the maternal role is one with which they have identified through their own mothers and have been socialized to assume since childhood. It provides a powerful avenue for a sense of identity and social acceptance. But while nurturing a baby has many rewarding aspects, it does little to address many women's continuing needs for a sense of self-esteem and a sense of recognition and power as an autonomous person. This is especially so these days, when motherhood is no longer viewed as the ultimate female role by many in our society.

---

[1]The current conservative trends in our legal and legislative systems seem to promote the interests of even the unborn fetus over those of the adult woman. There has been considerable publicity recently about the use of the legal system to enforce mothers' responsibilities to their children, such as the prosecution of pregnant women who endanger their fetuses through their own addictive behaviors. Conversely, disturbingly little legal attention has been directed to the prosecution of irresponsible fathers, such as the very high numbers of delinquent fathers who impoverish their children through failure to provide court-ordered child support.

Julie's mother

Some mothers may even come to resent the attention lavished on their babies by their families and communities. This focus on the child's needs may be particularly distressing to a mother who has experienced trauma or neglect as a young girl. When attention is lavished on the child at the expense of the child's mother and this situation is coupled with the child's enormous personal demands on the mother, we should not be surprised that many women are at times at least ambivalent about this all-consuming job and the child making these demands.

Motherhood highlights a woman's experience of finding her own needs increasingly submerged by the pressing needs of another. Her role of caregiver to others is in fact a lifelong expectation, as most women are taught early in life that their destined and most "feminine" role is that of nurturer, not only in families but also in the worlds of school and work. They are likely to find themselves accepting this role later in life, though it may be with ambivalence and with a host of their own remaining unmet needs.

While the traditional expectations of mother as primary emotional and physical caregiver to the children is well known, the psychological costs are rarely elaborated except in the literature of feminist social analysts (Braverman, 1989; Luepnitz, 1988). Statistics on the single parenthood phenomenon in the United States and the vastly unequal numbers of mothers with sole custody and inadequate child support lend further support to the vastly unequal caretaking expectations (and realities) of the mother's role in the family.

Caregiving, of course, extends across the life span and does not end for the mother when her children become more independent. The vast majority of adults who provide unpaid care for elderly relatives in their home are women.[2] Brought up from girlhood to value attachments to others, learning to please those around her and to suppress her own anger and needs for autonomy, a traditionally socialized young woman does not grow up, as a rule, feeling well equipped or indeed entitled to express her needs and to make demands for herself directly. A traditionally socialized woman with aspirations that conflict with her expected caregiving role or resentment about the unequal family demands on her energies would be hard pressed to find acceptable means to express her discontent. Not

---

[2]Caregivers frequently lose time from work, emotionally exhaust their own reserves, and assume a significant financial burden. Research on caregiver burdens has identified anxiety, depression, and feelings of guilt and resentment toward dependent family members as major issues for caregivers.

only might such a women feel immobilized to actively protest her dilemma, but she might also be quite emotionally needy for attention and caregiving herself.

Caught in such a bind, it is possible that the caregiving act itself might become distorted or perverted to meet some of a woman's own "unacceptable" needs (Leeder, 1990; Yorker, Kahan, & Jewart, 1992), for this role offers a "safe" outlet that guarantees approval and acceptance. The irony of the "perfect mother" who is later unveiled as a MBPS mom is perhaps not quite as mysterious in light of the multiple limitations imposed throughout her development on a woman's self-expression via more direct and assertive actions. This is especially so when her direct early efforts to be recognized were met with avoidance or neglect.

While many mothers do find socially sanctioned avenues for their competitive and assertive feelings, and either challenge traditional expectations or find indirect means for satisfying their needs for achievement, power, nurturance, and the like, they face obstacles on many levels. It has been suggested that women are more prone to depression, eating disorders, and other internalized, self-destructive behaviors at least partially as a result of their attempt to achieve some control in situations of psychological powerlessness (Bepko, 1989; Mirkin, 1990). And powerlessness for mothers not only derives from the submergence of personal needs inherent in caregiving, but also from the life-long realities of gender-based discrimination both inside and outside the home.

There has been a dramatic increase in the past few decades of mothers expanding their traditional homemaker role to include employment outside the home. Yet even when employed full-time, women often find themselves expected to perform an unequal share of domestic duties and household caretaking. In the workplace, discrimination continues to result in generally lower pay, lower status, and less authority for women.[3]

Not surprisingly, most of the mothers who engage in MBPS behavior are traditionally socialized women. If they do work outside the home, the majority seem to be engaged in "traditionally female" caregiving occupations such as nursing, childcare, or teaching where they continue to function in underpaid roles that have little glamour or power.

It is not just in their homes and families of origin that little girls

---

[3]While many men too work in jobs with low status and little autonomy, they can at least experience the societal privileges of being male in the other aspects of their lives.

experience a lack of recognition and learn about the invisibility of being female. When they enter the school system, young girls quickly learn the gender hierarchy in the educational world as they progress from the female-headed preschool world, up through grade school, and on to higher academic levels, "seeing fewer and fewer females in authority as we climb the educational ladder: fewer as faculty, fewer still as deans and presidents, and fewest of all in the fields of science, engineering, politics, business, foreign policy, or other specialties valued by the world at large" (Steinem, 1992, p. 116).

A recent report by the American Association of University Women and the National Education Association called *How Schools Shortchange Girls* (1992) documents a variety of ways in which our educational system discriminates against female children even in the earliest grades. This review of 20 years of research indicated that male students receive more teacher attention than girl students in the form of more instructional time, more hugs, more license to call out in class for attention, and more teacher response to their classroom participation. The report notes that boys received "more precise teacher comments than females in terms of both scholarship and conduct" (p. 69). Beginning at the preschool level teachers had a marked tendency to choose classroom activities and presentation formats in which boys excelled or which were most appealing to boys. The report also found pervasive sexual harassment or sex-biased peer interactions in the hallways and classrooms that was often treated by the administration as more of a joke than as serious misconduct.

Given these and many other overt and more subtle forms of gender bias in the education of our children (including bias in instructional materials, test development, and selection of famous figures as role models), it is little wonder that the initial academic advantage with which girls start in the earliest grades erodes within a few years' time. By junior high school, there are dramatic declines in the confidence of girls in their ability to succeed in the "male" domains of math and science and their career plans show similar alterations. Recent work by Brown and Gilligan (1992) demonstrated a very disturbing and consistent decline in young girls' confidence and self-esteem as they reach early adolescence. The *New York Times* (January 9, 1991, p. B1), reporting on a survey of 3,000 children, noted that Gilligan had "found that at the age of 9 a majority of girls were confident, assertive and felt positive about themselves. But by the time they reached high school, less than a third felt that way."

A woman with her own childhood history of being neglected

and "unseen," with an ambivalent relationship to her caretaking role but strong injunctions against acknowledging these feelings, with a physically or developmentally difficult baby and little support from an uninterested husband, might feel tempted to act out of some of her own needs for recognition, power, and nurturance even at the expense of her child. Her ability to meet some of these needs by winning admiration for her heroic efforts for her child and her attentive caretaking during crises of illness help set the stage, in a disordered few, for a dangerous and exaggerated imposturing of the caregiver role.

MOTHERS AS HEALTH CARE GIVERS

Embedded as it is in the larger society, our health care system too has been organized around the availability of mothers to serve as primary caregivers within and outside the family. In fact, the hospital, as a system, will not only appreciate a mother's attentive caregiving to her child, but is actually dependent on her active collaboration and sacrifices. Our medical system essentially *relies* on the availability of a homemaker-mother, with flexible time and a primary devotion to the needs of her child, in order to care for the significant numbers of chronically ill, developmentally delayed, and handicapped children (and adults) in our society. Our health system essentially requires the presence of at least one unemployed or otherwise "free" parent to take her child to appointments during daytime hours, learn and follow complicated medical procedures at home, monitor her child closely around the clock, and make important medical judgments.[4]

The personal difficulties associated with maintaining employment for the single, working mother of a chronically ill or disabled child are not an issue for health care administrators. Her impossible bind, of risking loss of job because of frequent childcare-related absences and thereby permanent loss of health insurance, or risking family and social disapproval for continuing to work and turning over most responsibility for the child to others, is rarely considered. The impossible time demands on mothers for extended caregiving are not a concern of those who prescribe the treatments.

---

[4]The United States was the only industrialized nation among more than 100 countries that did not, until 1993, have national parental leave policies providing job guarantees for new parents or those caring for family members with serious health problems.

MOTHERS AND CHRONIC ILLNESS

In our capacity as consultants and therapists in a large tertiary-care pediatric hospital, we have spoken with many mothers of chronically ill children who have had extensive contact with the medical world. Their observations and insights into the powerful feelings and projections generated by their relationships with physicians and health care professionals, and their awareness of the excitement and attractions of the hospital's social milieu highlight the vulnerability of mothers caring for sick children, especially when there is little family support.[5]

Several parents have talked movingly about the intense emotions stirred up in them by the demands of caring for a child with a chronic disease. Life is often an unpredictable roller coaster of relapses and remissions, interspersed with stable periods of good health. During the healthy times, daily living follows a fairly normal course. But when illness reappears, the profound disturbance of routine, coupled with deep emotional responses, takes its toll and extends beyond that crisis period. New levels of angst and emotional strain accompany the next period of stability. The lack of predictability becomes extremely stressful.

In describing their lives in the hospital world, mothers of children with chronic illnesses often use metaphors of war, battlefields, and comrades in arms to describe their struggles and relationships. They see themselves as isolated from the rest of society, which is literally true for extended periods of time. Parents have told us, with great emotion, of how infrequently other friends and family members could or would really be there for them during times of medical crisis. Extended family often appear anxious, bored, or unsure of what to say or do. The hospital environment is also isolating—with the news from the outside world blaring in on the television set but barely registering. For those mothers, time takes on a wholly different cadence. The doctor's visits or procedures become the important markers of daily life rather than family meals, shopping, or even the needs of a spouse or employer.

Many of these mothers describe, as their most intensely emotional relationships, those that develop with the various medical professionals who become such an important part of their lives. This

---

[5]Sometimes this lack of family support is genuine. But we have also found mothers, especially those of children with life-threatening illnesses, who feel directly responsible for their child's illness and resist letting other family members provide relief at the bedside when the child is hospitalized.

seems to be particularly true for single mothers or those with un-supportive partners.

Mothers have told us that issues that were too complicated and painful to discuss with family members and friends had been more easily shared with physicians and health care workers who had a common knowledge of medical concerns and an understanding of the reality of living under extreme emotional duress. A close bond can arise between parents and physicians, heavily weighted on the parent's side by the longing for such a shared understanding.

Some parents have described to us a sense of exhilaration in working side by side with physicians and medical personnel. The feeling of being seen as important and useful was unmistakable and occasionally quite explicit. One mother spoke movingly of the con-fusing feelings she would have when visits to a particularly un-derstanding and caring physician would bring bad news. Here was the person who most understood her son, and most understood what she was going through. The bad news he imparted would hit her like a ton of bricks, but then there was this other feeling—a feeling of wanting to stay and share her feelings with this physician. Not only did he care, but he had the knowledge to make everything better. She talked about how enticing it would be, during a remission, to have him sitting next to her on the park bench, watching her little boy playing in the sandbox, looking so normal.

Another mother said there was just too much time to think when all she had to do was "just be a mother." She confided having the fantasy of calling her child's doctor at the office, and sharing, just once, the small details of a normal day in her life. She didn't, of course, but she could understand how a parent's intense needs could get confused and caught up in an environment that felt so safe—not just for her son but for herself. In our hospital we have parents return to visit the nursing station or the intensive care unit, patronize the hospital cafeteria like a neighborhood restaurant, or go on to do hospital volunteer work after a child has died.

Some parents of chronically ill children described their stays in the hospital as the most interesting time in their lives, although it was often stressful and frightening as well. More than one parent told us of having a kind of excited feeling when telling friends and relatives about close calls, rescues, and the medically puzzling aspects of her child's illness. These made her unique, and increased the level of interest in her child, as demonstrated by specialist and student visits to the bedside, and hushed discussions in the hallway. In embarrassed tones one mother told us how different and exciting being a "part of the team" was, compared to the humdrum life she led, outside the hospital, in her suburban community. Again, we remind the readers that these are parents who are not in any way causing illness in their children but are simply struggling with normally demanding lives and the intense emotions aroused by their child's serious problems.

Several parents have talked about the social milieu of the hospital after the day shift goes home. Some described the grouping of "regulars" in the cafeteria or the parent lounge as a second family. Others talked about a kind of sharing across racial and social class lines that rarely happened for them outside the hospital. The child's illness was the great leveler. The severity and prognosis of each child's illness—the number of relapses, the number of surgeries—defined the new hierarchy. And watching others deal with illness and death allowed some mothers to play different roles. Some even talked of practicing responses in front of mirrors or to themselves after the last television went off and the hall lights were dimmed.

One mother talked of the mixed emotions she had when her child was discharged: happy to be finally able to go home, her child having survived another crisis, yet fearful of the lack of medical support, of being the only responsible person. There was also a kind of empty feeling, of missing the people she had gotten to know so "intimately, on the surface." There was a kind of sadness about having to return to a life in many ways more bland than life in the hospital.

And though these mothers did not subject their children to medical abuse and were clearly devoted parents, they probably shared many of the feelings we have described in mothers who do have MBPS. It is a telling fact that the medical behavior of a MBPS mother does not appear to be dramatically different from that of the "good mother" of a chronically ill child until late in the game when the "impostor mother" is finally unmasked. Both mothers make personal sacrifices of time and energy necessary to meet the ill child's needs. They are sensitive and hypervigilant to any indications of illness or relapse. They manage medication, suctioning, gastrostomy feedings, catheterization, apnea monitoring, restrictive diets, or whatever other home treatments are deemed necessary to the survival of the child. Their "enmeshment" with the child, and adept sensitivity to changes in child's color, breathing, and state of consciousness, are taken for granted by the medical caregivers and are critical to the child's survival. Multiple visits to specialists, extended overnight hospital stays, and active collaboration with medical personnel are commonplace.

In the normal course of the sick child's medical treatment the mother's sacrifices are expected and her personal needs become secondary. Her major satisfaction in her devoted caretaking of her chronically ill child, beyond the maintenance of the child's well-being, is that of being a "very good mother." But if she has little family support, her caregiving job can make her feel isolated from and unappreciated by the outside world. It is natural, then, that her intense collaborative relationships with medical staff and her sense of community with fellow "hospital mothers" would become important social reinforcements for her otherwise demanding and draining role. It is understandable that many mothers who at some time experience such a caretaking alliance with our medical system would find social stimulation and a sense of importance in this exciting world, as these mothers so movingly described. And it is really not so surprising that some small percentage of these mothers, with unsatisfying relationships at home, find the hospital world attractive enough to fabricate convincing medical reasons to remain in this exciting and nurturant place.

THE ABSENT FATHER

If MBPS was simply an unusual variant of a personality disorder without a gender dimension, then one would expect to see a significant number of men engaged in this type of relationship with physicians. Yet the gender-based statistics are staggering. Rosenberg's (1987) review reported a 100% rate of MBPS by mothers. Our more recent review identified only 11 cases of MBPS in fathers out of hundreds of reported cases. And several of these father perpetrators did not appear to fit the typical dynamics of the MBPS mother (see Chapter 1). Some appeared psychotic in their rather bizarre behaviors or reports of symptoms. Others seemed mainly to be motivated by the desire to develop "evidence" against their ex-wives in custody battles rather than seeking relationships with medical staff. At the least, none of the fathers described as engaged in MBPS behavior fit the model of the prototypical "perfect caretaker" attempting to win attention and admiration for their medical knowledge and cooperation.

The strong imbalance of caregiving demands on mothers is intimately tied to the lack of such societal expectations for many fathers. Goldner's (1985) analysis of trends in the social construction of gender roles in the family identified historical developments in the fathering role that have contributed to his often disengaged role. His assigned sphere of work in the world outside of home and family distanced him increasingly from the emotional life of mother and children as work became more industrialized over time and more external to home. While the "detached" or "absent" father is not nearly as roundly blamed for psychopathology in the mental health literature as the "enmeshed" mother, he too represents a predictable outcome of rigidified and restrictive gender roles. While many men do manage to fulfill their gender-determined roles of breadwinner and competitor in the world outside the home while remaining emotionally involved in the life of the family, many others drift toward detachment if not to total disengagement. The traditional American conception of the "protective father" is in many families highly incongruent with the reality of a father who is uninvolved in the life of his family, the emotional needs of his spouse, and the feelings and needs of his children.

The myth of the "protective father" in our culture is also belied by the significant degree of physical and sexual abuse to which many women and children are subjected (Schechter, 1982). The statistics are staggering and the consequences are devastating. Beliefs about male dominance and privilege fuel such abuse and have allowed abusive behavior to continue for so long that violence in the home is a fact of life for many women and their children. The real or implied threat to their health and safety if they should choose to step out of role or challenge a husband's or father's dominance adds to the sense of powerlessness for many mothers and daughters. And emotional neglect too can create chronic feelings of powerlessness.

Although in general, in our society, there seems to be significantly less primacy and value placed on the fathering role compared with the mothering role, ironically there is some general recognition of young boys' needs for the "other" (male) parent.[6] Yet despite at least an equal, if not greater, need for a girl's connection with the "other" parent, much less social concern is focused on fostering father–daughter relationships. Furthermore, it is not just fatherless girls who are missing out on this different kind of relationship. Research indicates that even in two-parent families young girls often experience a different quality of attention from their fathers than do their brothers (Maccoby & Jacklin, 1974). Fathers' relationships with their daughters from infancy often encourage more dependency.

---

[6]Several institutions and organizations are designed to foster this separate kind of relationship identification: Little League, Big Brothers, mentor programs for minority boys, among many others.

Maccoby and Jacklin (p. 362) report that boys are "handled and played with somewhat more roughly and receive more physical punishment. In several studies, boys were found to receive both more praise and more criticism from their caretakers." In addition, they found that fathers in general seemed to stress their daughters' conformity to traditional gender roles. Given that girls' traditional role is to be more passive and nurturant, and that boys seem to receive more active and more overt feedback, daughters may well experience their fathers as less interested and less attentive.

As girls reach adolescence, they often experience renewed interest in closeness with their fathers, even as developmental separation issues take on renewed significance. Yet they may continue to encounter less-than-satisfying relationships. According to McGoldrick's (1989) analysis,

> Commonly, the father–daughter relationship may be problematic in adolescence. Fathers often become awkward about relating to their daughters as they approach adolescence, fearing their budding sexuality. Given the frequently limited masculine repertoire for handling closeness, they may sexualize the relationship or they may withdraw, even becoming irritated or angry as a way of maintaining the distance they feel is necessary. They may need encouragement to engage actively with their daughters rather than avoid them. They may interact more easily with sons, where shared activities such as sports allow companionship without too many pressures for intimate relating. The unavailability of fathers for their daughters may lead daughters to develop an image of the male as a romantic stranger, an unrealistic image that cannot be met. (p. 216)

While the fact of emotional neglect and physical absence by some fathers is well known, other deviations in father–daughter relationships may be due to more active forms of paternal psychopathology. The flip side of the "mother-blaming" tendency in our mental health literature is the relative neglect of theory and research on paternal psychopathology and its contribution to child maladjustment. Phares (1992) explores the relative scarcity of research on fathers' influences on children's mental health problems. She concludes that unquestioned and often sexist theories and research assumptions based on outdated societal norms often result in the exclusion of fathers from this research:

> These assumptions cover a variety of areas, including assumptions that fathers do not have any role in child care, that fathers do not spend

significant amounts of time with their children, and that fathers are unimportant in child maladjustment. These outdated assumptions have influenced clinical child research designs and may have led, either intentionally or unintentionally, to the use of research as a way of maintaining the status quo. Bernard (1981) noted that fathers have been granted a dispensation against family participation. Her assessment of parenting research literature leads to the conclusion that anything a father gives to his children (e.g., nurturing, emotional involvement) is above and beyond the requirements of his role and therefore can only be investigated in a positive light. . . . Conversely, mothers are expected to devote most or all of their time to their children and therefore are seen as the only culpable party when a child develops psychological problems. (p. 660)

It is noteworthy that the fathers of the child victims of MBPS tend to mirror the fathers of the MBPS mothers; that is, they tend to be either physically or emotionally unavailable. While it is easy to focus on the culpability of the "overinvolved" MBPS mother who is running to the doctor repeatedly with fabricated symptoms, what do we make of her husband, living in the same house, who never visits the hospital, never makes his own observations, and takes little or no interest in the increasingly severe illnesses of his child? It is no accident that just as MBPS mothers are caricatures of "perfect mothers," so too their unseeing partners are extreme caricatures of "disengaged fathers." A family systemic view of the development of this perplexing syndrome would certainly point to the recurring issue of male abandonment. This can be seen in both the father's failure to fulfill his spousal and child caretaking role and in a longer historical view of the MBPS mother's own experience of paternal absence or neglect.

WOMEN AND THE MEDICAL ESTABLISHMENT

It is no mere coincidence that the medical world is the chosen arena in which these fascinating cases unfold. Women have had a long and ambivalent relationship to organized medicine, often serving an essential but subservient role in this male-dominated world. While intimately involved throughout history in the caretaking and healing of others, women have enjoyed little independent status or recognition for their skills. Their relationship with the medical establishment has often involved both a close, collaborative relationship and a struggle for control, elements reenacted in complex and damaging ways in every MBPS case.

Ehrenreich and English (1978b) document the long and gradual struggle in the early days of life in America between the female lay healers and the developing male establishment of organized "professional medicine" which over the course of several decades slowly wrested control of the healing profession:

> The female healer in North America was defeated in a struggle which was, at bottom, economic. . . . Healing was female when it was a neighborly service, based in stable communities, where skills could be passed on for generations and where the healer knew her patients and their families. When the attempt to heal is detached from personal relationships to become a commodity and a source of wealth in itself— then does the business of healing become a male enterprise. . . . The chief opponents of the female healer, the men who were drawn, from the late 1700's on, by the possibility of medicine as a lucrative career, were hardly "professionals" in the genteel, European sense, but they were no less exclusive. (p. 41)

At the same time these male physicians began to succeed in passing legislation restricting the practice of medicine to gentlemen educated by increasingly exclusive schools and licensed by their own closed professional societies. Only very small numbers of women by the turn of the century had managed to gain entry to the new "regular" medical schools, but they were faced with an enormous degree of discrimination and harassment, including highly restrictive entry, charges of being "unfeminine freaks," denial of internships, inability to gain positions in hospitals, and exclusion from professional medical societies. While in the latter part of this century the percentage of women in medicine has grown significantly, there are even now significant obstacles to full equality for women in the healing professions due to continuing discrimination and sexual harassment.

Doctoring remains, by and large, a male-dominated profession in which a healthy dose of paternalism characterizes the doctor's attitude toward the passive patient. Physicians are members of a highly respected, well-paid elite whose expert opinions are sought out and valued, even in areas beyond their immediate training and expertise. Pediatricians, for example, are the experts to whom mothers are expected to turn for all manner of advice about everything from temper tantrums and emotional development to routine fevers, colds, and nosebleeds, to serious developmental problems and life-threatening illnesses. Despite the need for a working partnership between pediatrician and parent in the healthy development and caretaking of the individual child, there is an enormous discrepancy between the prestige, power, and remuneration enjoyed by the professional baby doctor compared with that of the experienced mother-homemaker (Ehrenreich & English, 1978b).

Men eventually managed to take over the highest echelons of professional healing. Women did find an avenue as nurses, albeit in a subservient role, beginning in the 1870s. It is interesting to note that male physicians initially resisted the inclusion of women even in a secondary caregiving role as assistants to physicians and were quite resistant to the development of nursing schools and the employment of nurses in hospitals. In the early 1900s there arose a movement of women working as visiting nurses in the slums which became the backbone of the public health movement and allowed nurses some degree of autonomy, without direct physician supervision. But by the 1930s nurses had become well integrated into the "mainstream" health care system in a less autonomous role, and were providing a cheap, dependable labor supply for hospitals.

Women also serve in many other roles inside hospitals and health centers. As Imber-Black (1989) notes,

> In the health care system today, women are 70% of the workforce, while men remain the overwhelming majority of the leaders. Despite all of the changes in opportunities for women, in 1985, only 15% of the all physicians were women. . . . Women remain the overwhelming majority in the lowest paying and least protected positions in the health care hierarchy. For instance, poor women constitute nearly 100% of home health aides, receiving minimum wage and no benefits in one of the most difficult health care jobs. . . . Thus while many advances in women's issues as both workers and consumers have been made in the health care system, it remains a larger system whose historical context is rooted in sexist assumptions and whose present values reflect the classist and sexist divisions of the wider culture. (p. 339)

The historical roots of womens' complex and unsatisfying relationship to the medical establishment are not foremost in their minds when most mothers interact with health care personnel. Yet the power, authority, and charisma attributed to the physician as well as the complex feelings of competition or resentment a mother may feel toward medical professionals are inextricably linked to the gender politics and history of women in the medical world.

Further complicating the picture is the irony that for many women the caregiving of her individual physician may be the most nurturance she has experienced since childhood. Certainly, there are many kind, sensitive, and caring physicians. For a woman with early life experiences of loss or of neglect by those with power, now feeling burdened by her own caregiving obligations toward her own family and perhaps lacking the support of a spouse, who is either emotionally or physically absent, the kind interest of her physician will carry great importance. Further, the power of his or her medical interventions in contrast to her own feelings of powerlessness is likely to have enormous appeal. While the intensive contact with her obstetrician is time-limited, the mother's contact with her pediatrician may span the course of many years. If she has other children, she may very well have had several years of extended contact with this pediatrician, especially if the children required frequent visits. The physician appears to be interested in her, and is well-educated, caring, and important. Unlike most of the mother's other relationships with professionals and even with other physicians, this physician treats her perhaps less as the passive patient and more as an active and interested collaborator in the care of her child. Even though the mother's own caregiving activities at home are routinely invisible and taken for granted, the physician is one person who notices her good care and appreciates her for it, particularly when her child is most ill. Furthermore, by virtue of the social prestige afforded to medical caregiving, a mother can at least bask in the glow of reflected glory when her pediatrician, with her help, succeeds in healing her child. If the child happens to be born with some special medical problems (for example, prematurity, orthopedic problems, digestive problems), mother's contact with the pediatrician and with the extended community of hospital staff, specialists, and allied health professionals will be frequent. She and her child are drawn into this interesting and highly respected world of new people, new procedures, new ideas, and considerable attention to her child and her caregiving.

If this mother has reason to feel neglected and hungers for this appreciation, she may gradually find herself taking steps to remain in this exciting world, even at the expense of her child and/or the "truth." Through manipulating her child's health status and deceiving physicians, she can simultaneously experience the camaraderie and admiration of the health care staff as well as a sense of control that she finds otherwise unavailable to her in this important professional arena. Each new procedure or lab test ordered and each new medical setback suffered by her child further cements her position as a valued team member in a puzzling medical drama that might otherwise be closed to her. She can remain the "good mother" and share in the excitement and prestige of the medical world while exercising secret power over the physicians. The only cost—and it is, of course, a huge one—is the health and well-being of her child.

We, health care providers and family members, are at first disbelieving and later appalled by the revelation of medical abuse by seemingly devoted and loving mothers. Yet we must stop and think about the many little girls who grow up feeling invisible and powerless, and the modern-day institution of mothering which for many can be isolated and unglamorous, with relentless caregiving demands. We must imagine these seriously wounded mothers in the context of an exciting, respected, and patriarchal health care system that has restricted women's roles yet relies on and welcomes the self-sacrifice of the chronically ill child's mother. Is it, after all, such a mystery that a needy mother with a particular set of vulnerabilities and a certain character structure could "do such a thing" to her child? Perhaps the most disturbing aspect of our examination of the context of mothers, caregiving, and medicine is the likelihood that unless there is a radical change in many of our basic institutions and social expectations, we can do little to prevent countless future cases of this disorder, even with improved diagnosis and understanding.

"So Help Me Doctor . . .": The Physician and the Impostor

In mid-1981, in a San Antonio public hospital, patients in the pediatric intensive care unit began experiencing inexplicable emergencies. Babies were suddenly dying. There was one common thread: all the incidents were occurring on the 3–11 P.M. shift—while nurse Genene Jones was on duty. As the crisis escalated, the hospital conducted an internal investigation and confronted the horrible prospect that "one of its nurses" was taking lives. Unable to admit that even to themselves, and fearful of bad publicity and lawsuits, the hospital officials said nothing to the police or the district attorney about their suspicions of nurse Jones; they chose, instead, to remove Jones by "upgrading" the ICU staff.

Genene Jones was then hired by Dr. H., who had just opened a private office and who was a resident at the same hospital while this was going on and had knowledge of it.

If one simply counted patients, [their new] clinic's first week was slow (no more than two children a day). Two respiratory arrests in a single week! *(p. 133). [The ensuing weeks were worse—a child had a respiratory arrest while in nurse Jones' lap, receiving a "vaccination." This child was to die en route to a hospital with nurse Jones caring for her in the ambulance.]*

Jones told [the doctor], "You're the town's new pediatrician, a specialist. Why should anyone be surprised that we're seeing a lot of sick kids?" (p. 151)

For weeks, [Dr. H] had not merely failed to suspect, it seemed as though she had refused to suspect. (pp. 164–65)

—Elkind (1989) (See Appendix B for more details.)

The interplay between the physician and the Munchausen by Proxy mother is critical to understanding the dynamics of this syndrome. What aspects of the relationship prevent doctors from "discovering" what is going on? Is it a problem we all share in detecting lying, especially when the source is someone we have no reason to mistrust? Our experience leads us to believe that physicians' inability to detect MBPS goes well beyond the inherent difficulties we all have in detecting lying. This chapter will focus on the complexities of the dynamic that exists between an MBPS mother and her child's doctor.

In the case of Danny H. (discussed in Chapter 2), the doctor was a hospital-based pediatrician who soon realized that he had been involved with Elizabeth, Danny's mother, years before when another child, 20 months old at that time, had died of a suspiciously intractable and undiagnosed diarrheal disease. The physician was disturbed by this realization because Elizabeth was now presenting her older child who she said suffered from severe asthma, and who exhibited deforming and debilitating side effects from the medication he was taking for the disorder. The child's vertebrae were collapsing from long-term use of steroids (which diminishes bone calcium), he was not growing, and he was deformed. The rest of his body was alternately saturated with a dozen other mostly unnecessary medications, or contained subtherapeutic levels of needed medicine. He fought tirelessly for the hospitalization of this child to protect him from his mother, and later presented teaching rounds on MBPS at several institutions in order to raise the level of consciousness in the medical community to ensure more rapid recognition of the Munchausen by Proxy disorder. Yet 6 months after he exposed Elizabeth's MBPS, he missed the diagnosis in another highly suspicious case in his care. Moreover, another consultant who had seen many cases of MBPS also failed to diagnose the syndrome.

This second patient was an infant hospitalized for months because her symptoms could not be alleviated. Though clinically impossible amounts of fluid were pouring from her nasogastric drainage tube into a collection bottle, the physician, while suspicious, did not make the MBPS diagnosis.

It could easily be argued that this severe degree of "not seeing" is exceptional, and therefore tells us little about doctors and MBPS. We would argue otherwise. Often it is just such extreme cases that provide the clues we need to understand a particular problem's dynamic pathology. Indeed, "missed clues" to the diagnosis of MBPS far from being unusual, are the hallmark of this disorder. Careful scrutiny of how these cases actually unfold offers an opportunity for deeper understanding not only of the syndrome, but of ourselves.

It is to the world of the impostor that we must turn for this understanding. Impostors are not content to play out their mendacious roles in private: they must have an audience. For MBPS mothers, the required audience is a very particular one, a physician (and to a lesser degree the hospital staff and the public at large if they too can be manipulated). In this chapter we will try to explain why physicians may be especially vulnerable to the workings of the impostor.

One of us (H.A.S.) was faced with a case of a child from another city, hospitalized and surgically treated at our own institution, who was finally suspected of being a MBPS victim after more than two years of treatment. This child's symptoms disappeared during a "test" situation that separated her from her mother during a stay at our hospital. Though the test raised the suspicions of the doctors, they did not have enough evidence to convince a court in the child's locality of parental maltreatment. Months following the hospitalization, however, the mother admitted to injecting her child with feces on several occasions, thereby bringing her close to death, to gain her admittance to a local hospital. She admitted to this action, but she vehemently denied having caused her chronic vomiting problems during the whole previous year.[1] Despite being armed with the whole medical history, during an interview prior to a court hearing the author was drawn into her story and began believing that she had only injected substances into her child to get help for her family because they were experiencing serious marital difficulties.

A visit to this woman's home after her daughter was removed from her care revealed that her living room was decorated with pictures of her child taken years before, when she had tubes in many orifices of her body. She still carried around the child's Broviac catheter, which was found to be unnecessary after her removal from her care. Yet by the time the author's hour and a half interview was up, he found himself beset with doubts and had to talk to two colleagues to refocus on the clear-cut evidence of abuse in the case. He was then able to see that he had been lied to and subtly maneuvered into believing that this woman was devoted to her child and desperately wanted the girl back.

Like doctors, we psychotherapists are sometimes miserably bad

---

[1]This kind of partial admission is quite common (Meadow, 1990b).

at recognizing lies. Furthermore, because we have emphasized to our pediatric trainees and child therapy students the importance of not leaping to the conclusion that all children's problems are caused by their parents, we caution ourselves to maintain an *extra* degree of objectivity. In addition, we have the natural response and desire to believe the story of any parent who is dealing with the difficulties of a child's illness, and who risks losing that child if we disbelieve her.

Interestingly, sometimes the MBPS mother's lying is carefully constructed, but at times it is trivial and makes no sense at all, and therefore should be easily recognized as lying. For example, we saw a mother who was suspected of murdering three children. In an interview with us in the presence of police detectives known by the mother to be well versed in all the details of her case, she told several obvious falsehoods. For example, she wrongly stated the number of babies who had died in her care. One child protective services worker told us of a case of MBPS in which the mother denied her actions but was very cooperative otherwise. "When I thought back over the conversation, I would find discrepancies. . . . She would tell the law enforcement people that she was in therapy because of depression and she told me a different reason." Much like psychopaths, these MBPS mothers can be incredibly convincing, but at times their falsehoods seem almost automatic, characterized by "a sharp and quick perceptiveness [coupled] with a failure to protect against detection" (Greenacre, 1958, p. 362). If the varying ability of these mothers to lie cannot by itself explain the difficulty we have in suspecting and apprehending them, what other factors are operating?

THE "GOOD MOTHER" IMPOSTOR

In this chapter we will be looking more closely at the interpersonal world of these parents. To do so we must focus on the mechanisms whereby these perverse relationships with physicians are brought to fruition. We feel the process is best conceptualized as a very skillful imposturing or masquerading, with the individual dynamics we described in Chapter 5.

Much has been written about the dynamics of the impostor as psychotherapy patient. Greenacre (1958, p. 370) saw them as pressured to fraudulence, to make up for a "failure to develop an identity and sense of separate self." Lying plays two roles for such patients. It transforms unbearable reality and it creates a life of "castle building . . . in which the extremely egocentric individual is always the hero of [his or her] fantasy or the recipient of much deserved pity" (Hoyer, 1959, p. 207).

Fantasy is used frequently by children to deny painful reality. Reality, when transformed to reflect more closely the child's wishes, can relieve anxiety. Wangh (1962) describes a situation in which a proxy can be used to contain a child's anxiety. He describes a situation in which a frightened child evokes an image of her younger sibling needing comforting for her fears as a way of dealing with her own anxiety. Anna Freud (1936, p. 122) talked of the child's reversing of reality: "Thus [for the child] the "evil father" becomes in fantasy the protective [stuffed] animal while the helpless child becomes the master of powerful father substitutes."

For the impostor, however, fantasy by itself is inadequate to the task; it is necessary that *others be involved* in the impostor's fantasy. Thus mothers with MBPS call attention to themselves by being helpful in the hospital, by making promotional movies, or by appearing on television as objects of admiration or pity (see Eggington, 1990, and Elkind, 1989, for two startling examples). A child protective services worker described one mother thusly: "She was very cooperative as I continued to ask her questions about the case and explained some of the things that we would like to do. It was almost as though she *wanted* us to be involved. She wanted to be monitored. It seemed like the more people she could get involved with her, the happier she was." Perhaps convincing others to believe in her fantasy intensifies the value or "truth" of the lie for the MBPS mother. Further, if people can be convinced to believe that unreal things are real, then the obverse may also be true: menacing reality may be unreal. Lying is but one aspect of this complex process. Grinker (1961, p. 55), discussing his psychotherapeutic work with impostors, points to the impostor's need in therapy to be found "lovable" and yet also "unworthy as a revenge against early frustrating objects." Grinker also notes the impostor's need "to borrow some of their [doctor-psychotherapist's] attitudes" and to "*compete with him*" (our emphasis). Bursten (1973), writing about patients who use deception as a "mode of narcissistic repair," adds two more features that have relevance to the description of MBPS mothers: deceivers feel contempt for the people they deceive and exhilaration whenever their deceptions are successful. We have heard of a kind of excited gleefulness MBPS mothers sometimes exhibit at the moment their infants are in gravest danger. And lastly, as we found in our own MBPS patients, an impostor or chronic liar "when confronted by exposure will occasionally admit the true situation readily, but more often is untroubled and is only stimulated to further fabrication or *inadequate evasions*" (Hoyer, 1959, p. 207).[2] However unconcerned in appearance, the risk for the pathological liar or impostor to function in reality is "to raise the potential for increasing and overwhelming anxiety" (Deutsch, 1955, p. 491).

All of this material is reminiscent of important dynamics that occur in confrontation between MBPS mothers and physicians, social workers, court personnel, psychotherapists, and even police: the former imitate and compete with doctors, they exhibit a seemingly insatiable need to be loved and admired, they simultaneously feel contempt for those they deceive and exhilaration while playing out of the deception, and when caught or accused of performing their destructive charade on the bodies of their children they often offer weak, evasive defenses.

Little has been written about the countertransferential aspects of lying and its effects on the therapist in a psychotherapy situation. Even simple lying without all of the pressured demands for closeness found in MBPS cases creates major difficulties and can produce anger in the recipient. The problems created by lying in MBPS for the physician are exponentially greater than those found in a psychotherapy situation where the patient's resistance is anticipated from the beginning. The doctor unknowingly involved with a MBPS mother *must* rely on her veracity: her baby's life depends upon her truthfulness. But her lying is in the service of another cause: an inappropriate fantastical relationship with him. This relationship is one with which he is ill-prepared or equipped to deal, especially when it presents itself so covertly yet so powerfully. Any signs of dislike or distancing, or even not believing her story, however subtle on his part,[3] could cause the mother to up the ante of the deadly game being played out on the child's body, leading to potentially disastrous consequences. The mother often acts to make the symptoms more severe, to prove that

---

[2]Hoyer was writing about a case involving pseudologica fantastica, which, however, appears to us to be a clear-cut case of adult Munchausen syndrome. He points out, as is true here, that this is not delusional behavior and draws an interesting parallel to adolescent daydreaming, that is, living in a dream world of one's own construction. Of further interest is his reference to F. S. Inbau and J. E. Reid's *Lie Detection and Criminal Investigation*. (Baltimore: Williams and Wilkins, 1953) assertion that for the pseudolog, detection through use of the polygraph is not possible. To our knowledge, this has not been tried in MBPS.

[3]And doctors may also be prone to dislike and to distance themselves from parents of a patient when they feel a sense of helplessness in the face of the child's illness (Meadow, 1992).

she is right and the physician is wrong. Moreover, we believe that sometimes she inflicts harm on the child to take revenge on the doctor who disappoints her. The responses this relationship arouses are as powerful as they are confusing. An interview with a pediatrician who was victimized by a MBPS mother enriched our understanding of this process.

"The overwhelming reaction when I think back is sadness. I feel like I've gone over it hundreds of times in my mind, and I was the person who was in the best position to be able to recognize it and to be able to intervene. Over the course of roughly 3 years there were times when I suspected that she could have been harming Sarina and I tried to address it, and then there were other times that I felt No, this can't be happening. And things went back and forth for the entire three years, and the upshot was that Sarina died and that I ended up not having intervened. And I can find in retrospect a lot of things that made me suspicious and at least a half-dozen times when I tried to intervene and was unsuccessful. But the upshot was that I was in the best position and didn't intervene.

"There were two occasions during hospital admissions for diarrhea when I ordered toxin screens for possible laxative abuse. The first occasion was at Mt. O. Hospital. As I wasn't the person who made rounds consistently and didn't make rounds for the rest of the hospitalization, I only found out afterward that the toxic screen hadn't been sent because it was a special test that had to go a lab somewhere in Pennsylvania. They called and asked my partner. He said, 'Well, she's been in the hospital for a couple of days already, and it would be negligible.' So it never got sent. On another occasion we got a toxic screen at University Hospital, but the laxative level never got ordered. Why does the majority of the harm happen in the hospital? It's because there are so many people who are responsible that nobody's responsible. One just wants to get out of the room. And its easier to do when there is more than one person responsible.

"On more than one occasion we had tried to refer the mother and Sarina for an inpatient psychiatric evaluation, ostensibly for the child. But in point of fact it was because we were all concerned about the fact that mother came across as being very strange. And each time she adamantly refused, saying, 'They never concentrate on her, they always try to concentrate on me and I won't do that.'

"At one point I read a *Pediatrics* article describing closed-circuit monitoring of parents suspected of MBPS . . . and I called the Inpatient Research Board at University Hospital and talked with the director's partner. I asked if we could set up a closed-circuit monitoring system, like they had described in the article, to observe Sarina and her mom. I got turned down flat. They just said 'No.'

"Part of the problem with dealing with a case like this is the nature of the beast of a pediatric practice. You have 10 minutes, 15 minutes, to do an assessment, to hone in on what a problem is and to 'solve the problem.' And yes, if you're a good pediatrician you tend to keep your antennae up for hidden agendas and for what the real agenda of the visit is, if there isn't something that's really obvious. But the amount of interaction that you have at any one time with a parent or child is fairly limited and is in a very real sense oriented toward investigation first and then pedagogy. It's not at all open-ended so that you can investigate. I think that when I was talking with Sarina's mother and listening to her, I had the sense that something was not right with this person, and that she was either too close to me, or trying to engulf me, or overwhelm me, or all of these things. But there isn't a way in a pediatric practice to investigate that because we're not trained to be able to, and because, well, with a mother like this, it's just too difficult.

"Sarina's mother was overwhelming. She'd be your best friend for life if you were a physician. I shouldn't use the word but I'm going to because I know what it means and it fits: she 'split.' You were either part of her 'good self' or you were the worst physician in the world. Twice when I asked her if she was giving Sarina any medicines that I had not prescribed, she immediately burst into tears and cried, 'How could you accuse me of that?! How could you ever think that of me. She is my life!' She went out crying and was back in 2 days—telling me Sarina was having diarrhea again and asking what to do.

"You couldn't suspect her easily and you couldn't confront her. What I think was happening was that she was trying so hard to make me a part of her life, of herself, that the urge was to cut and run! While sitting in a room with her, the force of what she was trying to do to me was nearly overwhelming. She expected something that I felt I could never fill. She was trying so hard to make me a part of herself. And there was a resistance to sharing these feelings with a colleague—in part out of fear of how the mother would react, because she reacted to everything so intensely.

"I did share my worries with colleagues in my practice. It was distressing, and a number of people just wanted to simply wash their hands of the whole thing and say 'You can't come back to our office.' I found my role was to repeatedly say that—she is difficult, a real pain in the butt, but our patient isn't *her,* it's Sarina. We really have to focus on her. In retrospect, what was real was the mother's manipulation of Sarina's problems. I completely missed this part of the time, or I didn't miss it, but was impotent to do anything about it."

This physician's dilemma, his sensitivity, and ultimately his inability to act forcefully as well as our understanding of the dynamics at work with impostors tell us much about *what* is going on. But they tell us precious little about *how* it happens and *why* physicians and other caretakers are so susceptible.

THE DIALECTIC OF MOTHER'S SKILL AND PHYSICIAN'S SUSCEPTIBILITY

The work of J. Reid Meloy (1988) concerning the dynamics of the interaction between psychopathic personalities and their evaluators, lawyers, and therapists, is helpful in understanding how the physician gets caught up in and contributes to the unfolding of the mother–doctor dynamic. He describes a specific process "by which the psychopath consciously imitates or unconsciously simulates a certain behavior to *force the victim's identification with . . . [him],* thus increasing the victim's vulnerability to exploitation" (p. 140, our emphasis). The psychopath, he writes, has little capacity for empathy, but does have "an exquisite capacity for simulation and imitation" (p. 140).[4] People who are particularly vulnerable to the *affective simulation of the psychopath* include "individuals who deny their own narcissistic investments and consciously perceive themselves as being 'helpers' endowed with a special amount of altruism" (p. 140). Based on an uncanny reading of a particular helper's needs, the psychopath "induces . . . a sense in these caretakers that they are the embodiment of

---

[4]Meloy calls this process "malignant pseudoid-identification." For our purposes we will use the more common term, identification, which consists of a fantasy to be—or be like—another person for a particular reason.

goodness" (p. 140). The whole process, which can operate on an unconscious level, appears parallel to the kind of process that evolves with MBPS mothers and their pediatricians. Meloy's suggestion that mental health and legal professionals are more vulnerable to this manipulation by the psychopath "when the interactional content concerns their *competency, autonomy,* or *knowledge*" (p. 139; our italics), as we will see, is also particularly applicable to MBPS cases.

It is these three issues plus the issue of *caring* that are at stake for most of us in the helping professions. They create a veritable mine field for a physician faced with the skillful manipulations of the MBPS mother when she creates an "unsolvable" clinical problem. The far-reaching knowledge of matters medical exhibited by these mothers and the support they express for the work of the doctor ("Doctor, I know you're doing your best, stay with it, let's work together. We'll support you") combine to encourage the pediatrician's empathic identification with the mother. She begins to look like an appreciative colleague *and* an ideal mother. As one pediatrician remarked, "It's nice to have that support . . . [though] they are feeding your ego at the same time they are trapping you!"[5] Also involved, of course, is a not-so-subtle challenge to the professional identity of the physician so ensnared. The competitive challenge to his competency is heightened through direct criticisms by the mother of the pediatrician's colleagues who work in other major institutions where these mothers have previously "shopped."

If it were just the issue of the pediatrician's competency, knowledge, and autonomous decision making, things would be difficult enough. But add the issue of the doctor's "caring" and the bold and sometimes bald manipulation of "adulatory support" that these parents often express, and a situation is produced in which the question of his *caring* is now tied to his medical/clinical *performance*. Now, when things are not going well clinically, the doctor is left vulnerable to the *self*-accusation of not caring enough and the feeling that he needs to try harder. And this step seals "the trap." It is this intense inward focus by the physician, the self-blame for whatever is going wrong clinically in the case (the kind of doubt doctors and clinicians too frequently do not share with their colleagues), that is transformed

---

[5]Unlike most parents, MBPS mothers are capable of remaining completely calm just at the point when their baby's lives are in the most danger. As one pediatrician who has been involved with some 15 MBPS cases said, "Most parents who have a child with an illness and you can't come up with a diagnosis after many, many tests in a long period of time in which the child is not getting any better. . . . [Their] anxiety level goes up."

into self-doubts. These self-doubts in turn cause otherwise competent doctors to miss or misinterpret obvious clues concerning MBPS behavior. Moreover, there may well be an element of truth to the self-blame and self-doubt if the physician finds himself fleeing from the demands and needs of an "engulfing" MBPS mother through actual avoidance or the desire to "get rid of" the problem.[6]

Other complications arise from the fact that the physician is often performing on his "best" behavior with the child of a knowledgeable parent in his or her own field.[7] (One mother, a nurse, was able to get the doctors she worked with to prescribe new medications for her children by phone, at her suggestion.) A study by Meadow (1992) suggests that pediatricians find intelligent parents more likable, which suggests another reason that pediatricians might be vulnerable to an MBPS mother who appears medically knowledgeable.

The situation can rapidly deteriorate into a hopeless one in which the physician strives with increasing intensity to come up with a solution to a complicated clinical picture. The physician is missing the fact that the very lack of clinical sense in the case, and not the symptoms he is attempting to track down, *is* the problem. The chameleonlike conscious and unconscious processes described for narcissists, impostors, and "as-if" personalities, and the countertransferential clues they leave, would be difficult for even the well-trained psychotherapeutic clinician to detect out of the context of his or her office,[8] but the pediatrician starts out, and *appropriately so,* without the doubting and inquisitive stance of the trained psychotherapist.

In some cases the aggressive component of the mother's relationship to the doctor and her need to control and demonstrate superior-

---

[6]According to Meadow (1992, p. 701), "The doctor is most comfortable if he or she can perform a particular investigation or prescribe a particular treatment." When he cannot, he may withdraw.

We were told by a colleague about a hospital on the east coast where a young boy with upper airway disease was being overtreated with steroids. Though several physicians apparently suspected a rather classic case of MBPS, psychological consultants were never called nor were child protective agencies involved. We heard about the situation several years after the boy had died at age 10. One colleague said that the medical consultant in charge needed to see himself as "god-like" to his patients, and had difficulty admitting mistakes. But none of his colleagues had intervened actively, despite their suspicions.

[7]This is particularly difficult for nurses when they deal with MBPS involving a mother who is a nurse. Many are very distressed and feel that they will be less trusting of parents in the future (Blix & Brack, 1988).

[8]Renik (1993) and Glasser (1986) have written about the difficulties of discovery of such disorders even in the context of an intensive psychoanalytic psychotherapy.

ity is prominent. In the terms of the last chapter, in these patients the "sadism" is more prominent. This intense negative attention directed at the doctor can sometimes lead to disastrous consequences for the child. We need only point to the mother we mentioned in Chapter 1 who was very adept at getting physicians to do her bidding: she allegedly convinced her doctors to fit several children with Broviac catheters they did not need. Her aggressive lobbying for her charges' needs and her air of superiority in taking "very damaged" kids and proving the doctors wrong reflected this dynamic.[9] Her attitude led several physicians to distrust and dislike her. Unfortunately, in such cases the physicians are often relieved when these mothers move on to "better" doctors and institutions. We have seen tragic effects when important lab results were not followed up on after the parent had removed her child to another's care. As psychotherapists, each of us remembers such feelings about patients who abruptly left therapy or "got" themselves dismissed.

NOT JUST DOCTORS

A defense attorney with whom we consulted on an MBPS murder case was upset about some perceived negative feelings about her client one of us apparently displayed in our consultations with her. Despite the fact that she recognized that her client had basically refused to accept responsibility for the killing of her child, the attorney admitted that she had become "more personally involved with this client" than she usually is:

> "Since Sandra spent so much time in the hospital without being caught hurting Sean, I kept wondering if there couldn't be something else going on. I wondered if maybe somebody else was to blame. It was hard to accept that she had actually hurt her child—killed him.
>
> "One of the frustrations that I have had is that I think there are an awful lot of negative views about Munchausen by Proxy syndrome, even in the medical/psychological field. Dr. S.'s article was the most sympathetic that I read, and even when I interviewed him as an expert witness for the defense, and we got right down to it, he really thought my client was a dangerous

---

[9]As Sarina's doctors learned, even when the parent is very compliant on medical matters other areas of the forcefulness of her personality can create grave problems for the pediatrician and the infant.

person! Dr. S. didn't hold out much hope for treatment. And I found that very frustrating because I don't think this woman should be in jail.

"The psychologist who helped me with this case is one of the most compassionate people I know; she's helped me on death penalty cases, helped me keep people from going to the electric chair. Even she thinks this woman is very dangerous. And I have a problem with that."

It is not just pediatricians, judges, lawyers, and child protective care workers who are vulnerable to this particular dynamic.[10] Most of us are invested in and intensely convinced by an image of good mothering,[11] and are quite susceptible to skillful lying[12] and effective imposturing, particularly when they involve a "symbol" so close to our hearts. We cling to a belief in a universal "naturalness" of the early mother–infant interaction that does not fit with the facts. For example, many mothers do not show an intense "natural" interest in their newborn children. We easily lose sight of the amount of work that goes into the making of this relationship.

[10]One CPS worker, frustrated when an original suspicion did not sway the hospital personnel, told us: "Unfortunately, we didn't have that much cooperation from the first hospital. Because they weren't really sure what was happening and they had their own doubts about what was going on. They almost didn't quite believe it. So we had to put this case on hold and wait until another time.

"Finally I got the phone call about midnight one evening months later from our night worker. She said, 'We have this situation down here and the doctors and nurses want a protective custody put on and they said you were involved before.' I said, 'Oh for heaven sakes, tell them right away to get all the evidence and don't let the mother out of their sight and call the police. And for heaven sakes try to convince the police to put protective custody hold on it.' And our night worker did have a hard time doing that originally, because again the juvenile detective who was called from his home that night just couldn't believe it! He had never heard of such a thing, but at least he did do what our night worker and the doctors and nurses suggested."

[11]Korbin (1989) has written about mothers who abuse their children in more traditional forms of child abuse and factors that lead to an escalation wherein the child is killed. Foremost in her model is that when these parents signal others about what is happening, there is a general refusal in their social networks (and among physicians) to "see" the message, which reinforces their self-image that they are really good mothers. As she sees it, this in part happens because of cultural beliefs about human nature and motherhood.

[12]None of us is much good at detecting even simple forms of lying. In a study by Ekman and O'Sullivan (1991), judges, polygraphers, Secret Service agents, police officers, psychiatrists, and others were evaluated on their ability to detect lying, in a test situation where they knew that they were being lied to half of the time. Only the Secret Service agents were any good at the task (deciding correctly 65% of the time). The rest might as well have been guessing.

The crucial thing that physicians, therapists, and workers in the field of child protection could do to minimize the effect of these personal and social forces, unfortunately, is not one that comes easily, especially to physicians trained to function as autonomous if not omnipotent healers. It would require a willingness to share feelings of inadequacy or bewilderment with colleagues. The clinical facts in many of these cases often raise suspicions quite rapidly for those not personally caught up in these "dramas," and calling for outside consultations early on could spell the difference between life and death for a child. The complex social forces elaborated in Chapter 6, when added to the dynamics of these parents and the socialization of physicians, conspire to make this step a phenomenon that occurs late, if at all.

Psychiatric consultation–liaison programs, growing in number in children's hospitals, at least offer the opportunity for more frequent and earlier detection. But the barriers even in these institutions appear great and consultants, unless experienced, are also vulnerable. One observer (D. Herzog, quoted in Sugar, Belfer, Israel, & Herzog, 1991, p. 1020) in such an institution answers the question of how one is to begin in such cases by suggesting:

> As clinicians, researchers, and educators, we can respond to such cases and the inherent uncertainty by fleeing: leaving consultation work or not working with seriously ill patients and families. We can, on the other hand, embrace such uncertainty as part, parcel, and the challenge of our work. In such cases, this means promoting and maintaining an open, questioning attitude by all staff about how this patient and family are doing, what the history is, and how various "players" fit in with it, and there should be a willingness to openly discuss disagreement and change plans, if appropriate.

Working with this kind of case offers an opportunity for us all to learn much about the practice of medicine, the way we affect patients, and the way they affect us. It will take grappling with some thorny questions at societal, institutional, and personal levels, but the rewards, we believe, are well worth the risks and pain.

Surrender in the Family: Dynamic Issues Involving Older Children

Our own cases and those discussed in the literature indicate that there are differences between the presentation of MBPS cases involving infants and those involving older children. The dynamic picture in the case of an older child appears to depend very much on *when* the process started. We believe that when the *first* appearance of a child in "serious need" of medical attention occurs after the age of about 7 or 8, the clinical picture is dramatically different from those in which the process begins in infancy or early childhood and continues through adolescence. In cases beginning early but lasting for years, we see, to varying degrees, the rather incredible development of a collusive process between mother and child. At times this process can lead to quite independent self-harming behavior in the child, prompted by the child's need to maintain a strong emotional bond with the mother (see case of Danny H. discussed in Chapter 2).[1] Children who are closely allied with their parents will actively resist intervention by those who discover the fabrication.

When the process begins with an older child, that child often

---

[1] We do not have very good long-term follow-up in this disorder. Some children may develop Munchausen behavior, but this is not commonly found among our cases nor in the literature.

resists manipulation by the mother, which frequently leads to his or her withdrawal or even to profound psychological disturbance. At other times there is a kind of passive acquiescence,[2] but sometimes the child will take an active part in the "illness" charade. Further, the *family*, not just the mother, is often more actively involved in the dynamics of this group of older child cases. Careful study of these children and families could teach us much about psychological development. But, as we will see, the opportunities for such study are rare.

MBPS BEGINNING WITH AN OLDER CHILD

It is not unusual for MBPS mothers who begin the process with an older child to appear overtly psychiatrically disturbed, with caricatured illnesses, and open hostility. In many respects, they are more similar to adult Munchausen syndrome patients than to the mothers who induce illness in their infants. For example, a 28-year-old healthy-looking young mother of two appeared in a doctor's office wearing a portable oxygen tank with nasal catheters, reporting that she suffered from "emphysema, multiple sclerosis, hypothyroidism, and antibiotic poisoning" (Woolcott, Aceto, Rutt, Bloom, & Glick, 1982, p. 298). She had brought her 8-year-old in for similar complaints, and with the concurrence of her 50-year-old husband she requested a blood test to see if the child had multiple sclerosis. The father did not live with the family and was receiving a disability pension for "nerve problems." The child had been admitted twice for seizures and diarrhea, neither observed, and at age 4 for a thyroid disorder. There was also a complaint of chronic abdominal pain.

The mother's family history included a mother with schizophrenia and an uncle who was in a psychiatric hospital. She herself had been in several foster homes, had a history of numerous physical complaints, and had had her first hospitalization at age 14 for hysterical paralysis of her right arm. She also had been operated on for appendicitis, though the postoperative pathology report was normal, and she had been hospitalized for 7 months with a diagnosis of schizophrenia.[3] Both parents were antagonistic toward and mistrustful of the doctors. They denied any psychological problems in their

---

[2]Such behavior is sometimes seen in child victims of physical and sexual abuse by a parent.

[3]It is unclear whether she actually was schizophrenic or if this was a factitious disorder. Fabricated psychosis is not rare in adult Munchausen syndrome cases (see Pope, Jonas, & Jones, 1982)

daughter, who was doing well in school despite having missed 40 days during the previous school year. They had a younger son who was delayed in speech development resulting from "blood on the brain at birth," for which they were suing the hospital. The florid nature of the presentation, the history, and the negative interaction left little doubt about where the problem lay. While not seen very often in MBPS in which infants are the proxy victims, such overt disturbance of the mothers and fathers with MBPS who present with older children is not unusual. In many ways such obvious signs of MBPS ease the burden of doubt that so often accompanies medical staff confrontations with people suffering from this syndrome. However, as we will see, this can be quite a mixed blessing.

The 8-year-old daughter in this case was quite exceptional compared to most children who find themselves in this predicament in that she appeared friendly and intelligent, was communicative, and did not report any physical problems. Woolcott et al. (1982) reported that she apparently had good peer relationships and her only wish was that her parents would allow her to play with other children during recess. She also showed few of the signs of the kind of disturbed relationship to reality most children caught in such a predicament exhibit by age 7 or 8. Unfortunately, she remained with her parents, who sought help elsewhere after being confronted. It is one of the many ironies of this disorder that despite such floridly disturbed presentations there is often great delay in doing anything about the problem because little actual illness is induced. Though these children are usually physically untouched, they are vulnerable to serious psychological harm.

Roth (1990) describes several cases of MBPS behavior beginning after the proxy-victim child was age 10. The case of Benjamin offers a particularly clear picture of the family dynamics when an older child is involved.

Benjamin was 11 years old when he first complained of pain in the right hip. This was tentatively diagnosed by the physicians as "juvenile rheumatoid arthritis." He recovered completely and was quite well for 3 years. During this time his mother kept insisting that his legs were abnormal and that he should be receiving medical treatment. When he was 14 ½ years old he began to complain of pain in several of his leg joints, associated with increasing difficulties in walking. He was hospitalized on a number of occasions and underwent various tests, in spite of an absence of laboratory or clinical evidence supporting active organic disease. When Benjamin was 15 years old he developed hysterical paralysis requiring a prolonged stay in a psychiatric ward.

The patient had been adopted at 20 months by a couple in their late 40s, living on a kibbutz. His elder sister by 3 years was also adopted, and near the time of Benjamin's hysterical illness was about to leave home for army service. The relationship between mother and daughter became increasingly distant and strained over the year before the daughter's departure. During the same year preparations were also being made on the kibbutz to send Benjamin and his peers to a boarding school. There was no evidence of open conflict between the parents, but the mother complained that she felt isolated within the family, commenting: "I feel as if I do not belong to this family." She was an anxious woman with prominent paranoid traits. The relationship between her and her son was strongly, mutually dependent. A turning point in Benjamin's recovery followed progress in the mother's therapy, in which she was able to deal with her anxieties. Nonetheless, she still insisted that use of his previously paralyzed leg "would lead to irreparable damage because there is something wrong with this leg." During the course of his therapy she commented on her inability to see him mature and leave home. Throughout his hospitalization Benjamin was withdrawn, depressed and socially isolated. He manifested separation anxiety when his mother had to leave. After 2 years of therapy he chose to discontinue the meetings. . . . (Roth, 1990, pp. 162–163)

In the four cases Roth described, the mother experienced the loss of contact or loss of a relationship with another child prior to the onset of this "doctor-shopping" behavior. Three of the children she described were over 10 when the behavior started and one was almost 5. The mothers refused treatment or withdrew early and the outcome was uniformly poor. One child appeared at age 18 for psychiatric help after years in foster placement because of an abusing home environment. He had attended a neurology clinic suffering from chronic headaches. Benjamin, after 2 years of therapy, was located and evaluated at 19 years of age. While he had been accepted in the army to do compulsory service, his social functioning appeared "minimal and largely formal. He remained exceptionally close to his parents and opted to live at home with them, an unusual choice in his social context" (Roth, p. 164). One mother described in a U.S. report (Woolcott, Aceto, Rutt, Bloom, & Glick, 1982) after bringing her 17-year-old son to many doctors in three states without success, called 10 years later to report that a doctor in another city had found a heart defect. Her 27-year-old son was unable to attend school or work.

Herzberg and Wolff (1972) described several families who persistently sought medical help for recurrent "fevers" in their teenage children, all of which turned out to be factitious. The authors described these adolescents (aged 11–17) as playing a role not just for the doctors and not just for the mother (4 out of 5 of whom had "troubling chronic illnesses of their own"), but often for "warring" parents as well. In this respect, they differ from infant cases that are characterized by an actively involved mother and an absent or excluded father.

The most dramatic aspect of this group of patients is the way the child is usually inducted into serving the needs of his or her family. In other conditions we have seen *folie à deux* involving several family members including children (for example, a family delusion of parasitosis) but MBPS does not involve a delusional system. While the mothers of these children are often paranoid and sometimes delusional, the children themselves are not. Though at least two of the adolescents described by Herzberg and Wolff were causing the high temperatures themselves, none were psychotic and none could be seen as being involved in this process solely for personal secondary gain. The group of adolescents they interviewed appeared "serious, controlled . . . unusually cooperative . . . and [were] precocious conversationalists. They seemed depressed, but unlike their parents appeared to be quite indifferent to their chronic illnesses. All were informed medically and two (both females) wanted to become physicians" (p. 207).

DYNAMIC FORMULATION

Can we begin to understand how and why a child would become a part of such a family dynamic to the point of falsifying symptoms? Object relations theory, particularly the school that has focused on the family and especially the adolesent in the family, offers a very useful framework for understanding this process. Zinner and Shapiro (1989), describing family therapy with an adolescent as the identified patient, start with the parent's choice of a marital partner, suggesting that a delusional person will seek out a spouse who will "complement and reinforce unconscious fantasies" (p. 111). When a child is conceived, from pregnancy onward, covert parental coercions interact with the child's constitutional givens and "fix him as a collusive participant in the family's hidden agenda. In most families the time of adolescence calls for the questioning of the family's expectations, as the independence of one of its members threatens a built-up, carefully constructed balance" (p. 111). Based on their clinical work with families of children entering adolescence, they describe how a family triangle could lead to an "overly close, at times symbiotic relationship of one parent with a child" (p. 104). At this point an older child or a young adolescent walks a "fine line between fulfillment of their own strivings for an autonomous identity, or [serving] the needs of a parent" (p. 117). In their investigations of family dynamics when an adolescent is involved, they were "deeply impressed with the power that parental anxiety holds in tipping the balance" (p. 118) in the direction of either autonomy or dependency.

We feel that where there is a parent who has used somatization or even participated in adult Munchausen syndrome behavior themselves, the temptation is great to now involve her child in contacts with doctors when under severe stress. Obviously, the older the child, the more cooperation or collusion is needed in order to engage the child and the medical system in the disorder.

ADOLESCENT COLLUSION

In attempting to answer how to account for the extent to which adolescents may collude in this activity, Zinner and Shapiro (1989) (discussing a host of behavioral and emotional problems seen in moderate-to-severe adolescent disturbances, but not MBPS issues) suggest the following:

> Our view is that there are a variety of motivations and coercions for the adolescent's collusion with parental [projections]. Among these are the opportunity for impulse gratification . . . and . . . selective parental reinforcement of attributes of the adolescent which conform to parental projections. We believe however that the motivation which may need to be most reckoned with is *the adolescent's fear of object loss which might ensue were he not to act on behalf of the parents' defensive organization.* (p. 117, our emphasis)

The parents involved in MBPS, needy and anxious as they are, look to their children for closeness to protect themselves from unfufilling and/or difficult marriages. When they suffer a loss, perhaps of one of their own parents (as was typical in the cases described by Hughes [1984] of chronic abdominal pain; see Chapter 1), or face a threatened "abandonment" by a husband or an older child, their anxiety level increases dramatically and they may attempt to cope by becoming obsessed with a child's illness.

The way in which the collusions are generated is postulated to be through a process of projective identification. As recent reviews (see Goldstein, 1991) attest, there are many views of this mechanism, but in its .most basic form, as first described by Melanie Klein (1955, p. 58) projective identification is a "combination of splitting off parts of the self and projecting them onto another person *and* the feeling of identification with other people because one has attributed qualities or attributes of one's own to them." Anna Freud (1936) had earlier described the concept of "altruistic surrender." As Zinner and Shapiro (1989, p. 113) describe it, "Here the self finds in others a 'proxy in the outside world to serve as a repository' for the self's own wishes [and] provide vicarious gratification of the projected impulse." Implicit in Anna Freud's formulation is the willingness, conscious or not, of the recipient of these projections to collude in providing this gratification. Without this collusion, the process fails.[4] In these "older" child cases what is projected varies in complex and fluid ways and involves not just the child but the relationship between the parents as well. As Zinner and Shapiro (1989) found in their work,

> The nature of the projected material, in so far as the relations of parents to adolescents are concerned, contains highly conflicted elements of an object relationship with the parent's own family of origin. In these situations, the parent's projection of elements of his own previously internalized relationships serves not only a defensive function, but also a restorative one to bring back to life, in the form of the offspring, the parent's own lost objects, both good and bad. The adolescent may be perceived at one time as the parent's parent, and at other times as the child who his parent once was. Thus in the same family a child can be both parentified and infantalized. (p. 116–117)

Our clinical data and the literature unfortunately do not allow us to elaborate many examples of this latter theoretical and almost obvious point concerning the multigenerational transmission and nature of these projections. However, a somewhat dramatic example of this kind of projection can be surmised from one of Herzberg and Wolff's (1972) cases:

> [Sarah and her mother and two grandmothers suffered from severe arthritis.] Initially the mother expressed only concern for her daughter and denied any for herself. Her denial was obviously very thin, since she readily revealed intense dependency and hostility toward her very suspicious and distant husband (a mechanically oriented man, who said that he wished he could "fix" his daughter). Mother also not infrequently

---

[4]Many (Stern, 1988; Zinner & Shapiro, 1989) have suggested that this mechanism is part of the process of normal development from infancy onward, involving mostly nonpathological projections on the part of the parent.

sobbed and said that she feared she herself would soon end up in a wheelchair crippled with arthritis. Her disease had its onset at age 28 and she, like her husband, looked about 10 years older than her actual age of 36. Interestingly, Sarah, who was 13 years old, localized her fever in her joints. She described how her mother took her temperature (usually 106°F although always normal on examination in the doctor's office) and sat in a corner watching it rise.

At age 4 she had become preoccupied with details regarding her infant brother's operation for an intussusception, where a segment of bowel telescopes into another causing a blockage of the bowel. She dated the onset of her interest in being a doctor to that event. Sarah felt very close to her brother's surgeon at that time, a young house officer who was later selected by the mother as the family's pediatrician. Sarah's symptoms, notably, began within a week of her menarche.

Mother had described 11-year-old Sarah as the most independent, self-sufficient and most physically mature of her children, having reached puberty ahead of her 13-year-old sister. She clung desperately to Sarah who as the strong child and emerging young woman was "selected" for the role of her own "mother."

Sarah's father, a hostile and paranoid man, was nonetheless grateful for the definitive report that his daughter was healthy, but that he and his wife required couples therapy to permit Sarah eventually to grow and separate from them. It was then that the previously compliant and "interested" mother became most upset with the recommendations. (pp. 208–210)

Sarah's assigned role was clearly as caretaker, even "parent" to her mother. It is likely that her interest in doctors related to some need for confirmation, or to some shared attachment with her mother to the young medical house officer. That Sarah appeared mature, bright, independent, is clear, but it may also represent her accepting a projected and terribly anxiety-provoking wish from her mother's own psyche. It was anxiety provoking, one could speculate, because of what her likely forbidden wishes from her own childhood were (with a sick mother and two sick grandmothers of her own, a "mechanical father," and a young doctor–father substitute). In so far as mother needed doctors and Sarah could and would play both the role of an independent caretaker of mom and dependent patient of doctors, helping her mother find doctors who were enlisted in seeking the source of her fevers, she was an almost too-good-to-be-true partner in her collusion. No wonder mother was upset at her daughter's clean bill of health.[5]

---

[5]This speculation, though based on very limited data, fits much of the material we have pieced together from information on a number of patients.

It is clear that involving a child in a collusion of this magnitude, especially if the "club" used is the threat of object loss, causes great damage to the developing psyche even if no physical harm is done.[6] Unfortunately, despite the bizarreness and severe psychopathology involved, courts and social agencies are very reluctant to act in these cases, allowing for the likely development of permanent damage.

WHEN THE CHILD HAS BEEN INVOLVED FOR YEARS

We have pointed out that there is little follow-up of the children involved in MBPS. In the last section we presented the very difficult situation in which older children find themselves. The family dynamic places these children in the midst of very disturbed systems of relationships. But what of the child who is involved from infancy, and in whose eyes the mother appears to be a nurturing and loving parent?

The case of Danny H., discussed in Chapter 2, may be informative in this regard. The process in his case began in infancy with food allergies and "serious asthma." Initially the child was a passive recipient of too much medicine and a diet restricted to breast milk. He ended up taking 14 different medicines. The side effects of the steroids alone were very distressing: head and stomach aches, dizziness, compression fractures of the spine, and physical disfigurement. Eventually he likely began to realize that his food allergies were bogus, for as a young child be began sneaking food on his own with no ill effects. Nor did he have any diarrhea when the doctors, their suspicions mounting, gave him a surreptitious trial of "allergy-causing" foods.

Yet when he was taken from home by the police and hospitalized in a psychiatric unit, he colluded with his mother in contining to take large doses of steroids thought to be smuggled in to him. He and his mother were said to be intensely "enmeshed," Danny adopting a sick role when in family sessions the mother would pretend to withdraw, and mother ending up herself in an intensive care unit when there was a threat that Danny would get better—or be taken from her.

[6]Such children are subject to depression, withdrawal, and retarded social development. At least two authors also describe the development of conversion symptoms, one a paralysis requiring long-term psychiatric hospitalization (Roth, 1990), and the other conversion blindness (McGuire & Feldman, 1989). The former appeared in the service of "proving" to the doctors she was ill, the latter, in a sibling, appeared as an attempt to halt the mother's illness—producing behavior.

One is tempted to think in terms of "symbiotic psychosis"—or a *folie à deux*—except that neither was psychotic. In one of the most profoundly disturbing sequelae of any case we consulted on, Danny was sent home by the courts over the vociferous objections of his doctors and therapists. They all felt his life was in danger. As predicted, soon after leaving the hospital he began having asthma attacks again, as he was exposed to known allergens and was at times *under*medicated. But the events on the night he arrested, after his mother was overheard telling him that he could not breathe, may have come about from the most incredible collusion of all. Voluntary occlusion of his vocal chords was a postulated mechanism and may have accounted for the difficulty the anesthesia resident had in intubating him (Freedman, Rosenberg, & Schmalling, 1991).

The evidence seems clear that Danny was not part of a *folie à deux*. Not only did he sneak real food, but he was happiest during the times when he was allowed to attend school and play with other children. Despite numerous absences from school, he did well in school prior to the arrest. Though immature and tied to his mother, he made progress in the hospital. And just days before the respiratory arrest, 4 months after discharge, he warned his therapist of the danger he was in by playing out the story of "The Boy Who Cried Wolf" in a sand tray.

The refusal of the courts to actively protect Danny led to an escalated campaign by the doctors. Combined with the child's (now aged 10) growing sense of possible separateness, it threatened the intense collusive process between mother and son, leading mother back to her dangerous game, with an intensity that inevitably spelled disaster. Now 19 years old, with neurocognitive damage and functional limitations, Danny is again totally dependent on his mother.

OUTCOME FOR OLDER CHILDREN

Godding and Kruth's (1991) paper on 17 children subjected to MBPS behavior in an asthma clinic suggests a "good" outcome in six cases. The children's average age was 7 (the range was 4–12). But we are *not* told when the behavior—of causing illness by undermedicating or causing real harm by seeking unnecesary procedures—began. It is therefore difficult to assign these children to either grouping in this chapter. All of the children were said to come from a disturbed psychosocial background, and 11 mothers were said to be depressed. There is not enough data to evaluate the significance, nor even the meaning, of what the authors called "good outcomes" for six patients.

The cases of McGuire and Feldman (1989) (see Chapter 1) need only to be recalled to give us pause. It does seem that the child involved at an early age is placed in much more physical danger all along the way. The child involved at an older age is at grave risk for psychological damage. In terms of the destructive effects attributed to MBPS behavior, even this must be said with a caveat. This latter group of children were likely reared in an environment generally more openly disturbed, at least on the surface, for years on end.

In summary, while the infant plays a clear-cut role for the mother in relationship to the doctor, the older child involved in MBPS plays more of a dynamic role within the family. However, in keeping with the very consistent dynamic issues found in this disorder, these older children also serve as a vehicle for the mother's connection to the physician. This connection, coming as it does from more severe disturbance, leads to a course more similar to the one described in cases of adult Munchausen syndrome behavior: a rapid dismissal from medical treatment and frenetic wandering to yet another medical setting. The long-term psychological damage to the child may be greater.

PART III

MANAGING THE PROBLEM

CHAPTER 9

Psychotherapeutic Work with MBPS Parents

"I am having trouble having Sandra placed on probation because no one in this area has any expertise with this illness, and it's hard for me to find someone who can take her into treatment. Everyone I talk to about the possibility of long-term treatment says 'We don't have enough data,' or 'For the few cases we have had, we don't think it was very successful.' I find that extremely frustrating, even though I realize there are probably not enough of these cases around and written up in the literature for people to really have expertise with Munchausen by Proxy syndrome. But it's incredibly frustrating that I can't find her any help."
— Defense attorney discussing her client

Often the [case] management was hampered by differing perceptions among professionals, particularly concerning the nature of the abuse itself, and the psychological condition of the mother. Wide differences of opinion sometimes occurred because of the mothers' ability to deceive, and to present as perfectly normal women. Many mothers who had already attempted to foster an over close relationship with a pediatrician and nursing staff, now attempted this with their social worker, health visitor, general practitioner or psychiatrist. Where two workers managed a case in close cooperation, this helped to reduce the potential overdependence and influence on the individual professional.
— Neale, Bools, & Meadow (1991, p. 330)

Hundreds of papers describing a fascinating variety of Munchausen cases have been published, but few of these papers offer much information about psychotherapy and the healing process. To a large degree, this vacuum is due to the unwillingness of identified Munchausen patients to seek therapeutic help, to use words rather than physical symptoms to express their pain, and to achieve the insight and skills necessary to discard Munchausen behaviors. When confronted with their fabrications and referred to a mental health professional, many flee to another physician; and those who are ordered to undergo therapy by the courts often go through the motions without commiting to the process. The overrepresentation of papers on adult Munchausen syndrome and Munchausen by Proxy syndrome in the medical rather than in the psychiatric literature also helps to explain why in-depth psychological data is lacking.

TREATMENT OF ADULT MUNCHAUSEN SYNDROME

A handful of reports have appeared detailing the psychological treatment of some adult Munchausen syndrome patients. Although we believe there are significant differences between adult Munchausen syndrome and Munchausen by Proxy syndrome, the fact that a significant number of people manifest both syndromes lends interest to the therapeutic work done with the adult disorder. Schoenfeld, Margolin, and Baum (1987) present an extensive history on the 4-year course of psychotherapy of a 23-year-old adult Munchausen syndrome patient. Their treatment consisted of combined dynamic and supportive therapy augmented by antianxiety and antidepressive medication. They described their patient's underlying personality as "immature personality with schizoid traits" (p. 611). They felt that the key aspects of the treatment included the act of confrontation during one of the patient's many crises, the use of the patient's children as a spur to generate treatment motivation, and the corrective experience of working with a nurturing female therapist. Interestingly, the patient eventually found employment in a "paramedical position," which the therapists viewed as positive "sublimative activity"! There is no long-term follow up.

Mayo and Haggerty (1984) present a detailed psychoanalytic discussion of a 16-month-long treatment of a female adult Munchausen patient, although the patient eventually dropped out of therapy. The therapy was organized around the theme that the patient's "parents' failure to acknowledge her dim memories of paternal incest left her feeling unreal and insubstantial" (p. 573). Therapy focused mainly on narcissistic issues during which time seven known hospitalizations were triggered by perceived abandonments (actually, vacations) by the therapist. The authors felt that this case demonstrated the significance of "current abandonment experiences in the activation of factitious behavior" (p. 575). They recommended the value of the therapist maintaining consistent, steady interest in the patient and devoting empathic attention to the subjective content of the fabrications rather than the objective reality of the material. Finally, they opined that the therapist needs to "expect and tolerate the continual return of factitious illness" (p. 576).

Another single case of an adult Munchausen syndrome patient is described by Stone (1977). This 26-year-old woman patient was described as a unipolar depressive with borderline personality organization and narcissistic and antisocial features. Her high degree of denial and splitting was not amenable to outpatient psychotherapy. She was only confronted about her simulated illness after transfer to a locked unit. Although the patient eventually checked herself out of the hospital against medical advice, she did eventually resume treatment with another therapist. The author concluded that "if anything positive is to happen, it will only come through timely, vigorous, and repeated confrontation about the true nature of the patient's illness and about his [or her] vengeful, exploitative, antisocial attitudes" (p. 253). O'Shea and McGennis (1982) presented two cases of male adult Munchausen syndrome patients treated as inpatients in Ireland. In each case, their therapy involved "nonjudgmental acceptance of his past history and the fostering of a sibling-type relationship with the therapist" (p. 17). They initially tolerated a significant degree of dependency, only gradually encouraging individuation. They stressed the need for a sensitive selection of communication techniques, including humor and body language, appropriate to the fairly primitive level of the patient.

Fras (1978) briefly described two outpatient adult Munchausen syndrome cases—one a therapy dropout and one a 5-year-long psychotherapy case—but the description of the course of treatment in both cases is limited. He recommended a very supportive, cautious psychotherapy aimed at maintaining a relationship with the patient and not challenging patient denial too vigorously for a long period. Again, it is interesting to note that the "successful" patient, once she stopped her self-induced diabetic problems, chose a medical career: she became a nurse!

Several papers describe more circumscribed treatments designed specifically for adult Munchausen patients. McDonald, Kline, and Billings (1979) described the use of sodium amytal interviews to elicit more information from their patients. While they found that the drug had no treatment value with their two patients, it did prove useful as a means of obtaining more truthful history from their patients and a better understanding of their cases.

Jamieson, McKee, and Roback (1979) used the Hollender-Hersch technique designed to help patients with factitious disorders. This technique involves two psychiatrists who split their roles into "helper" and "confronter." Their goal was to develop a supportive alliance with the patient while increasing the patient's reality testing and not reinforcing her self-destructive urges. They described a 4-month course of treatment that appeared to work well; however, the patient seemed to be producing symptoms again at 2-year follow-up.

Brody (1959) described the treatment of three adult polysurgery patients treated with 3 years of psychoanalytic group psychotherapy. Behavioral approaches have been tried by Solyom and Solyom (1990), Klonoff, Youngner, Moore, and Hershey (1983), and Yassa (1978). These approaches utilize a range of procedures from aversive therapy to biofeedback, reinforcement of wellness, paradoxical therapy, and denial of privileges for symptomatology.

TREATMENT OF MBPS

The literature on the treatment of MBPS patients is even more limited. Many of the papers detailing psychotherapeutic treatment of adult Munchausen syndrome patients describe work done with adults hospitalized in psychiatric or medical facilities for periods of months or years. But most MBPS mothers are *not* inpatients (medical or psychiatric) and therefore are more difficult to work with in any intensive, ongoing psychotherapy. Opportunities for long-term work with these patients typically occur either in court-ordered, outpatient psychotherapy mandated by a judge in order for the mother to regain custody of her child or children, or more rarely in situations in which the parent experiences an acute psychiatric crisis (becomes suicidal, psychotic, or the like) following exposure of her fabrications.

Thus a very limited literature exists detailing the process of treating MBPS. One very early paper by Lansky and Erickson (1974) predated even the naming of the syndrome; the authors described the outpatient treatment of a couple in which the wife was abusing the child with caustic agents and medication. Nicol and Eccles (1985) described a fairly detailed court-ordered 1-year psychodynamic therapy with a MBPS mother. They found their patient to be intelligent, motivated to understand her behavior, and able to bring painful material to her therapy sessions. The two major affective states addressed in therapy were remorse and depression. The patient had a particularly ambivalent relationship with her father and her abusive behavior seemed to have been triggered when her idealization of him was shattered in young adulthood. Moreover, this mother grew up in a family culture of exaggerated illness behavior. The therapist's task was described as "uncover[ing] and interpret[ing] these fantasies and behaviors to the patient" (p. 348). At a 15-month follow-up, no further abuse was known to have occurred. A more limited discussion of a mother's treatment was offered by Kravitz and Wilmott (1990). Lyall, Stirling, Crofton, and Kelnar (1992, p. 373) indicate that in one case "family psychotherapy was only partially successful. A subsequent child in the family died of 'sudden infant death syndrome,' and after two years the family moved out of the area."

What is missing in this scant literature is information about the experience of the therapist in working with such patients. The parent involved in MBPS, in particular, tends to evoke intense feelings in all the caregivers who come into close contact with her for the many reasons described in Chapter 7 and the psychotherapist is no exception. While some authors such as Fras (1978) have hinted at the need to remain free of personal or professional biases against these patients in order to remain effective, little has been said about the therapeutic dilemmas these patients can evoke in their therapists. Furthermore, our formulations of the underlying dynamics and conflicts in these patients have been quite limited, resulting in few clear directions for psychotherapists beginning work with them. Most therapists see only one or two of these mothers as patients in the course of a long career, so virtually no one can claim great expertise in the treatment of MBPS.

THERAPY CASE HISTORIES

What follows are descriptions of treatment by two psychotherapists who were willing to share, in their own words, recollections of their respective work with two different MBPS mothers. Of particular interest are the unique problems these patients posed for the therapists and the choices they made in responding to these dilemmas.

Psychotherapy with Iris

"Iris was a 29-year-old mother of two children when she was referred to me by the court for MBPS.[1] She was accused of

[1]This case is based on interviews we conducted with Dr. G., a male psychologist at a publicly funded clinic on the East Coast. He treated Iris for 2 years.

pulling out some of her youngest daughter's IV lines and injecting substances under her skin over the course of 8 months while
her daughter, Linda, was hospitalized for asthma. During that
hospitalization Linda had a suspicious cardiorespiratory arrest.
Iris had no criminal charges pending, just child custody issues. I
was called by the mental health chief and asked to see this patient
because I had a reputation for seeing difficult and exotic cases. I'd
never actually heard of MBPS—I'd heard of Munchausen syndrome when I worked in an adult psychiatric hospital—but I
didn't have a clue as to what MBPS was. It was explained to me
and I prepared myself by reading several articles.

"Iris, when I met her, told me she 'didn't understand' the
MBPS diagnosis—but a number of people seemed to think she
had this disease. She said that these were smart people so they
were 'probably right'! She seemed baffled, shocked, and angry at
the accusations even while she partially admitted she 'may have'
done something wrong, unbeknownst to her.

"I've worked with a lot of men involved in sexual offenses and
her attitude kind of reminded me of these men. They use denial
and always present themselves as the victim. Sometimes they
have been victimized as children, but it's still a diversion away
from their own responsibility. Iris tended to do that. But at least
she would allow me to pull her back to examine what was going
on inside of her.

"My agreement with the protective services agency overseeing
the court-mandated therapy was that I was only to be the therapist, not the evaluating doctor. I would provide reports of Iris's
progress in therapy. I conferred with her attorney. But it wasn't
my job to decide when and if her daughter would be returned to
her custody. Iris had very little money, so our agency allowed
her to pay for treatment with a minimal fee. Her attendance was
very good and she only missed a few appointments. She wasn't
too dependent though, and I can only recall one time when she
called me in crisis—following a car accident.

"Iris was a tall and bouncy person. I tended to get drawn into
her talking about how terrible it is to have your child removed.
And at times it did seem to me that maybe there was too much
hysteria around her Munchausen behavior, like they wanted
to accuse Iris of *everything* that had gone wrong in the hospital
with her daughter's care. I guess I was giving her the benefit
of the doubt, while realizing that it's a thorny problem to sort
out the actual destructive interventions Iris made from other er-

rors and normal medical complications that arose, independent of her. I could see why the hospital would *want* to hold her responsible for things for their own purposes yet . . . who knows?

"My background as a therapist is partially psychodynamic and psychoanalytic. But mainly I'd describe my approach to Iris as supportive, as that of providing an atmosphere where she could open up about herself and her experiences, where she'd be willing to tell me the truth or would be able to come to some discovery of what actually *did* happen, since she claimed not to remember.

"She wasn't that interested in intensive exploration. I didn't really learn a tremendous amount about her early family relationships. I do know that Iris's older sister was bedridden with a neurological disease when Iris was young. Iris was the main family member caring for her sister. She described her father as an excessive kind of guy. But it's not clear that he was all that loving. Iris herself had an interesting medical history including having been hospitalized at about age 9 for a toe infection, and as a teenager for scoliosis. Otherwise she didn't seem to have a lot of physical complaints while I worked with her.

"Iris's history was that she became pregnant with Linda while she was living with her parents and dating a much older man. She later married him during the pregnancy. From her description, it sounds like he was never much of a father. He ended up leaving Iris when Linda was still very young, and about a month before she started her MBPS behaviors. Around the same time, she had also lost a job that was very important to her.

"In talking about that time, Iris could acknowledge that she was in a very bad way. She felt angry at the doctors because they weren't paying enough attention to her daughter, and this MBPS would be a way of getting more attention for her. She wouldn't admit to any anger toward Linda but it was acceptable for her to couch her justification for MBPS, *if* she actually did this, as a way of getting more attention for her child. She professed much love for this child and actually did seem to love her very much.

"I felt that she had a lot of anger she was denying. On the surface she was a Pollyannaish-type person, but there were times when I saw a lot of anger in her. When her defenses failed and she was under a lot of stress, that anger came out and she became explosive. She never really did anything terribly destructive and she never got directly angry at me. But, of course, I never gave her much reason. She listed to what I had to say and tried some things I suggested. But she never really admitted to remembering tampering with Linda's lines. I felt she was either lying to me or in such a dissociative state that maybe she needed extra help. I hit upon the idea of presenting her to Dr. B., a colleague of mine who was a renowned expert in hypnosis. She went willingly, and I presented the case. Dr. B. interviewed her but didn't feel she could be hypnotized.

"I also had access to psychological test data from independent examiners. Dr. D.'s testing was very impressive and convincing, but I sort of felt she had a lot of anger at my patient, and my patient certainly didn't like Dr. D. So I had a feeling that this psychologist's recommendations were somewhat overdrawn.[2] She recommended that Iris not be allowed to have custody of Linda pretty much ever again. She said that Iris was a very dangerous mother for this child.

"It was hard for me to see her as a dangerous person, and was especially so for the child protection agency. Iris was cooperative, she did the whole thing, therapy seemed to go well. Her visits to the foster home went very well. Linda was evaluated and also seen with Iris and her new boyfriend. Linda was thriving, mother was attentive, and the new boyfriend seemed like a very nurturant, paternal kind of guy.

"Eventually Iris regained custody of Linda. Therapy with me was no longer mandated, but she continued with me for several more months. But Iris's relationship with her boyfriend fell apart shortly before we terminated therapy several months later. I think the boyfriend got frustrated with all of Iris's demands. She'd been having this insomnia problem and was prescribed some common sleep medication. She took it and started having fainting and visual problems. She couldn't be alone and had to be driven everywhere. She was put on several other medications and gradually the problem subsided. I have no idea how real these medical problems were.

"We terminated therapy because Iris rather precipitously de-

[2]The evaluating psychologist was not blind to Iris's diagnosis of MBPS. Because of the intensity of feeling that child abuse can generate, we have made it a practice to request raw data (from the examining psychologist) which can then be evaluated blindly by other psychologists. We also strongly recommend the use of personality and projective instruments that are sensitive to the denial and more characterological problems common in these patients.

cided to move to Minnesota. She said it was to get away from her problems at work, but actually she was going to be moving close to her ex-husband and his family. Her decision to move was pretty impulsive. I advised her to see a therapist in Minnesota, but I doubted she'd see someone. And I've never heard from her again.

"Looking back, I don't think that I ever really broke through the denial, so I don't feel that my therapy was really that successful in helping her come to terms with what really happened. It was helpful in a supportive way and I tried to at least get her to be aware of the fact that when she's under a lot of pressure it's possible that she could do things that might be destructive. My final diagnosis was that of factitious disorder. I felt she had a personality disorder with mixed passive-aggressive and dependent-histrionic features.

"In retrospect, I think I might have been a little more confrontive, but frankly I don't know if that would have helped or hurt."

Psychotherapy with Stephanie

"Stephanie was a 19-year-old married caucasian woman transferred to me after first being seen once by an intern at our clinic.[3] I was under the supervision of a psychoanalytically oriented psychiatrist, who assigned the case to me. I had never before heard of MBPS and had no clear idea of what to expect. Stephanie's initial history was very unclear. She was being accused, by a well-known medical center, of administering poisons to her 2-year-old daughter, contaminating her stool specimens, and inducing bleeding and a variety of other symptoms in this young child over the course of a year.

"Stephanie was being mandated by a children's protective services agency to see me in therapy. She was also going collaterally, with her daughter, Donna, to see a child psychiatrist. I made it clear to the protective services agency that I would not tell them much more than whether she attended therapy. The child psychiatrist would be responsible for making decisions about reunifying Stephanie with Donna.

---

[3]This case is based on interviews we conducted with Dr. R., a male psychiatrist at a public outpatient clinic in the midwest. He treated Stephanie for 2 years.

"The therapy spanned a period of 2 years: first I saw Stephanie twice a week for about 5 months, then once weekly for a year, and then about every other week for 6 months.

"When Stephanie first came to me she was clearly in a lot of distress about Donna's placement outside the home. She presented as a friendly and notably bright and bubbly young woman. While she partially acknowledged MBPS, she claimed that there were only two isolated incidents and that the courts were overreacting. She was angry about what had happened at one of the hospitals and claimed that the hospital's own incompetence had resulted in some of Donna's medical problems. She seemed to sincerely believe this. As a matter of fact, I don't think that the hospital ever really did definitively prove that she had caused at least one of the incidents of bleeding. The tests were never conclusive. But I took the stance that 'whatever the cause may be, let's focus on *your* problems.' That helped her focus in therapy on the conflicts she had with all the important people in her life rather than on the MBPS per se.

"Stephanie was the eldest of six children. She described a fairly calm and uneventful childhood, although she came to see that she had a very idealized view of her mother. She felt very insecure and inferior by comparison with her mother, especially given all the problem she had had with her own pregnancies, and her kids' behavior problems. She often found herself feeling overwhelmed inside, yet needed to present to the world the image of being competent and in control. Yet she sought impulsive, destructive solutions when in this tense, overwhelmed state.

"Stephanie idealized her father too, but was very angry and resentful of him because she felt he was more accepting of and lenient toward her brothers. The males in her family had had a coalition from which she felt excluded. And even though she claimed to feel so close to her mother, it didn't seem to make up for these feelings of exclusion. In the session after she first talked about how envious she had been of her four brothers and how resentful she continued to feel toward her father due to his rejection, she cried. She said later that that was so disturbing to her that she had to deliberately remind herself of all her positive feelings about him in order to calm down—graphically describing a splitting phenomenon to neutralize the bad feelings.

"Prior to our therapy, she couldn't seem to deal with anger at all. Later she became much more aware of these feelings and better able to figure out how to deal with them.

"The fact that Stephanie's husband was not sufficiently available as a support for her played a big role in the development of her symptoms. One major insight that developed in the course of therapy was that she came to see her husband as not meeting her needs. She became increasingly dissatisfied with him and began contemplating getting out of the marriage. Initially she had been grateful that he stayed with her despite all her legal troubles, but she began reflecting on the many ways he had let her down in their relationship. For example, she had been hospitalized for several weeks on bedrest due to back surgery and her husband would call up complaining about his troubles with their oldest daughter and begging/demanding she come home.

"Another relationship that seemed to contribute to Stephanie's MBPS was her relationship with one particular pediatrician whom she needed to see frequently because of all the medical problems. The MBPS started during her time working with this first physician. Subsequently, she left and some other pediatrician took over for her with whom she had a less intense and conflictual relationship. But then all of her feelings got transferred to me, her therapist.

"Stephanie also developed a very conflicted, paranoid relationship with Donna's child psychiatrist. I couldn't tell how much was projection and how much was based on reality. I had the sense that this man really didn't like Stephanie and was taking a much more suspicious, mistrustful attitude toward her than I. Maybe this stance was warranted. I became aware, over time, that my own tendency to be sympathetic was countertransferential. Stephanie presented herself in a way that made me very sympathetic *despite* what she had done and despite her denial and minimization.

"The child psychiatrist felt there would be a continued risk until Donna was old enough to report any continued abuse, while I was beginning to be supportive of Stephanie getting increased parental privileges. I felt that my own efforts in therapy were being undervalued, but then . . . I couldn't be sure that the other psychiatrist wasn't right!

"There were some puzzling things that happened even while Stephanie continued in therapy with me. Her older son, who had *not* been removed from her custody, ended up having some minor surgery done. Their previous pediatrician had never felt this boy had clear-cut pathology but the surgery was planned by a second doctor. I spoke with her and told her of my concerns and those of the first pediatrician. She still felt the procedure was appropriate. Also, the boy ended up on medication for "seizures." I was never sure it was really necessary. Stephanie certainly had a lot of trouble with this son. Yet interestingly, it was her younger daughter she hurt. One pediatrician thought she was doing the same thing with her son. There certainly were a lot of other unexplained things going on with the child. But Stephanie had a clearly different kind of investment in this daughter than in her son. She experienced a symbiotic fusion with Donna. She used to say, 'It's like we were the same person.'

"Stephanie had a lot of trouble with the interpretation that her anger toward her son was transferential, or a displacement of her feelings toward other earlier men in her life. But she described identical feelings of being excluded from the world of her husband and her son and the world of her father and brothers.

"Diagnostically, I'd describe Stephanie as having a self-object disorder. Essentially, she had a narcissistic personality disorder. She wasn't grandiose or entitled, but her problems revolved around self-esteem regulation and self-image management. It wasn't very clear *why* she developed this way. The psychopathology in her parents didn't come across at all—it sounded like they were basically okay and Stephanie was overreacting to normal parental inadequacies.

"There was some speculation that Stephanie also had adult Munchausen syndrome, given her history of frequent doctor visits with complaints that couldn't be nailed down. She'd had unexplained shoulder and neck pain, surgery for varicose veins, unexplained hearing loss, and a couple of operations for recurrent disc problems. She admitted she liked to go to the doctor for the 'comfort.' This pattern started in adolescence although I was never able to elicit any history of medical or hospital experience in her early life or in parental history. Also, at some point in therapy, I had Stephanie hypnotized by a local hypnotherapist, but it didn't help reveal anything more about the patient's abuse of her daughter and how or why it was done.

"The last time I saw the patient was about a year ago when treatment ended. Stephanie did get her daughter back before therapy ended, and I think she probably ended up leaving her husband. I have no other follow-up available. There were never any criminal charges filed against Stephanie as far as I know.

"Advice I'd have for other therapists working with MBPS patients is to beware of the intense countertransference that can develop. Negative transference can get in the way of dealing with these people as patients with a problem rather than as "bad" people. There's also the danger of going the other way and feeling gratified that you're the only person who understands, who feels sympathetic to this poor victim of the system. I suppose in the end I saw Stephanie as a 'screwed-up' person who was doing the best she could, a woman who actually did have her values and standards and ideals. I always felt she was being as honest as she could."

These two cases highlight many of the common dilemmas for psychotherapists faced with a parent engaging in Munchausen by Proxy behavior. They tend to be very different from the inpatient psychiatric patients described in the adult Munchausen syndrome literature. Neither patient described in this chapter was voluntary or particularly motivated to understand her behavior. Thus the therapists faced the problem of how confrontative to be versus how supportive and accepting, in order to establish a working alliance. Even more interesting is the fact that both therapists, despite having educated themselves about the syndrome and the typically "victimized" and believable presentation of these mothers, had periods of difficulty maintaining therapeutic objectivity. Both found themselves at times almost accepting the denials of their patients as to the accusations of medical abuse, feeling strong countertransferential pulls toward sympathy with these likeable and insistent patients.[4] Both even felt annoyance and resentment toward other mental health professionals consulting on their cases in more critical ways, and felt confused as to their own perceptions and judgments. Both felt they had made reasonably good therapeutic alliances with their patients, yet both simultaneously sensed the limitations of these bonds and the difficulty they found in confronting the core issues directly. Both noted an upsurge in some questionable illness-oriented behaviors in their patients in the later period of the therapy, but were unsure of how to interpret these behaviors. And both therapists ultimately lost touch with their patients after termination, so they were unable to judge the long-term impact of treatment once their patients left town.

Certainly, these two cases, in conjunction with the literature, point to several useful recommendations for therapeutic work with MBPS parents.

---

[4]We know of numerous other examples of this countertransference effect, the results of which can have serious consequences for the child.

RECOMMENDATIONS FOR THERAPY

The Therapeutic Frame

The role of the courts in mandating and monitoring the therapy is crucial if many of these patients are to receive any treatment at all. Even for parents who acknowledge their MBPS behaviors, voluntary agreements with child protection agencies are seldom powerful enough to motivate a parent to invest herself in psychotherapy and attend regularly.

The therapist has a difficult balancing act to accomplish: providing indications of therapeutic progress to legal authorities and doing so without jeopardizing patient confidence and confidentiality. The contracts developed by the therapists described here, to provide limited information to the court and leave the assessment of the patients' readiness to regain custody of the children to other parties, were important in gaining their patients' trust.

Countertransference Issues

MBPS patients are masterful at evoking the sympathy, doubt, and narcissism of their caretakers. Not only should a therapist prepare himself or herself by reading extensively about the syndrome before embarking on a course of treatment, but ideally the therapist should have access to ongoing consultation or supervision with colleagues (preferably someone familiar with the disorder) in order to deal effectively with countertransference issues. Since other therapists are also likely to be involved (for example, child's therapist, spouse's therapist, psychological examiner, and so on), it would be helpful to establish collaborative relationships, within the bounds of appropriate confidentiality, so as not to become split off into opposing camps. While we clearly lack an adequate body of psychotherapy data to make generalizations or to draw conclusions, it does seem likely that there will be important differences in the patient–therapist relationship based on the gender of the therapist, with male therapists perhaps being more susceptible to intense transferential issues with MBPS mothers, if our theories of the syndrome's dynamics are accurate.

SUMMARY

Very little encouraging data is yet available on successful therapeutic work with MBPS mothers. Unfortunately, their skill at imposturing and in fabricating believable stories can be utilized to consistently deny their actual harming behavior and/or to falsely convince therapists of their motivation for change. It is very difficult if not impossible for a therapist to gauge the patient's sincerity and truthfulness and to successfully challenge her defensive structure when she is an involuntary or reluctant patient.

Given these constraints, as well as the fact that personality disorders are notoriously difficult to treat—as they represent longstanding defects in character that may not create much anxiety or discomfort in the patient—we must set realistic goals. We believe that psychotherapy with MBPS patients is more likely to be successful if focused on the goal of altering the symptom of medical attention-seeking behavior rather than attempting deeper, long-term change in personality structure.

While there is not much literature to guide us, our theories of the dynamics of this disorder and the social context of MBPS (see discussion in Chapters 5 and 6) suggest that it would be useful in therapy for these patients to explore their early as well as current feelings of neglect and how their relationship(s) with medical staff may enact these earlier relationship issues. Exploration of relationships with significant figures in their childhoods as well as current adult relationships, especially spouses, is likely to reveal patterns of experienced abandonment and deprivation. In reality, most of these mothers appear to have little support or attention from their partners (see Chapter 1), who themselves would likely benefit from psychotherapy. Helping these women to articulate their present feelings and assisting them in directly and assertively expressing their needs for support and recognition to their husbands, partners, and families may be one way to help free these mothers from the vastly more destructive reliance on their "sick" child as a means of keeping the physician close. Family therapy incorporating significant family members, and, if possible, bringing the husband or partner back into the family as a functioning parent, can be an important component to successful change of the mother's behavior. Success in therapy will ultimately depend on the individual dynamics of the patient, her willingness to acknowledge her fabricating behavior and its destructiveness, the responsiveness of other family members to the need for change in the family system, and the therapist's ability to work supportively with the patient without being deceived by her cheerful surface presentation. With the majority of MBPS mothers, this is a highly challenging task for even the most experienced therapist.

Psychological Testing
of MBPS Patients

Given the problem of fabrication by MPBS mothers, not only regarding their children's medical condition, but also regarding their own medical and personal histories, psychological tests offer one of the few available tools for collecting objective, quantitative data about such patients. In our experience mental health professionals who perform court-ordered assessments of MBPS parents *without* the aid of psychological tests—and projective tests in particular (tests that assess less conscious psychological material)—are at major risk for being deceived by the parent's often skillfully maintained facade of normalcy.

Unfortunately, psychological testing requires cooperation by the examinee and several hours of active participation. Many clinicians initially involved as consultants to pediatricians stymied by MBPS cases often lose control of the cases and access to data about the parents once the parent is accused and the legal system is activated. Often many other mental health professionals (for example, the pediatric consultation-liaison psychiatrist, the child's assigned therapist, the court-appointed evaluating psychologist, the mother's private psychotherapist, and so on) are involved, and they work at cross-purposes because of poor coordination of data, limited financial resources for thorough evaluation, and legal constraints on the sharing of data due to confidentiality issues and ongoing legal proceedings. In addition, since the majority of MBPS reports in the literature are written by pediatricians for medical journals, articles on MPBS tend to emphasize the unfolding of the medical mystery and offer limited data from evaluations of the mother and limited interest in or familiarity with psychological test data, if it is available at all.

Despite the wide variability in manifestations of MBPS, parental dynamics reveal a remarkable consistency when viewed from a clinical standpoint. At present we possess no standard profile of the MBPS parent; thus today the collection of psychological test data is ordered more as an aid to psychological treatment of the parent and assessment of the overall degree of psychopathology than as definitive evidence of the diagnosis of MBPS. If efforts were made to develop such a profile (assuming there *is* one), it would serve as an extremely useful tool in helping support the diagnosis of these mothers in the courtrooms, especially in the many cases based on circumstantial rather than eyewitness evidence. Such a profile could help point the way to the most relevant treatment approaches for these patients and could also guide us in reassessments of these mothers' progress following a course of psychotherapeutic treatment.

ADULT MUNCHAUSEN SYNDROME TEST DATA

Despite all these obstacles, a number of reports in the literature do allude to the use of psychological testing in specific cases, and some provide data. Most of the available data are contained in the adult Munchausen syndrome literature which may provide clues to the pathology in the by-proxy disorder, given the overlap in the two syndromes. Because some adult Munchausen patients are hospitalized for extended periods in medical or psychiatric units, they have provided a more accessible pool of examinees than have the MBPS mothers.

Table 10.1 presents a summary of the test data available on adult Munchausen patients in the literature. Most of the quantitative data derives from adult intelligence tests; most of the projective test results are interpreted and summarized rather than quantitatively presented. With the possible exception of the cases discussed in Pankratz and Lezak (1987), none of the patients was tested with a complete neuropsychological test battery despite some suggestions of possible brain dysfunction. The scarcity or unavailability of detailed data for all tests (for example, Wechsler Adult Intelligence Scale [WAIS] subtest scores, Minnesota Multiphasic Personality Inventory [MMPI] T-

TABLE 10.1 Summary of Test Data of Adult Munchausen Syndrome Patients

Authors	Tests administered	Quantitative data	Interpretations
Stone (1977)	WAIS	Verbal IQ 111 Performance IQ 108 Full Scale IQ 110	Considerable scatter; some personalized, bizarre responses.
	Rorschach	None	"Preoccupied with percepts involving decayed, decomposed, or otherwise mutilated bodies" "Confusion regarding identity was marked; sexual and aggressive impulses were commingled and primitive"
Howe, Jordan, Lockert, & Walton (1983)	WAIS	Verbal IQ 114 Performance IQ 123 Full Scale IQ 119	—
	Bender	None	Adequate, no organic involvement.
	"Personality data"	None	"Projection, somatization and acting out are her preferred defense mechanisms. Impulse control . . . deficient and ineffective"
O'Shea, Lowe, McGennis, & O'Rourke (1982)	WAIS	Verbal IQ 86 Performance IQ 78 Full Scale IQ 82	Only Digit Span fell significantly below average.
	MMPI	All T-scores >70 F − K Index = +32	Dramatic "fake bad," a "naive malingerer"
	16 PF	10 of 16 factors were extreme	—
	Maudsley Obsessional-Compulsive Inventory	None	"Significantly troubled by checking, slowness, repetition, and doubting"

(cont.)

TABLE 10.1 (cont.)

Authors	Tests administered	Quantitative data	Interpretations
Lidz, Miller, Padget, & Stedem (1949)	Wechsler–Bellevue	Verbal IQ 114 Performance IQ 80	—
	Hartford–Shipley Scale	Vocabulary: 17 Abstract: 12 Conceptual Quotient: 71	—
Victor (1972)	MMPI, DAP, TAT, Rorschach	None	"There is very strong evidence of conflicts in the sexual area probably dating back to early father–daughter relationships." "Elaborate defensive system which includes denial of feelings, somatization, fantasy, fulfillment, and passive withdrawal"
Pankratz (1981)	Rey Osterrieth Complex Figure		"Severe problems in perceptual organization"
Sussman, Borod, Cancelmo & Braun (1987)	WAIS-R Wechsler Memory Scale	Full Scale IQ 76 Memory Quotient 79	"Persistent deficits in attention, concentration, & visuospatial organization were evident"
	MMPI	F-Scale–110 T-score Extreme elevation of all scores, esp. PA & SC	Possible invalid profile in "fake bad" direction
Barker (1962)	Summarized 7 cases	IQ range: 64–125	4 of 5 cases had verbal IQ > Performance IQ
	Rorschachs, TATs, Picture Frustration Studies, Phillipson's Word Association Tests	None	Interpretations drawn from this group were "not informative."

(cont.)

TABLE 10.1 (cont.)

Authors	Tests administered	Quantitative data	Interpretations
Spiro (1968)	WAIS	Full Scale IQ 109 minimal scatter	—
	Rorschach, TAT		No evidence of psychosis
	MMPI		Consistent with diagnosis of sociopathic personality disorder
Cramer, Gershberg, & Stern (1971)	*Patient 1* Wechsler-Bellevue	Verbal IQ 112 Performance IQ 103 Full Scale IQ 109	No evidence of thought disorder
	"Projective and graphic material"	None	"Revealed a woman who was infantile and narcissistic, with a low frustration tolerance" Hysterical character disorder
	Patient 2 Wechsler-Bellevue (six exams done)	Verbal IQ 107–125 Performance IQ 92–109 Full Scale IQ 100–118	Progressive deterioration seen over the six administrations
	Patient 3 TAT	None	Preoccupation with death, loss, deprivation
	Patient 4 Wechsler-Bellevue	Full Scale IQ 86	Signs of organicity and gross deficit in body imagery
Pankratz & Lezak (1987)	Presented 5 patients	No quantitative data	All cases had good verbal skills and fund of information but "the more obvious verbal skills obscured deficits in conceptual organization, management of complex information, and judgment"

scores, and Rorschach Structural Summary) makes pattern hunting very difficult.

The available WAIS results show the greatest variability. Reported scores range from below-average to above-average on the Full Scale IQ, with "minimal" to "considerable" scatter. Where data are available, it appears that Verbal IQ generally exceeds Performance IQ.

Of the four MMPIs presented, at least two raise questions about invalidation in the direction of "faking bad," the excessive endorsement of items indicating psychopathology in a rather naive attempt to appear highly disturbed. This was noted in the extreme T-score elevations of all scales and a high F-K Index. The response to duress and/or a "cry for help" might also explain these elevated MMPI profiles. Alternatively, such profile elevation may reflect rather florid histrionic elaboration of emotional and physical complaints.

Signs of impaired brain function were mentioned by some authors (Pankratz, 1981; Sussman, Borod, Cancelmo, & Braun, 1987; Cramer, Gershberg, & Stern, 1971; Pankratz & Lezak, 1987) either on intelligence tests or on a specific visual motor task (the Rey Osterrieth Complex Figure Test). One paper (Howe, Jordan, Lockert, & Walton, 1983) reported Bender test results as evidence of no brain impairment, with no other neuropsychological data. From the available data, few of these particular studies appeared to employ a comprehensive assessment of the patient's neuropsychological functions.

Perhaps the most consistent data come from the reports of projective test results (for example, The Rorschach inkblot test and the Thematic Apperception Test [TAT]). While Barker (1962) reported that his summary of seven sets of projective data was "not informative," and Spiro (1968) reported no evidence of psychosis, there were some consistencies in the remaining projective data. In general they (Stone, 1977; Cramer, Gershberg, & Stern, 1971) reported themes of preoccupation with decay, death, and loss. Identity confusion as well as sexual and aggressive impulse control issues came up several times. Defense mechanisms of acting out, projection, somatization, and denial were all described.

In summary, the adult Munchausen test data, limited as it is thus far, describes subjects exhibiting a wide range of intellectual ability, with generally stronger verbal than nonverbal abilities. The question of neuropsychologic impairment cannot yet be addressed given the lack of adequate comprehensive assessment data; cause and effect relationships also remain unclear. Projective data suggest that adult Munchausen patients are struggling with primitive sexual and aggressive impulses that they attempt to control through denial, somatization, projection, and/or acting out. When given an opportunity to describe their psychological state on a seemingly straightforward self-report measure (the MMPI), there may be a tendency toward deliberate exaggeration in the direction of pathology, resulting in potentially invalid profiles, or a reflection of genuine personality pathology.

MBPS PARENT TEST DATA: LITERATURE REVIEW

The Munchausen by Proxy syndrome parent test data that has been reported in the literature (see Table 10.2) is even less amenable to meaningful summary. The three identified papers (Rosen et al., 1983; Griffith, 1988; Bools, Neale, & Meadow, 1992) provide a less coherent perspective than the adult data because they take different approaches: two focus on individual measures, one on family systems measures. While none of the papers provides actual MMPI subscale data, they report at least three valid MMPI profiles (Rosen et al., 1983; Griffith, 1988) that are not psychotic but emphasize denial of distress and perhaps deceptive or manipulative efforts to look healthy. This is in interesting contrast to the tendency of the reported adult Munchausen syndrome patients to "fake bad" on the MMPI. The third MMPI is reportedly low in Pd (the Psychopathic Deviate subscale), but higher in the Psychotic scales. The one reported battery that included projective test data (Rosen et al., 1983) described the "complete denial of any aggressive or sexualized material" and the use of dissociation of affect and reaction formation as defenses. Most of the other individual measures were paper-and-pencil self-report measures and yielded results in the "normal" range.

In the paper by Bools, Neale, and Meadow (1992), the results were based on an evaluating clinician rating scale derived from a detailed patient history and/or personal interview. This method of scoring by trained clinicians resulted in ratings of fairly nonspecific personality disorders in 90% of the Munchausen by Proxy mothers in their sample. It should be noted that this British clinical team had access to extensive and detailed social, historical, and psychiatric data on their patients and were likely more aware of the presence of serious, if subtle, parental psychopathology in MBPS mothers than the average mental health professional lacking their degree of experience. Their access to very detailed histories of their patients' past

TABLE 10.2 Munchausen by Proxy Syndrome Parent Test Data

Authors	Tests administered	Quantitative data	Interpretations
Rosen, Frost, Bricker, Tarnow, Gillette, & Dunlavy (1983)	MMPI	None	Within normal limits—pattern of "trying hard to deny any upset or distress"
	Rorschach, TAT	None	"Complete denial of any aggressive or sexualized material." Major defenses: reaction formation, dissociation of affect
Griffith (1988)	*Wife 1* FACES III	None	Chaotic adaptability, enmeshed cohesion, moderate overall dissatisfaction
	Global assessment Scale	40	—
	Hamilton Depression Scale	8	Normal
	MMPI	None	"Suggesting . . . egocentric, deceptive & manipulative characteristics with tendency towards emotional reactivity but not indicative of a psychotic disorder"
	Whitely Index	17%	—
	Husband 1 FACES III	None	Structured, enmeshed family structure, low level of dissatisfaction.
	Global Assessment Scale	65	—
	Whitely Index	2%	—
	Wife 2 Global Assessment Scale	45	Normal
	Hamilton Depression Scale	6	Normal
	Hamilton Anxiety Scale	10	—

(cont.)

TABLE 10.2 (cont.)

Authors	Tests administered	Quantitative data	Interpretations
	MMPI	None	Valid profile "Elevated mania and schizophrenia scales suggesting inner turmoil" Very low Pd
	Whitely Index	20%	
	FACES III	None	Rigid adaptability, low dissatisfaction, separated in cohesion
	FES	None	No elevation, depressed subscale: *Conflict*
	Husband 2 Global Assessment Scale	72	—
	Whitely Index	5%	—
	FACES III	None	Separated cohesion, rigid adaptability, high dissatisfaction
	FES	None	No elevation, depressed subscale: *Conflict*
Bools, Neale, & Meadow (1992)	Personality Assessment Schedule	Range of scores: 10 to 106 $\bar{x} = 51$ Median $= 46$	18 of 20 mothers were diagnosed with a personality disorder (mainly histrionic, borderline, or avoidant).

behavior and extensive psychiatric histories is also in marked contrast to the limited personal history often provided directly by the mother to the evaluating clinician in a typical MBPS assessment. Thus, the use of clinician ratings of psychopathology in a Munchausen by Proxy syndrome parent, without the use of sensitive psychological test instruments or extensive experience and familiarity with the syndrome, might be considerably less useful to the average clinician in identifying and understanding the personality problems of these patients.

This very scant data currently in the literature suggests that Munchausen by Proxy syndrome mothers may utilize more denial and dissociation than adult Munchausen syndrome patients while making a more conscious efort to appear psychologically healthy and functional. However, more subtle and indirect measures of assessment seem to yield the clearest evidence of psychopathology.

MBPS PARENT TEST DATA: PSYCHOLOGICAL TESTS

In our efforts to further unravel the complexities of the dynamics and personalities underlying MBPS, we have obtained detailed psychological test data on 12 Munchausen by Proxy syndrome mothers seen by a number of our colleagues (see Table 10.3). The difficulties in obtaining thorough and extensive test data were made clear to us in the effort it took us to gain access to even this limited material. While more extensive batteries (including thorough intellectual, personality, and neuropsychological testing) would have been very valuable for purposes of research, we had access only to the limited test data utilized by the psychologists for purposes of their treatment needs or mandated for court evaluation. Given that these clinicians were generally operating without an existing theoretical model or test profile, their selection of test instruments was largely based on personal preference and familiarity.

Intelligence Tests

The actual Wechsler Test subscale scores are presented in Table 10.4. These results reflect a low-average to borderline range of intellectual functioning.

We cannot generalize our findings of generally low intellectual functioning to the larger population of MBPS mothers because our sample represents a specific group of mothers who either willingly submitted to testing or were court-ordered to submit to these procedures. It is quite possible that mothers of higher intellectual functioning and/or social class may not be caught as readily, may be less cooperative, or have access to legal representation that helps them to avoid court-ordered psychological assessment.

In any case, in our sample we found that the seven patients were about equally divided between those with higher Performance than Verbal IQ and those with the opposite pattern, but only two differences were of any magnitude (though not statistically significant). In

TABLE 10.3. MBPS Mothers' Test Data

Patient	Mother's age	Child's age	Mode of abuse	Test available
1	32 yr	3 yr	Poisoning	Rorschach TAT
2	19 yr	16 mo	Suffocation	WAIS-R Rorschach TAT
3	24 yr	1 yr	IV tampering	WAIS-R MMPI Rorschach TAT
4	20 yr	18 mo	Poisoning	WAIS-R MMPI Rorschach TAT
5	29 yr	2 yr	Induced vomiting	MMPI TAT
6	30 yr	1 yr	Poisoning	WAIS-R TAT
7	28 yr	15 mo	Fabricated reports of seizures	MMPI Beck Depression Index
8	31 yr	14 yr	Fabricated symptoms	MMPI
9	33 yr	2 yr	Induced vomiting	MMPI
10	25 yr	5 yr	Fabricated seizure reports	MMPI, WAIS-R
11	29 yr	10 yr	Fabricated illness	MMPI-2, WAIS-R, TAT
12	21 yr	6 mo	Fabricated apnea	MMPI-2, WAIS-R, TAT

terms of subtest scores, the majority of examinees had quite low Information scores, indicating a poor fund of information. Similarities was also a relative weakness for four of the seven examinees, suggesting difficulties in verbal abstraction and concept formation.

In the Performance subtest area, Picture Arrangement (a task of sequencing cards depicting stories about people) was the highest subtest score for several of the subjects. This finding suggests that these women can successfully focus on sequencing information about social relationships and interactions. They seem to have greater difficulty using visual and spatial skills. Five of the six subjects had

TABLE 10.4. Summary of WAIS-R Intelligence Test Data

PATIENT 2

Information SS	5	Picture Completion SS	8
Digit Span SS	8	Picture Arrangement SS	10
Vocabulary SS	4	Block Design SS	7
Arithmetic SS	7	Object Assembly SS	3
Comprehension SS	7	Digit Symbol SS	5
Similarities SS	3		
		Verbal IQ	80
		Performance IQ	78
		Full Scale IQ	78

PATIENT 3

Information SS	7	Picture Completion SS	9
Digit Span SS	10	Picture Arrangement SS	11
Vocabulary SS	7	Block Design SS	5
Arithmetic SS	7	Object Assembly SS	7
Comprehension SS	4	Digit Symbol SS	10
Similarities SS	6		
		Verbal IQ	85
		Performance IQ	89
		Full Scale IQ	85

PATIENT 4

Information SS	5	Picture Completion SS	5
Digit Span SS	7	Picture Arrangement SS	11
Vocabulary SS	7	Block Design SS	6
Arithmetic SS	5	Object Assembly SS	7
Comprehension SS	9	Digit Symbol SS	10
Similarities SS	6		
		Verbal IQ	79
		Performance IQ	83
		Full Scale IQ	79

PATIENT 6

Information SS	6	Picture Completion SS	11
Digit Span SS	8	Picture Arrangement SS	9
Vocabulary SS	9	Block Design SS	10
Arithmetic SS	7	Object Assembly SS	5
Comprehension SS	11	Digit Symbol SS	12
Similarities SS	9		
		Verbal IQ	89
		Performance IQ	99
		Full Scale IQ	92

(cont.)

TABLE 10.4. (cont.)

PATIENT 10

Information SS	3	Picture Completion SS	4
Digit Span SS	6	Picture Arrangement SS	6
Vocabulary SS	6	Block Design SS	5
Arithmetic SS	7	Object Assembly SS	1
Comprehension SS	6	Digit Symbol SS	8
Similarities SS	4		
		Verbal IQ	74
		Performance IQ	69
		Full Scale IQ	71

PATIENT 11

Information SS	9	Picture Completion SS	7
Digit Span SS	11	Picture Arrangement SS	6
Vocabulary SS	9	Block Design SS	7
Arithmetic SS	10	Object Assembly SS	8
Comprehension SS	10	Digit Symbol SS	10
Similarities SS	9		
		Verbal IQ	95
		Performance IQ	84
		Full Scale IQ	89

PATIENT 12

Vocabulary SS	4	Picture Completion SS	5
Similarities SS	7	Block Design SS	6
		Verbal IQ (prorated)	77
		Performance IQ (prorated)	72
		Full Scale IQ (prorated)	74

considerably higher Picture Arrangement than Object Assembly scores, supporting a relative strength in at least a superficial level of social adeptness, despite weaker performance in skills involving more abstract visual–motor and spatial material. Also, half of the subjects attained higher Picture Arrangement than Comprehension skills, suggesting that their ability to correctly size up social interactions may exceed their ability to express and perhaps even comprehend the more abstract concepts and principles underlying social rules and expectations. Thus they are likely to appear more socially adept than they really are in terms of a mature, abstract understanding of the social world.

Personality Tests

Table 10.5 presents the MMPI raw data available on nine patients. While it is difficult to summarize and compress even this small number of MMPI profiles into a single meaningful description, the following themes from the profile configurations emerge: a rigid, denying defensive style with underlying suspiciousness, marked immaturity, rebelliousness, and lack of social conformity or outwardly conforming behavior. These profiles point to repressed hostile and aggressive features. The generally low Social Introversion scores reflect an outgoing style of shallow, superficial relationships that may further mask repressed hostility. These nine patients differ in the degree of acting-out tendencies, the degree to which they use physical symptoms to express their conflicts, the degree of internalized pain, anxiety, and anger, and the degree of possible concurrent depression and energy they manifest. There seems to be a proclivity to cover over negative feelings with a rigidly positive veneer. These profiles further suggest notable self-centered, narcissistic inclinations with impaired capacities for intimacy and reciprocity with others. It can be speculated that patients with concurrent depression and anxiety rather than paranoid tendencies would have a better overall prognosis for psychotherapy and eventual successful reunion with their children. Patients who are experiencing the internal discomfort of anxiety and dysphoric feelings are generally more motivated to gain insight and relief through psychotherapy than persons who project their negative feelings onto others.

The most striking consistent finding in these nine MMPI protocols was in the high negative F – K Index (they averaged an index of −14), which is used as a measure of profile validity. Virtually all the patients seem to be either significantly lacking in personal insight, highly defensive, or—potentially—deliberately attempting to "fake good" and deny pathology as much as possible, raising questions about the profile validity. This tendency toward "faking good" is likely to have suppressed the overall profile more toward the non-pathological range of scores. In some cases this validity scale configuration with a relatively flat clinical profile may be associated with underlying psychotic trends. The degree of psychopathology in the protocols, therefore, is likely higher than indicated by the absolute elevations (high points) of the MMPI T-scores, although the configuration of clinical scales still yields important data. While the fact that these evaluations were court-ordered could to some degree ex-

TABLE 10.5. MMPI Test Scores

PATIENT 3

T-scores:

L	F	K	Hs	D	Hy	Pd	Mf	Pa	Pt	Sc	Ma	Si
50	45	67	47	52	63	62	47	50	49	52	53	41

$F - K = -21$

Welsh Code = 34–9286/7510:K–L/F

PATIENT 4

T-scores:

L	F	K	Hs	D	Hy	Pd	Mf	Pa	Pt	Sc	Ma	Si
57	46	59	51	43	58	57	57	59	41	47	48	40

$F - K = -16$

Welsh Code = 63451/98270: KL/F

PATIENT 5

T-scores:

L	F	K	Hs	D	Hy	Pd	Mf	Pa	Pt	Sc	Ma	Si
36	46	57	44	52	49	62	51	62	58	44	49	49

$F - K = -15$

Welsh Code = 64–7259/30 18:K/F:L

PATIENT 7

T-scores:

L	F	K	Hs	D	Hy	Pd	Mf	Pa	Pt	Sc	Ma	Si
46	48	55	60	51	63	52	42	52	51	54	68	39

$F - K = -13$

Welsh Code = 931–846 27/5: 0#K/FL

PATIENT 8

T-scores:

L	F	K	Hs	D	Hy	Pd	Mf	Pa	Pt	Sc	Ma	Si
67	52	72	48	49	56	71	53	53	51	57	62	41

$F - K = -20$

Welsh Code = 4'9–83 65 7/210:K'L–F

PATIENT 9

T-scores:

L	F	K	Hs	D	Hy	Pd	Mf	Pa	Pt	Sc	Ma	Si
60	55	46	54	38	56	48	59	47	40	69	70	49

$F - K = -5$

Welsh Code = 9'8–5 3 1/046 7:2#L–F/K

PATIENT 10

T-scores:

L	F	K	Hs	D	Hy	Pd	Mf	Pa	Pt	Sc	Ma	Si
55	53	66	48	54	51	60	41	47	52	57	45	67

$F - K = -17$

Welsh Code = 0–48273/1695:K–LF/

(cont.)

TABLE 10.5. (cont.)

PATIENT 11

T-scores:

L	F	K	Hs	D	Hy	Pd	Mf	Pa	Pt	Sc	Ma	Si
57	37	70	49	42	51	54	65	45	44	48	47	35

F − K = −24
Welsh Code = 543189 672:0#K'L/F#

PATIENT 12

T-scores:

L	F	K	Hs	D	Hy	Pd	Mf	Pa	Pt	Sc	Ma	Si
74	100	50	74	60	84	84	62	90	72	88	82	62

F − K = 3
Welsh Code = 6*8 349''1 7'05 2−F*L'K/

plain the motivation of the examinees to try to appear psychologically healthy in order to regain custody of their children or escape prosecution, these F − K Index scores are probably still diagnostically significant given that the clinical scale configurations give other supporting evidence of high denial and antisocial tendencies.

All but one of the profiles have all subscales in the moderate range, with no T-scores exceeding 70. The profiles tend to show elevations in the Character scales rather than the Psychoneurotic or Psychotic scales. The subscales that show the most consistent high scores are 6, 3, and/or 4, known respectively as the Paranoia, Hysteria, and Psychopathic Deviate scales. The Paranoia scale was constructed to reflect pervasive suspiciousness, interpersonal sensitivity, defensiveness, and—for extreme scores—misperceptions of social situations reflecting frank paranoia. The Hysteria scale was designed to help identify patients who use the defense of the conversion form of hysteria—the use of physical symptoms as a way of coping with stress and adult conflicts—as well as marked repression and underlying dependency needs. The Psychopathic Deviate scale was designed to measure the amoral and asocial tendencies of persons with psychopathic personalities, but may also be associated with narcissistic proclivities.

All but one patient had relatively low scores on the Social Introversion scale, reflecting their generally gregarious, outgoing social style with fairly shallow, superficial relationships. The Social Introversion scale was designed to measure withdrawal from social contacts and responsibilities. It is of interest that the MMPI profiles of

Patients 7, 8, and 9 differed most from the others in their elevation on subscale 9, the Hypomania scale, which measures emotional excitement, flight of ideas, and overactivity. This scale may also reflect narcissistic self-enhancement. These patients also happen to represent three of the mothers who fabricated symptoms rather than actively induced illness in their children. High scorers on scale 9 have been described as expansive, outgoing, uninhibited, self-centered, energetic, and impulsive. The elevated scale 9 of Patient 7 in conjunction with an elevated scale 3 and low scale 0 describes a person who can be characterized as boastful, exhibitionistic, reactive in the face of frustration, and unable to delay gratification due to undercontrol of her impulses. Yet another mother who fabricated her symptom reports, Patient 10, reflects the opposite pattern of high social introversion and low hypomania. In her case, the relative elevations in scales 4 and 8 (Psychopathic Deviance and Schizophrenia) seem to best account for her impulsive, nonconforming pattern of behavior, as well as perhaps underlying dysphoria and social distancing.

Projective Tests

Thematic Apperception Test (TAT)

Individual TAT responses prove even more challenging to condense into a meaningful qualitative summary. Taken as a group, the TATs of the eight patients made available to us could generally be characterized as having brief, constricted stories, a characteristic of respondents who are either resistant to the task, defensive, or possessed of limited intellectual ability. Given the generally low-average to borderline intellectual functioning of several of these patients, and their concerns about the legal implications of their evaluations, it is not surprising that they did not volunteer a great deal of projective material. There was a range of pathology from mothers with very loose associations and rather violent and sometimes bizarre material (Patient 2) to those with highly controlled, Polyannish stories with magical problem resolutions (Patient 3). What did emerge from the stories as a whole was an undertone of dysphoric feeling (mainly described as "frustration," "dissatisfaction," or "sadness" about loss). There was also some awareness of parental expectations that the (child) protagonists of the stories passively resist, resulting in guilt, shame, frustration, and anger. In only one of the protocols does the character actively take charge of her situations and resist authority: "knowing she's going to get in trouble . . . but she feels she has to do it." This same protocol also describes a conscious act of deception: a child "pretends" to cooperate with his mother so he can get his way. This mother likely felt somewhat more able to take charge in her life, even if through rebellious, deceptive, and utimately self-defeating behaviors.

Several of the other protocols describe characters who passively try to resist doing what is expected of them but ultimately are presented as helpless in terms of having an impact on events in their stories. In an interesting contrast to this passive helplessness, *half of the protocols contained stories of characters whose murderous or suicidal impulses got out of control and resulted in unintentional murder.* For example, one patient described a woman who chokes a man to death but "the thoughts running through her head is she wished she didn't (sic) have done it." Another patient told a story about another loss of control involving both sexual and aggressive impulses: "He killed her. He didn't mean to but he did . . . killed her by accident. He did whoopee too much. That's it. Cops find him, he goes to jail, and get a long sentence. He feels messed up." Another example is the patient who described murderous feelings that got out of control when a small disagreement between husband and wife escalated into the husband bludgeoning the wife to death. "After he realized that she was dead he couldn't believe what he'd done." These patients seemed to vacillate between states of passive helpless resentment and the fear of explosive anger with unintended murderous consequences.

The quality of object relations is quite striking in several of these protocols. There is a marked *absence of warmth and relatedness between characters in almost all of these stories.* Events happen in the stories with little elaboration of causality, motivations, or relationships. One patient (1) refused several times to predict the endings of her stories: "I'm not good at endings. I told you that. Nobody knows what tomorrow will bring." Several of the stories relied on an extremely stereotyped, idealized view of love and relationships. For example, one patient cited Katherine Hepburn and Spencer Tracy and Susan Hayward and Clark Gable as the characters in two of her stories. Another patient described her male character in a story as Humphrey Bogart.

Finally, some of the stories seemed to suggest a perception of men as more nurturing and supportive figures than women, as in the stories of Patient 6. Some of the other protocols had very little in the way of nurturant figures, male or female, except for a "miraculous healer" who is a male cleric or physician (Patient 4, Patient 5) healing an otherwise incurable illness.

Five of these TAT protocols were presented to a psychologist who is an expert in TAT interpretation, Dr. Drew Westen, director of psychology at The Cambridge Hospital in Massachusetts. He examined these protocols, blind to the patients' status as MBPS mothers. He summarized the group of responses in these words:

> By and large, the records suggest minimal capacity to invest in other people, minimal complexity to representations of people, minimally developed sense of causality in the social realm and a rather bleak (though not always grossly malevolent) object world. Themes of badness, loss, and deformation (or sexualized aggression) are prominent. Defensively, most of the responses are "shut down," as the subjects appear to be clamping down on associations to painful experiences, perhaps of abuse, and to their internal lives more generally. Denial is prominent, and many of the protocols have a childish quality, although it is difficult to know how much this may reflect age or intellectual factors as much as psychopathology or emotional issues.

Rorschach Tests

The Rorschach test responses generally indicate cognitive slippage, the use of primitive defenses, difficulty modulating emotion, efforts to avoid affect, and passive-aggressive tendencies. These descriptions are quite consistent with the MMPI and TAT findings. A rather rigid, "shut-down," defensive style is found, with denial of affect and immaturity. Outwardly conforming behavior masks more hostile and aggressive features, which seem to find expression in passive-aggressive ways. While these patients seem able, superficially, to size up and function in social interactions, cognitive testing suggests that their abstract conceptual ability is somewhat deficient, just as the TAT suggests that in object relations their poor elaboration of causality, motivation, and interpersonal relationships results in a social world of limited complexity. Table 10.6 summarizes the significant findings.

The small number of available Rorschach test protocols means that this summary description is very tentative and, in conjunction with our other test data, only an exploratory effort that may help us develop hypotheses about the dynamics of MBPS mothers.

In general, while these Rorschachs suggest that the patients' tests cannot be categorized as psychotic, they do display impaired perceptual accuracy, resulting in a rather unusual, idiosyncratic way of organizing their thoughts. There are no significant findings on particular indices such as the Depression, Suicide Constellation, or

TABLE 10.6. Summary of Significant Rorschach Findings (Exner Scoring)

Variable	Patient 1	Patient 2	Patient 3	Patient 4	$\bar{x}$
F + %	.50	.46	.58	.40	.49
X + %	.54	.45	.50	.38	.47
X − %	.15	.35	.25	.31	.27
3r + (2):R	.31	.10	.25	.23	.22
Afr	.30	.35	.60	.44	.42
L	.86	.72	1.00	3.33	1.48
Ma:Mp	2:1	0:2	1:4	0:0	
FC:CF + C	0:1	2:2	1:3	0:0	
C'	0	2	4	0	
S	3/13(23%)	10/31(32%)	7/24(29%)	0/13(0%)	21%

Schizophrenia index and no consistent findings on special scores such as Aggression, Morbid, and more Thought Disordered scorings.

There is a consistent finding in the Structural Summaries that suggests underlying patterns of contained anger and passive aggressivity. This was indicated by a significant number of White Space (S) responses by three of the four patients resulting in an average of 21% White Space responses for the four protocols. Some of the protocols also reveal a higher number of passive to active Human Movement responses (Mp > Ma), suggesting more passive interpersonal inclinations and passive ideation. (See Table 10.6 for highlights of the Structural Summaries.)

Most of the Affective Ratios are low to average and some of the lambdas are high, while in most the FC to CF + C ratio is weighted on the side of CF + C, suggesting poorly modulated affect, especially in emotionally charged contexts.

Certainly, there are individual differences across the four patients' test results reflecting differences in these patients' personality organization. Some of the protocols have no human content (supporting their difficulties in interpersonal relationships) and some have no Achromatic Color responses. There are a few Sadism responses (reflecting the patient's emotional excitement to descriptions of hurting or injuring) and one patient has some Fabcoms (implausible combinations of blot details suggesting more severe thought disorder).

One general finding was that all of the patients indicated difficulties responding to Card 4, often thought of as the "Father Card." Patient 1 made devaluing statements ("This one is dumb"), as did Patient 3 ("Someone very tall, not some*one,* some*thing* very tall . . .

(?) . . . too ugly for someone") as did Patient 4 (she stared transfixed at this card as if in a trance—"What's the purpose of this part? . . . I just don't see what this has to do with anything . . . it looks like a face of a sea serpent . . . I watched a movie with my kids"). This finding is of particular interest, given our theories of these mothers' experiences of disillusionment and neediness in relationships with powerful male figures.

These protocols were submitted to an expert in forensic Rorschach interpretation, Dr. Carl Gacono, from Atascadero State Hospital in California, for scoring and interpretation. He was blind to the diagnosis of MBPS. He gave the following impressions of the data:

> These are mainly protocols of patients with chronic problems, although Patients 2 and 4 may have some situationally induced problems. All of them have low self-esteem and all have cognitive slippage as well as depression and aggression problems. Rather than pathological narcissism, egocentricity may manifest in passive dependent or demanding behavior. Affect is particularly problematic for this group. Problems modulating strong affect such as depression and anger are indicated. Poor affect modulation contributes to cognitive slippage and scores indicate moderate to severe thought disorder. As a group they attempt to manage affect through avoidance and distancing.
>
> These subjects rely on primitive defenses that are only marginally successful. All use devaluation typical of character disorders. Interpersonal difficulties are apparent. . . . The women's responses to Card IV ("father card") may in part offer hypotheses concerning their disturbed object relations. Poor reality testing, primitive defenses, and unusual content elaboration on Card IV are consistent with patterns of women who have been molested, abused, or could be a partner in a battering relationship.

It is interesting that both of the outside experts brought in to examine these results and "blind" to the MBPS behavior speculated that the subjects might be victims of abuse—sexual molestation or battering—which could help explain their "clamping down on associations to painful experiences." While this history is certainly a possibility for any or all of these women, this information was not revealed by more than two of these patients in the histories they provided and is not identified in the histories of most reported MBPS mothers.

CONCLUSION

If overt sexual or physical abuse are not prominent features in most of these cases, we are once again struck by the profound impact on these women of their early experiences of undervaluation and emotional neglect, within a society that reflects this devaluation of women on a larger scale. This experience of lack of recognition, not uncommon in the lives of many women, is apparently capable of contributing to a personality disorder with a high degree of denial and defensiveness, passive agression, and cognitive slippage. Behavior as bizarre and destructive as MBPS may be one tragic outcome.

While no single or simple psychological test profile yet emerges of the "classic" MBPS mother, we do feel an impressive consistency in the patterns of these mothers' limited store of information (with the exception of medical knowledge), poor abstract conceptual ability, superficial social skills, and outgoing behavior. This is coupled with a rigid, denying defensive style masking an underlying rebelliousness, emotional immaturity, self-centeredness, lack of social conformity, and intense passive resentment. This is the profile of a patient who is likely to be very resistive to psychotherapy and therefore very challenging to treat.

CHAPTER 11

Legal Issues and MBPS

In our experience it is difficult to convince courts of the diagnosis and degree of ongoing risk.
—McGuire & Feldman (1989, p. 292)

We found the courts reluctant to take action even when we felt there was a preponderance of evidence.
—Atoynatan, O'Reilly, & Loin (1988, p. 9)

Lawyers representing children and parents have rarely even heard of the syndrome. . . . The capacity of the judge to differentiate between the forms of Munchausen syndrome by proxy and the risk to the child may be the only difference between effective and disastrous court intervention.
—Kinscherff & Famularo (1991, p. 49)

In the late 1960s, years before pediatricians became aware of Munchausen by Proxy syndrome, a 7-month-old boy adopted by a U.S. Army family was taken to the hospital after he turned blue while playing with an adopted sister. In a pattern that was to become familiar a decade later, the child was subsequently admitted to six different hospitals with respiratory and/or cardiac arrests. Though he appeared fine during his stay in the hospital, his medical crises usually occurred within 24 hours of discharge. During the boy's last hospitalization 2 weeks prior to his death, his sister was admitted after she too stopped breathing. This child had a history of "apnea" dating from 4 months of age. Investigation by the FBI eventually revealed a pattern involving the deaths of *six* other children.[1] The mother, it was also discovered, fabricated stories concerning threats against her family and reported multiple recurrent medical problems in her own history.

She was tried for first-degree homicide in a trial that lasted for 5 months and produced 9000 pages of testimony (40% of which dealt with psychiatric issues). The jury was permitted to hear evidence concerning the deaths of the other six children because there was not enough evidence in any single case to prove "beyond a reasonable doubt" that they were "not accidental or attributable to natural causes . . . but rather to the hands of the mother" (DiMaio & Bernstein, 1974, p. 753). When the judge's decision to allow evidence concerning all the woman's children to be heard was appealed to the U. S. Supreme Court, the justices ruled in the prosecution's favor. The Court in this case allowed the admissibility of "prior acts," stating that in "the crime of infanticide . . . evidence of repeated incidence is especially relevant because it may be the only evidence to prove the crime" (DiMaio & Bernstein, 1974, p. 753). A defense of insanity in this case was not allowed.

With the introduction of the clinical description of MBPS and the publication of numerous case reports during the past 15 years, it might seem logical to suppose that all U.S. jurisdictions would treat this problem with some degree of uniformity, but this has not been the case. Quite the contrary, approaches vary radically from jurisdiction to jurisdiction. Some MBPS cases are treated as civil cases, others as criminal cases; and in criminal cases different kinds of charges can be filed depending upon the nature of the abuse. Each kind of charge has an attendant burden of proof; any attempt to terminate parental rights also involves a burden of proof.[2] We have also found that lack of familiarity with the disorder, scarce financial resources in many jurisdictions, and even political considerations play an important role in decisions about whether to charge a MBPS mother with criminal wrongdoing.

---

[1]"From 1946 to 1969 nine infants and small children had suffered a minimum of 20 episodes of cyanosis while in contact with or under the care of Mrs. W. Seven of these children died. Of the dead, . . . three were her own . . . one a neighbor's child, and the last Paul [the patient described above]" (DiMaio & Bernstein, 1974, p. 751).

[2]These latter issues are beyond the scope of this chapter, but are similar to issues involved in charges of child abuse and termination of parental rights. (See Schetky and Benedek, 1992, who note that in general there has been a trend toward criminal treatment of offenses within families.) Prosecutors have wide discretion regarding filing charges.

We cannot emphasize enough that these legal issues must be viewed in the context of the social and psychological obstacles already described in this book. District attorneys and judges may be somewhat more hardened in their views of "human nature" and human propensities than pediatricians; however, they seem as unable and unwilling as those in the healing professions to bring themselves to believe that a seemingly caring and adoring mother could repeatedly inflict painful harm on her helpless infant. Kinscheriff and Famularo (1991), for example, report on such judicial blindness:

> [A mother] secured at least two unnecessary major neurosurgical procedures and had been discovered injecting contaminated fluids into the child's IV line during a hospitalization. She never acknowledged the MBPS. Nonetheless, attorneys for the state child protective services were willing to agree to placement of the child with her mother if she would begin psychotherapy. The Court agreed and placed the child with another relative but permitted continued supervised contact and residual rights. During "supervised" visitation the mother again allegedly attempted to poison the child. (pp. 46–47)

It should come as no surprise to those who deal with such issues that cases of child physical or sexual abuse rarely end up in the criminal courts, even though they often involve children old enough to testify about their own torment. It is rarer still that a case of MBPS finds its way into court.

Nonetheless, those of us in the healing professions have a legal obligation to make the justice system aware of suspected cases of MBPS. As Newberger (1992, p. 148) notes, "all states require all professionals who have responsibility for the care of children to report situations in which they suspect or believe that a child is a victim of abuse." DeAngelis (1992, p. 106) also warns that "the legal requirement to report supercedes all claims to confidentiality. Those who report and/or are involved in the evaluations and investigations are granted *immunity* from any civil action provided their report is reasonable and made in good faith." Moreover, Newberger (1992, p. 144) points out that there is now an extensive body of case law which defines a professional liability risk for not reporting."[3]

While criminal prosecution of parents with such disturbances may not be the best approach, until we have better studied the implications of lesser forms of legal intervention on the well-being of

---

[3]It has been very painful for us to discover that many physicians are reluctant to report their suspicions even in blatant cases of MBPS.

the child, prosecution is often necessary to guarantee the child's safety. With follow-up studies, such as those being conducted by Meadow and colleagues, we may soon be able to better predict which children continue to be at risk.

It is difficult to craft a chapter on legal issues that would be suitable for a readership that we hope includes a broad spectrum of professionals, such as child mental health workers, pediatricians, social workers, law enforcement officers, defense and prosecuting attorneys, and judges. All these groups need legal and ethical guidance for dealing with MBPS, but there are major differences in the kinds of information that each professional group would find most useful. Doctors and hospital workers, for example, need to know more about what to do at the bedside than in the courtroom. But in a society noted for its litigious leanings, the physician also needs to understand the legal significance of his or her actions or inactions. These problems are compounded by the newness of this syndrome, its peculiarities, and the wide variation in jurisdictional responses to cases of MBPS. Therefore, we have divided this chapter into two sections. The first looks at what needs to be done and can be done in the hospital or doctor's office; the second examines the issues as they emerge in the legal system.

IN THE HOSPITAL OR DOCTOR'S OFFICE

Physician Attitudes

The gathering of evidence in MBPS cases, where eyewitness report and confessions are unusual, poses many interesting legal and ethical questions. The essential issue involves ensuring a principled balance between protecting a preverbal, helpless infant and safeguarding the civil liberties and due process protections of the suspect parents. In the case of an infant, there are three important elements that the pediatrician/social worker/psychology consultant ought to know. These are: (1) the importance and admissability of indirect evidence, for example, documenting a lack of symptoms when the mother is not present; (2) the acceptability of the use of professional opinions (of doctors, nurses, social workers, and so on) as evidence; and (3) surveillance using surreptitious monitoring techniques. Overarching these practical considerations and contributing to the challenges of establishing good evidence is physician discomfort with the detective role and physician aversion to involvement in the legal arena.

The majority of pediatricians place primary value on their healer role and ther relationship with the family: they have little preparation or taste for the requirements of gathering "admissable" evidence. Unlike other child abuse situations, their role does not end when they contact child protective services about a suspected MBPS case; indeed, bringing a suspected MBPS mother to the attention of the legal system may signal the beginning of a prolonged and frustrating process of evidence gathering, testimony, acrimonious relations with the press and defense attorneys, continuing involvement as the child's physician, and acting as advocate and consultant to various social agencies. We have seen examples of physicians backing away from cases when medicolegal issues appear to be emerging.

Admissible Evidence

For the concerned health care provider who believes that a patient is being subjected to covert abuse by a parent, the place to start is at the bedside. The easiest method for establishing abuse, though it has potential attendant risk for the child, is careful documentation of the child's symptoms in the presence and in the absence of the suspected MBPS mother. This becomes important particularly if the mother is not directly observed harming her child, and when the child's illness cannot be explained by any medical tests. In these cases, demonstrating that the child appears to be well while in the hospital *in the mother's absence* is of enormous legal value. If, as often is the case, the mother is almost always present, such a test situation is obviously difficult to create. In a case we consulted on where the mother eventually admitted to poisoning her child with household detergents, the mother agreed to absent herself from the hospital for 4 days. Some mothers are much less resistant than expected when asked to comply with such a test situation. The observations made during that illness, when the child was admitted for intractable vomiting, were crucial in convincing us and the courts that the mother suffered from MBPS. She very believably claimed that the administration of chemicals to the child occurred under stress because her family was "falling apart." However, her child was noted to be seriously ill prior to her family's difficulties and to do much better during the mother's absence from the hospital for several days.

This little girl was born prematurely and suffered from chronic vomiting for 2 years. As is often the case, a *possible* cause, gastro-esophageal reflux, was discovered after an extensive work-up, and led to surgery. As is equally common in these cases, the child continued to be symptomatic after surgery. The court and the consultant were convinced by the observations of the pediatric gastroenterologist that indicated that the mother (who disclaimed any role in the child's vomiting) was lying and suffered from MBPS. The child was removed from the family and continues to be free of all symptoms 2 years later.

Importance of Documentation

It is difficult to overemphasize the importance of careful documentation by the attending and other physicians faced with such grave suspicions. Tort negligence theory may be useful as a way of explaining how a child is hurt. In tort practice the plaintiff must be in the care of the defendant and the injury must be one that could not occur without some form of negligence. The evidence usually includes sufficient material of human experience to warrant the conclusion. In child abuse where the mother is being charged with the responsibility for injury to the child, the prosecutor can use this approach to dismiss other possibilities of how the injury could have happened. *Very* detailed evidence must be presented so that all other reasonable possibilities for the cause of the illness appear extremely unlikely. Though a young child is usually within the exclusive control of the parents, and although illnesses that are tied temporally to a parent will raise suspicions, this is not enough. As Rypma (1990, p. 49) notes, "Expert testimony on the dynamic issues involved would then be critical once the attorney has effectively foreclosed all reasonable explanations for the illness." The judge/jury should be left with only one reasonable explanation for the child's illness: the mother caused it.

Use of Professional Opinions

Careful record keeping and documentation of methods used to find the source of noxious input are extremely important, but so are the *opinions* and *suspicions* of the medical personnel involved. For example, hospital records that include opinions about what might be causing a child's illness have been excluded from the category of "hearsay" (see *People vs. Phillips,* 1981).

It should also be noted that limitations on privileged communications such as those between doctor and patient may apply. In general, where a child's health and safety are involved, states have

granted an *exclusion* to the privileged communications doctrine usually applied to physician–patient relationships. As Rypma (1990, p. 51)
points out, the "admissibility of physican–patient communications
coupled with mandatory reporting of child abuse laws may even
provide a tool for prosecution given the possibility of an initial denial
. . . followed by [an] admission by the abusing parent to a therapist in
a psychotherapeutic relationship."

Privacy and Surreptitious Surveillance

Surely the most controversial issue in the gathering of evidence of
illness-causing behavior involves surreptitious surveillance. Hidden
video recording can prove enormously valuable in such cases, but
such surreptitious actions raise many ethical and legal issues and often
incur the resistance of at least some of the staff as well. Regarding
adult Munchausen syndrome patients, Sadler (1987) has argued strenuously that the rights of individuals to confidentiality need to be
protected, even though these patients are fabricating their illnesses.
Meropol, Ford, and Zaner (1985), on the other hand, contend that
family, insurance companies, and other doctors ought to be told, as
these fabrications are not neutral acts (that is, they affect others). We
have not understood this aspect of the debate over privacy in adults,
as "factitious disorder" is a recognized, diagnosable illness and therefore, when strongly suspected, ought to be recorded in the medical
chart and reported to appropriate agencies. Meropol, Ford, and Zaner
(1985, p. 280) have argued that "because the doctor–patient relationship has been initiated by fraud, the privilege of confidentiality is not
absolute and may be breached as necessary for the well being of other
persons." They point out that such "fraud" is now illegal in the state
of North Carolina. However, they warn, and we strongly concur,
that this does *not* justify "invasion of personal privacy" (for example,
room or bag searches). Informed consent or legally obtained search
warrants are required for that particular step.

When a Child's Life Is in Danger

Where a child's life is in danger, the rules should be different. To
what degree they should be different is under debate and varies from
jurisdiction to jurisdiction. Investigations of child abuse, physical or
sexual, can be instituted with the faintest of doubts by just about
anyone in some states. But the telltale signs of the usual forms of child
abuse frequently make detection and proof less problematic once the

suspicion of abuse is raised. MBPS often raises problems of detection that are exponentially more difficult. Nonconcealed close human observation of a child in the hospital is difficult and far from infallible, and when the induced illness is of the magnitude of suffocation or sepsis (as it often is), the child is at grave risk. In our experience, reports to the child protective service are usually futile in the absence of hard evidence. Fathers, who might be a source of useful information for discrepancies in the mother's stories, should be interviewed but rarely are. Some vehemently defend their wives if they are not already colluding with them in the harming of their children. Direct confrontations, as Samuels et al. (1992) and Epstein, Markowitz, Gallo, Holmes, and Gryboski (1987) point out, often produce entrenched denial. Several case studies (Kinscherff & Famularo, 1991) and our own experience have demonstrated that such confrontations often do not lead to a cessation of the endangering behavior. Confrontation may even cause the parents to intensify their efforts to demonstrate that the child is really ill or may cause them to change doctors or flee to another area.

The tension is clearly between protecting the life of the infant, who usually cannot speak for himself or herself, versus maintaining the constitutionally guaranteed rights to privacy and due process of the parent. As Kahan and Yorker (1991) summarize, the Fourth, Fifth, and Sixth Amendment rights of protection against unreasonable searches and seizures, against self-incrimination, and guaranteeing legal assistance, plus the Fourteenth Amendment's due process clause, usually exclude evidence that is surreptitiously obtained from use in subsequent criminal trials. Note, however, that the U. S. Supreme Court has held that "evidence obtained illegally by a private party (not acting under the direction or employment of a law enforcement agency) is admissable" (see *Burdeau v. McDowell,* 1921; Kahan & Yorker, 1991). Physicians or other hospital personnel may qualify as private parties for purposes of this exclusion. Child protective service workers are in government employ and therefore are in a more ambiguous role and may not be considered private parties in this regard.

Kahan and Yorker clearly feel that, as in adult Munchausen syndrome, searching a mother's purse or her belongings at home or in the hospital can only be condoned with an appropriately obtained search warrant where probable cause can be shown. They point out, however, that the legal debate over whether in-hospital closed circuit video monitoring would constitute a violation of Fourth Amendment protection seems to fall on the side of protecting the baby, even without a legally obtained search warrant. Southall et al. (1987), writing from England, where the right to privacy is less broadly defined, take a strong stand defending the use of police-managed video surveillance and the breech of confidentiality: "A paediatrician's responsibility is primarily to ensure the survival and health of the child . . . [and] . . . it is often the absence of concisely documented information which leads to unnecessary difficulties"[4] (p. 1640). Southall and colleagues were strongly criticized in the English press but were defended by Meadow (1987) in an editorial in the *British Medical Journal*. "Critics," he said,

> were forgetting the identity of the patient. If that 2-year-old, who had had periods when his air supply was cut off and he had had to struggle to get air, had been asked if he wanted to be filmed so that the cause of those episodes could be found, he would have answered "Yes." Some will believe that the mother should have been confronted with the allegation before being filmed. . . . I do believe in prior confrontation because sometimes the mother will stop her actions and accept help, but accusing a mother of bizarre and dangerous actions is difficult when you are uncertain of her guilt. Some mothers whom you confront deny their actions and continue them whether they are putting a hand over their baby's nose and mouth, making the toddler sick and adding blood to the vomit, or injecting contaminated solutions into their child's intravenous infusions. . . . Full admission rarely follows other forms of confrontation even when that confrontation is supported by strong forensic evidence. (pp. 1629–1630)

Williams and Bevan (1988), writing for the faculty of law at Sheffield University, suggest useful guidelines for video surveillance involving a two-stage procedure. The first stage should consist of "a clinical judgment on the case by a very small group consisting of the consulting pediatrician concerned, a second appropriate consultant colleague,[5] a social worker with statutory authority who deals with child abuse, and a senior nurse involved in the child's care" (p. 780). They would be charged with evaluating all the "evidence" available and deciding whether secret surveillance is necessary and appropriate. Williams and Bevan point out that all "the alternatives to surveillance should be considered" (pp. 780–781).

[4]For a very detailed description of how the British group carries out video surveillance in cases of suspected suffocation, see Samuels, McClaughlin, Jacobson, Poets, and Southall, 1992.

[5]We feel strongly that this consultant should be a person with extensive knowledge of this syndrome.

The second stage of the procedure should be designed to

> include notification of the decision to the hospital administration. It would also involve alerting the nursing staff who must be briefed well so that any doubts they have about the wisdom of secret observation can be dispelled. For those who remain opposed to the proposal, it should be made clear that individuals can opt out of the exercise without fear of the consequences. However, it should be made equally clear that anybody opting out *must still maintain strict confidentiality.* (p. 781; our italics)

Consultation with the family's general practitioner is *not* felt to be useful and may be inappropriate because of the conflict of loyalty which he or she would then feel. We were recently called to consult on a case in another hospital when a consultant in pediatrics could not convince a family practitioner colleague to look for toxins in a child who was having bouts of unexplained diarrhea.

Opinions about whether to inform the police vary. It is unclear whether an appropriate search warrant for hospital surveillance is the better route or whether a "private party approach" is more appropriate. Rosen and colleagues (Rosen et al., 1983; Rosen, Frost, & Glaze, 1986; Frost, Glaze, & Rosen, 1988) have reported that the video evidence gathered in two separate MBPS cases was admissable in court, (Rosen, et al., 1983; Rosen et al., 1986; Frost, Glaze, & Rosen, 1988), resulting in two convictions, one for murder. But Zitelli, Seltman, and Shannon (1987) warn against overzealous use of such surveillance, and suggest that great pains be taken to focus surveillance *only* on the child. They caution that the "physician must be wary . . . not to intrude . . . on the parents' legal rights" (p. 917). Underlying our concern is the lack of knowledge and inability to appreciate the potential for parental causation of a child's serious recurrent illnesses on the part of the protective and judicial system. Samuels, McClaughlin, Jacobson, Poets, and Southall (1992) reported on 14 cases in which covert video surveillance (CVS) was employed. Though there was a strong suspicion of abuse, it was felt that the "information upon which [it was] based [was] usually insufficient to guarantee that a court would separate the child from its parent." Clearly this procedure was not being used excessively or for trivial cause; the authors report that "to date no child has undergone CVS . . . and [been] found to have a natural (nonabuse) cause for their cyanotic episodes" (p. 168).

The median surveillance period in the cases described by Samuels et al. was 24 hours. In all 14 cases the parents attempted suffocation in the hospital in close proximity to the staff. It was felt that they did this in order to demonstrate to the physician and staff that the "symptoms" were real.

Without major educational efforts, cooperation from protective services and warrant requests for this type of surveillance are unlikely to be successful. An example of this problem is the child with stunted growth and repeated presentation as a "failure to thrive" patient (this case is detailed in Chapter 1). It took months to have the child removed by county authorities, during which time the child reported he had been induced to vomit at home, but ate voraciously and gained weight in the hospital.

Given the potential for severe risk in this disorder, the helplessness of the infant, and the great skill of the parent at hiding the abuse, we think that surreptitious surveillance is sometimes necessary. After all, physicians often screen for toxins from blood drawn for other tests, without parental consent. Telemetry, involving video monitoring of children, is becoming a common part of medical practice, particularly in hospitals. It has been argued that this type of surveillance does not involve entrapment by enticing the parent or in any way changing the environment in a fashion that might induce behaviors. This is particularly true if equipment can be used to focus solely on the infant.[6] The possibility of losing a criminal case because of evidence so obtained would, to most physicians, pale next to the possibility of losing a child. We feel that as MBPS becomes firmly recognized as a disorder, surveillance will be seen as part of the standard treatment for documenting the abuse.

Since many of these cases end up in family court, rather than the criminal justice system, and usually involve the temporary removal of a child, the privacy violations associated with covert surveillance seem like a small price to pay for potentially saving the life of one or more children. While it is possible that the hospital and the physician could be sued for violating the rights of the parents, such suits are very unlikely to be successful given the aforementioned protection for good faith reporting of child abuse, especially when the evidence for the suspicion of MBPS is strong. Constitutional lawyers may, however, see this issue differently.

In a case we heard about where a couple was acquitted of what appeared to several experts as clear-cut Munchausen by Proxy behavior, the pediatrician was sued by the parents for libel. Their

---

[6]A recent FBI journal article (Fiatal, 1989) on the subject interestingly suggested video surveillance *without* sound recording as further protection for the parent.

attempt to go to trial was summarily dismissed by the judge when the facts of the case were presented. In one case the mother sued a university hospital (*Fitzgerald v. Stanford University Hospital,* 1992) for $7 million for negligence in the treatment of her child which resulted in a respiratory arrest and subsequent brain damage. A psychiatrist was allowed to testify as an expert witness on MBPS after a "403" hearing on the admissability of evidence regarding the syndrome in this civil malpractice suit.[7] He testified that the mother's behavior played some role in the girl's medical emergency. The jury agreed, voting 10 to 2 for the defense. The two members who voted for a negligence verdict did so, according to the defense attorney, because they felt that the university had not adequately protected the child from her mother's illness-causing behavior.

IN THE COURTROOM

There are two important courtroom issues related to this disorder: the possibility of using sibling-illness data and/or prior medical histories of the child and parents in helping to frame the case that the behavior fits the syndrome, and the admissability of expert testimony about MBPS.

Use of Medical Histories of Victim Siblings

While generally inadmissible in trials, evidence of prior bad acts have been allowed in MBPS cases. In an early criminal case (*People v. Tinning,* 1988, discussed by Egginton [1990]), attempts to show intent or motivation "rather than propensity," by the use of sibling data, were originally denied. Only after defense *erred* and tried to make an argument about a rare genetic disorder as a cause for the other children's demise, was the prosecution allowed to admit findings concerning the deaths of other children in the family. However, as we mentioned earlier in this chapter, there is precedent in the federal courts (DiMaio & Bernstein, 1974, p. 753) "that when the crime is one of infanticide or child abuse, evidence of repeated in-

---

[7]While MBPS will be found in the appendix of DSM-IV (i.e., it is in need of further study), and psychiatrists usually are called as expert witnesses, it is our opinion that pediatricians with some knowledge or experience with this syndrome also qualify.

cidence is especially relevant because it may be the only evidence to prove the crime."

In a related matter in a California criminal case (*Estelle v. Mc-Guire,* 1991) a man was convicted of second-degree murder for his daughter's death. The court allowed evidence of the "battered child syndrome" even though the defendant had not been directly linked to the earlier abuse of his daughter (*San Francisco Chronicle,* 5 December, 1991) The Supreme Court supported the California court's ruling that "when offered to show that certain injuries are a product of child abuse, rather than accident, evidence of prior injuries are relevant" (*Estelle v. McGuire,* 1991). As this disorder gains acceptance as a syndrome, it will be increasingly likely that such standards of admissible evidence will apply in these cases as well.

Accumulating data in the literature suggests just how important the histories of sibling involvement can be. As we mentioned earlier, Meadow reported on 32 children with fictitious epilepsy. These 32 children had 33 siblings, of whom 7 died SIDS deaths (Meadow, 1984b). In another report on recurrent suffocation in 27 families, Meadow (1990b) found that of 27 siblings, 8 had died and 1 had suffered brain damage from "suspicious causes." Such information is most convincing to courts, and especially juries, of the potential dangers to a particular child. And it may lead, as it did in at least one other case (DiMaio & Bernstein, 1974), to a conviction.

Admissibility of Expert Testimony

The success of admitting expert witness testimony in evidence has varied. In the case of *People vs. Phillips* expert testimony on MBPS was found "helpful to the jury and judge because the syndrome is rare and not within the realm of common experience" (Rypma, 1990). In the Phillips case, expert testimony was admitted even though at the time MBPS was not a psychiatric disorder recognized in the DSM III (third edition of the *Diagnostic and Statistical Manual* of the American Psychiatric Association). Evidence was admitted based on these experts' opinions because it relied on studies that had appeared in professional journals. The principle involved here, although it did not apply in *People v. Phillips,* is known as the Kelly-Frye standard, that is, "a scientific principle or discovery" becomes "demonstrable" when the material from which the principle is derived has been "sufficiently established to have gained general acceptance in the particular field in which it belongs." This usually requires a qualified expert to give an opinion based on the reliability of the data (*People v. Frye,* 1923, cited in Cleary (1984). Kempf (1990) points out that there are several inherent difficulties in establishing the reliability of a diagnosis like MBPS, particularly with psychiatric testimony, which "is generally not associated with 'objective' clinical laboratory results but focuses on behavior and perceptions" (p. 13).

MBPS poses problems that go beyond the usual order of magnitude found in child abuse cases. However, as the syndrome becomes increasingly well known to jurists and public alike, we anticipate that some of these hurdles will be lowered and that future prosecutions and depositions appropriate to the complex factors involved will become more and more the rule rather than the exception as they now are.

Diminished Capacity and MPBS in Criminal Prosecution

Given our clinical findings and our psychological test data, it is unlikely that a plea of not guilty by reason of insanity or temporary insanity is likely to be successful if offered by defendants in these cases. Test data rarely demonstrates evidence of a psychotic process, and the clinical material shows a substantial amount of premeditation. But in some states the courts have moved away from narrowly defined diminished capacity requirements (*People v. Gorshen,* 1959) to one where, though intent could be demonstrated, the jury could also consider whether a person's mental disability interfered with his ability to meaningfully reflect on his actions. Should such complexity become the standard, we will need to develop through long-term study, better understanding of the natural history of this disorder. In particular, if rehabilitation and family reunification is the goal in what appears to be treatment-resistant families, how can we guide the courts in providing for the "best interest of the child" standard? While the ongoing debate concerning the value of maintaining the biological connectedness of a child to his or her family is beyond the scope of this book, we can make some educated guesses on an approach to this problem based on our clinical experience.

To recapitulate, legal precedent affords medical personnel wide latitude to investigate suspected cases of MBPS and to act on informed opinions when the life of a child is threatened by another's hand. While there are many roadblocks to bringing the process of this unique form of child abuse to a halt, these are gradually being removed with increasing awareness of the syndrome. We also feel strongly that longer term studies on the process, course, and outcome in MBPS should prove invaluable in striking a reasonable balance between privacy rights and child protection, and between punishment and treatment of the parent offender.

Management of
MBPS

*"My frustrations had to do with the legal system and I have tried
to control my anger. But I have been made very angry by the
whole process, because this case was treated much more gently
than any other case. It was pretty much a foregone conclusion,
after the mother admitted to Munchausen, that she would get
probation in court. To me this was very serious child abuse. And
the law was not handled evenly and it made me very, very
angry.*

*"I think really I'm kind of ashamed that my fury came out in
ways I didn't want it to. I'm still furious about the way this was
handled through the courts, but I probably could have done harder
work on behalf of the mother. But I found myself kind of
immobilized, probably by anger, about how this woman's child
abuse was glossed over."*

—A juvenile court social worker discussing her
frustrations in taking a MBPS case through
the legal system

*". . . I don't think this woman should be in jail. I don't think
that helps her at all and I don't think it helps society. As I
understand it, the only way she could be in a position to do this
again is if she were the primary caretaker of either a child who
was helpless or maybe a helpless elderly person. I think she can
be kept from being in that position and I think she needs
psychological help. I don't think there is any way she can get
that in prison."*

—Defense attorney who represented a MBPS mother
in a murder trial

As we have seen, Munchausen by Proxy syndrome takes a significant toll in human suffering and social and financial costs, and poses a range of major risks to the child victim—from school absences and unnecessary treatments all the way to disablement or death. These very serious dangers demand that we develop more rapid identification of MBPS cases and more effective responses. These cases also take their toll on the many physicians, other health care professionals, child protection workers, psychologists, lawyers, judges, and others who work with them. A more structured approach to managing these cases could reduce some of the stress felt by all who must cope with MBPS patients and clients. A good start would consist of the development of guidelines for an effective medical, child protective, and therapeutic response to suspected cases.

Effective, systematic response to this problem must occur at many levels: recognition, confrontation, child protection, medical education, and prevention. With greater awareness of the problem in our pediatric community, a more rapid and more effective response by doctors and child protection agencies, and better conceptualization of the psychopathology and its treatment, we could spare lives as well as prevent a great deal of psychological and physical mobidity.

In this chapter we would like to present a detailed picture of how to assess and manage this syndrome. The combined experience of many hundreds of pediatricians and physicians in this country and elsewhere has helped to uncover the many signs useful in identifying the syndrome and to map out paths to follow in planning an effective response. As we will see, the design of a meaningful intervention that (1) takes into consideration the protection of the child, (2) the treatment needs of the parent, *and* (3) can be supported on a long-term basis by the courts is one of the greatest challenges posed by this disorder.

GUIDELINES FOR SUSPECTING AND IDENTIFYING MBPS

While no single indicator provides adequate evidence of factitious illness, an accumulation of positive indicators should serve as a serious warning to health care professionals. The following discussion (based on Meadow, 1980, 1982a; Guandolo, 1985; Jones et al., 1986; Kaufman et al., 1987) summarizes the most commonly noted signs that should raise suspicions about MBPS:

• A child who presents with one or more medical problems that do not respond to treatment or that follow an unusual course that is persistent, puzzling, and unexplainable.

• Physical or laboratory findings that are highly unusual, discrepant with history, or physically or clinically impossible.

• A parent (usually the mother) who seems medically knowledgeable and/or fascinated with medical details and hospital gossip, seems to enjoy the hospital environment, and often expresses interest in the details of other patients' medical problems.

• A highly attentive parent who is reluctant to leave her child's side and who herself seems to require constant attention.

• A parent who appears unusually calm in the face of serious difficulties in her child's medical course while being highly supportive and encouraging of the physician, or one who is angry, devalues staff, and demands further intervention, more procedures, and the like.

• The suspected parent may work in the health care field herself or profess interest in a health-related job.

• The signs and symptoms of a child's illness fail to occur in the parent's absence. (Hospitalization and careful monitoring may be necessary to establish this causal relationship.)

• A family history of unusual or numerous medical ailments that has not been substantiated and raises questions about the reporter's veracity.

• A family history of similar sibling illness or unexplained sibling illness or death.

• A parent with symptoms similar to her child's own medical problems or an illness history that itself is puzzling and unusual.

• A suspected parent with an emotionally distant relationship with her spouse. The spouse often fails to visit the patient and has little contact with physicians even when the child is hospitalized with serious illness.

• A parent who reports dramatic, negative events, such as house fires, burglaries, car accidents, and the like, that affect her and her family while her child is undergoing treatment.

• A parent who seems to have an insatiable need for adulation or who makes self-serving efforts at public acknowledgment of her abilities.

GUIDELINES FOR VERIFYING MBPS

If MBPS is suspected, several important steps should be followed so that the diagnosis can be verified or rejected in a speedy fashion. The literature (Kaufman et al., 1987; Rosenberg, 1987, 1992; Meadow, 1985; Epstein, Makowitz, Gallo, Holmes, & Gryboski, 1987; Jones et al., 1986; Sanders, 1991; Light & Sheridan, 1990; Siegel, 1990; Sugar, Belfer, Israel, & Herzog, 1991) suggests that the concerned physician should take the following steps:

• While much MBPS illness-producing behavior may take place in the hospital setting, hospitalization may be the only way to thoroughly evaluate the ill child, observe parent–child interactions, and develop a plan for effective surveillance.

• Convene an interdisciplinary meeting of all involved professionals as soon as possible to share information, compare impressions, and develop a group consensus on a viable plan. It is even more important to convene such a meeting if specialists from different medical centers are involved. If such a meeting cannot be arranged, phone contact should be established with involved physicians at the hospital and at other centers.

• Involve social service and psychological staff as early as possible for consultation and evaluation of a suspected Munchausen by Proxy case. If staff at a medical center have no familiarity with MBPS, they should contact professionals experienced with this disorder to initiate at least a telephone consultation. It is not at all uncommon to find staff split over whether a parent is harming her child. The availability of a consultant can be crucial to seeing that a fair and informative evaluation is carried out. As Sugar, Belfer, Israel, and Herzog (1991, p. 1020), remind us, "The child and adolescent psychiatrist often provides the glue that keeps the medical/nursing team working together in such a case. The psychiatrist has a major role in facilitating communication among the various care providers and assisting these providers in managing feelings that can adversely affect care."

• Obtain thorough, detailed medical histories for the patient and other family members, including parents, living siblings, and deceased siblings. Details of the histories should be carefully verified with actual medical records from *all* physicians and hospitals; death certificates and autopsy reports should also be examined. Claims by the parent of lost records or deceased or relocated physicians should not be accepted at face value. Medical records from other institutions are best evaluated *in person* to ensure review of all material, including nursing notes and oversized material that would not usually be included in a photocopied record sent to an outside doctor. As Duffy (1992, p. 410) reminds us, "Physicians should be castigated for not reviewing old hospital charts or for failing to create a life table of disease that might identify a constellation of abnormalities over a period of several years. The converse of this failure is the tendency to substitute the old record for a fresh encounter with the patient. This shortcut may prejudice the physician's thinking and force the diagnostic conclusions into previously suggested pathways."

• Obtain thorough social histories *from other family members*. Inaccuracies or outright falsehoods in social history may provide valuable findings to bolster evidence of medical fabrication. Interview the father (or the partner of the suspected parent) as early as possible to check for suspicions, to verify information, and to clarify family dynamics. As Meadow (personal communication, August, 1992) wisely remarks, "Many husbands have complained that the paediatrician never tried hard enough to see them and that if they had been interviewed and asked about the illness events and about what was happening, the abuse would have been detected much earlier and its extent diminished." Meadow also notes that "mothers and sisters of the perpetrating mothers are worth their weight in gold. So often they provide the information about the perpetrating mother and the insight into her behaviour that enable one to be sure about what is happening and also to identify ways of helping." He concludes, "the members of the extended family are useful not only for clinching the diagnosis [by establishing that illness events that have been reported did not happen], but also in providing insight and understanding of the mother and her behaviour." Another researcher went as far as to suggest that he would seek a court order if the father refused to meet with him.

• Provide continuous surveillance of the suspected parent and the patient in the hospital or enforce a period of separation so that the child's behavior and symptomatology can be observed carefully in the absence of the suspected parent. In some cases intensive care unit admissions may be necessary to maintain adequate supervision. Do not attempt this latter step unless there is enough evidence to obtain a hold order if the parent decides to flee with the patient. During such separation situations staff should schedule regular sessions with the parents, noting their reactions and concerns. It *cannot* be overstated that the child needs very attentive care both physically and psychologically during such separations.

• Encourage nursing staff to pay close attention to parent–child interactions, especially regarding feeding, diapering, and handling of invasive lines and hospital equipment. Nurses may be in a better position to recognize some of the telltale signs of MBPS behavior in the mother, so training for nurses in recognizing this syndrome is important.

• Institute controls so that a suspected parent does not have access to her child's medical records; if the parent insists on access to records, make sure this access is carefully supervised. Parents should never have the opportunity to tamper with nurses' observation records, charts, and the like.

• Limit the child's intake to hospital food only. Do not allow the suspected parent to bring in any foodstuffs. Observe the child patient at meal times to make sure the parent does not interfere in any way with the child's eating or drinking.

• Medication should be administered to the child only by hospital staff.

• Do thorough toxicology screens, looking in particular for emetics and phenolphthalein in cases of vomiting and diarrhea even when there is evidence of mild gastrointestinal disorders such as dumping or reflux. Check blood, urine, and stools, and take levels of all prescribed medications to check for overdosing. Ask for a pharmacist consultation if available. New, useful laboratory techniques are being added to our armamentarium of diagnostic strategies all the time. Rosenberg (1992) cites several new techniques, including analysis of calculi with infrared spectrophotometry for diagnosing factitious urinary stones, thin layer chromatography and mass spectroscopy to uncover ipecac poisoning, pharmacokinetics, and sleep disorder laboratory work-ups for apnea patients.

• Recognize, however, that laboratory tests cannot identify many different agents and that the range of potential falsification is beyond most screening tests.

• Carefully store laboratory samples until the best plan is developed for sophisticated analysis.

• Make an effort to personally interview every reported witness to any illness episode to seek verification or disqualification of parental reports. Try to carefully differentiate true *eyewitness* observations from the reports of family members or hospital staff close by during an incident in question, who relate what the parent *said* happened. It is crucial to determine whether a witness to a child's apnea or seizure, for example, was present when the episode *began*.

• Keep careful, legible documentation of all suspicions and all steps taken by medical staff to verify a MBPS diagnosis.

• If possible, obtain psychiatric and psychological evaluations of both child and parent, utilizing projective as well as objective psychological tests administered by psychologists familiar with this syndrome.

• We need to pool our knowledge and experience in order to develop *clinical profiles* that can help us to distinguish the characteristics of true illness from the same symptoms when induced. See Appendix C for an example of the data useful in distinguishing true apnea from induced suffocation.

• The fact that these children often have a previously *explained* disorder should not deter suspicions. Previously explained disorders in MBPS make it harder to suspect falsifications, *but* they do not negate the presence of past and current *un*explained disorders. If this problem is as common as our study of neurologists and gastroenterologists suggests, we will need to develop profiles and consultation systems that will enable us to react more swiftly and thereby avoid the draconian methods entailed in surreptitious surveillance.[1]

GUIDELINES FOR CONFRONTING A MBPS PARENT

Once the evidence of MBPS becomes compelling, confrontation with the suspected perpetrator is necessary. Now the health care system must shift into a very different treatment mode.

"Milder" cases of exaggerated symptoms or parental amplification of a child's bona fide medical problems pose the greatest dilemmas for medical staff in terms of timing and means of intervention. Staff may question whether there is adequate hard evidence or even much value in directly confronting the parent, especially if the "harm" done to the child consists merely of excessive medical visits. In general, we encourage physicians to first attempt to engage these mothers (and their partners as well, if at all possible) in supportive psychotherapy, perhaps in sessions paired with weekly medical check-in visits. However, the success of such efforts is often limited by the mother's denial of any personal distress and insistent focus on

---

[1]We are planning a study in a large HMO to track all visits/hospitalizations in a computer data base. Much as has been done for apnea (SIDS versus suffocation), we plan to compare the presentation of children who are MBPS victims with a particular symptom (for example, chronic diarrhea) with children who have a genuine disorder. Through this study we hope to develop algorithms, much like those available for apnea, to make detection easier (see Appendix C).

the child's medical symptoms. If the parent's medical overutilization does not show some improvement and if the parent fails to make a therapeutic connection with the psychotherapist, the use of the child as proxy is likely to continue and even intensify, particularly as the physician begins to more openly express doubts directly to the parent. At this point the active involvement of the local child protective agency becomes necessary, even if there is inadequate cause for the immediate removal of the child from the home. The mere presence of the child protection agency as a new actor in the case can provide the physician with more leverage to bargain with the mother, and can also prevent the family's flight to another medical center.

The literature (Siegel, 1990; Jones et al., 1986; Rosenberg, 1987; Sanders, 1991), provides many useful guidelines for the parent confrontation:

• The local child protection agency and/or the police should be brought into the case even before the parent is confronted. A police hold order concerning the child can prevent the parent from fleeing with the child victim only to resurface elsewhere to begin a new round of child-endangering activities.

• Have the spouse or other family members present when the suspected parent is confronted, both to assess spousal/family complicity and to weigh the potential for spousal/family support for such interventions as child protection and mandatory psychotherapeutic treatment.

• Tell the spouse/family clearly and directly what is suspected. The goal of the meeting is not necessarily to extract a confession (although that would be helpful) but to inform those involved that MBPS behavior has been exposed, that new steps are going to be taken to protect the child, and that help for the MBPS mother will be forthcoming.

• Once an MBPS mother is confronted and exposed, she should begin to receive psychological help immediately. Since there may be a risk of suicidal behavior (threats are not uncommon), arrangements should be made for crisis assessment of the perpetrator parent and her partner after confrontation.

• Custody of the child immediately after confrontation with the parents should be in the hand of social services personnel who should have a preexisting plan for short-term protection of the child. Removal of any siblings is also important pending thorough medical evaluation of sibling health status and potential risks of reunification. Rapid response, while posing certain risks, is recommended.

• Emergency placement of the children should generally *not* utilize the homes of relatives or family friends, for such people are likely to deny the reality of MBPS in the mother. Adequate protection of the child from exposure to the suspected parent and from continued abuse cannot be guaranteed under these circumstances.

GUIDELINES FOR LONG-TERM MANAGEMENT OF MBPS PARENTS AND CHILDREN

While the identification of MBPS and the parental confrontation are the most dramatic aspects of care for these patients, the most challenging phase is that of long-term management and treatment of child and family. Several authors (Waller, 1983; Rosenberg, 1987, 1992; Jones et al., 1986; Griffith, 1988) have offered useful recommendations for long-term care:

• It is critical that child protection workers, attorneys, judges, and other involved people have a working knowledge of MBPS. Mental health professionals and physicians involved in a case have a responsibility to educate these other professionals and provide appropriate reading material for their edification. Even a few good summary articles on the syndrome can be very helpful. (Appendix A categorizes MBPS articles by prominent signs and symptoms of illness.)

• A major goal of long-term management is to provide for review and establishment of the most appropriate medical and psychological treatment of the child. Ongoing monitoring of the child's physical and emotional status in the absence of deception or medical abuse will finally clarify the child's true health care needs.

• The child's primary physician should remain in charge of the child's health care only if he or she is convinced of the diagnosis. If at all possible, the number of additional specialists and treating physicians should be reduced to an absolute minimum and should ideally involve the original treating physician(s) involved in the uncovering of the MBPS.

• Criminal prosecution of the abusing parent is an option, as is family court action on custody. Criminal action may provide more leverage for enforcing appropriate child protection measures and may also allow for longer parental monitoring through probation.

• The courts must consider the issue of family loyalties in long-term placement of the child. Placement in the custody of an ex-husband or grandparent, for example, may well allow the abusing parent to have continuing access to the child and continuing opportunity to sabotage the child's progress in health status and emotional growth. Even children in foster care may continue disturbing relationships with their parents. Neale, Bools, and Meadow (1991, p. 329) point out that

> in a number of cases [of foster placement] the mothers continued their over-dependence, over-involvement and over-control, bombarding the children with letters, phone-calls, presents and money. The children were put under much stress and the mother's behaviour disturbed the foster placements.

• Court-ordered review of all medical records as well as periodic physical examination of all the siblings is important.

• The parent(s) should be mandated by the courts to remain in long-term psychotherapy *with therapists knowledgeable about this disorder.* Psychotherapy for any affected children, ages 3 and over, should also be provided.

• A decision to return the child to the parent's home or the parent to the family must be based on a thorough psychological/psychiatric evaluation of the parent and her progress in psychotherapy as well as the quality of the parent–child relationship. The overall psychopathology of the parent, not simply the absence of MBPS behavior, must be taken into consideration in the decision to return the child to the parent.

• Ideally, there should be long-term supervision of these families even after reunification with the abusing parent, for periodic review of medical utilization and child's health status. Neale, Bools, and Meadow (1991, p. 331) point to harrowing examples of continuing abuse in this respect.

PREVENTION OF MBPS

Prevention of MBPS is probably one of the most difficult and challenging issues we face. Our free-enterprise health care system encourages open access to caregivers and institutions limited only by the patient's ability to pay for services. Even Medicaid encourages such behavior. With no centralized control of health care utilization, our system allows parents to shop widely for different physicians and hospitals whenever they exhaust the investigative skills of or lose faith in their current doctor. It is interesting to speculate about whether the recent trend toward managed health care and more carefully monitored controls on utilization by health insurers will result in less doctor shopping and abuse of the medical system as the whole health care system becomes increasingly cost-conscious. Our experience indicates that large HMOs, even those with computerized patient data, are far from immune to the problem of MBPS, particularly when all medical visits and hospitalizations are prepaid.

For families with limited income and mobility, the possibility of effectively monitoring their health care patterns is somewhat greater. Local areas could potentially develop flagging systems for alerting hospital personnel, via medical charts or computer screens, about "overutilizers" or children with multiple suspicious emergency room or clinic visits. A "red flag" might alert a physician to do a more-thorough examination, pursue psychiatric/psychological consultation, and be less-liberal in prescribing medication or yielding to parent-requested tests and procedures. Such a system requires clearly defined sets of rules delineating adequate grounds for suspicion and requires trained medical staff to make judgments of when to flag cases for possible MBPS behavior. The ethics of such action is currently unclear and must certainly balance the child's need for protection with the potential invasion of privacy and risk of misdiagnosis of this disorder.

A new development that could revolutionize our system of medical information management was proposed in the spring of 1992 by U. S. Secretary of Health and Human Services Louis Sullivan on behalf of the Bush administration (Rich, 1992). They proposed developing a national electronic medical network to computerize medical billing and record keeping on a nationwide basis, a system that holds out the possibility of a dramatically more powerful means of centralizing information and tracking and flagging potential health care system abusers such as MBPS mothers. But here too the practical and ethical problems will be enormous.

Training pediatricians to recognize the signs of MBPS is another important contribution to early detection, if not prevention, of MBPS. Stancin's (1990) survey of pediatric residency training programs revealed the lack of a formal, consistent, or structured training experience in MBPS. She made several recommendations to improve residency training in this area, including formal didactic, clinically focused instruction early in training with emphasis on the range of subtypes of MBPS and specific protocols for residents for identifying, reporting, and managing these challenging cases. Detailed, structured maternal interviews such as the one developed by Siegel (1990) would be quite useful to residents and pediatricians alike in assessing suspected cases and gathering useful information. This need for training applies also to child protection workers, nurses, and mental health professionals (Blix & Brack, 1988).

Another problem seen repeatedly in Munchausen by Proxy cases is the phenomenon of invalid medical diagnosis and questionable histories perpetuating themselves from admission to admission as each physician accepts at face value the information obtained from previous charts. While it is impossible for physicians to independently verify each item of data in a patient chart, medical professionals need to cultivate more skepticism about medical records. Residents in training need to be taught to avoid the very common phenomenon of fiction becoming "fact" through sheer power of repetition. Whenever an oral medical history sounds unusual or a written medical record looks suspicious, it is essential to speak directly to a prior caretaker.

A related problem is the need for more thorough medical investigation of parental requests for medication for treatment of symptoms not directly observed by physicians. The authors are familiar with the case of a MBPS nurse who obtained multiple prescriptions for her child, some inappropriate, simply by calling pediatricians. Mothers who are nurses, who are otherwise medically sophisticated, or who are experienced caregivers of medically fragile children are particularly likely to have the skills and credibility to successfully order up a range of drugs, virtually on demand. It is, of course, the physician's responsibility to assess the bona fide medication needs of the child.

An important recent preventive suggestion is to develop multidisciplinary teams or task forces on MBPS in order to more effectively coordinate our response to these cases. An example is the task force in the Cleveland, Ohio, area described by Sturm and Roberts (1991) encompassing social service providers, pediatricians, public school staff, child protection workers, court representatives, and attorneys. Task forces such as this can collaborate on clinical and legal approaches to individual Munchausen by Proxy cases as well as collect data, establish general policies, and provide formal and informal support and education to a wide range of professionals likely at some point to become involved in cases involving factitious illness. The presence of such an ongoing group in a community not only maintains a high level of awareness about the syndrome, but may enable faster, more confident diagnosis by health providers seeking consultation and validation of their almost unthinkable suspicions.

Markantonakis (1989) has suggested that we develop a nationwide registry of convicted MBPS parents so that they cannot as easily continue their deceptions by moving to another part of the country once court supervision comes to its inevitable end. This registry might function like the registry of convicted sex offenders used in California for the purpose of maintaining law enforcement agencies' awareness of such offenders when they move into a new community. Aside from the obvious privacy and civil liberties intrusions that such a registry would entail, however, there is also the problem that many MBPS parents are not convicted of a criminal offense but instead are dealt with in juvenile court, where records may be sealed. Kinscherff and Famularo (1991) propose the development of an "information bank . . . maintained by the National Center for Disease Control . . . modeled after similar banks for missing persons and known child abusers," which presumably would list diagnosed MBPS parents even if they were not convicted of felony child abuse.

It should be of serious concern that at least some MBPS parents who are not successfully rehabilitated, even if they lose permanent custody of their "proxy" child, may eventually establish residence in new areas of the country and have more children or assume a responsible role with children, meanwhile escaping any surveillance regarding the status of their new children's health.[2] We have no statistics and no idea how prevalent this problem may be, but it certainly must exist. This problem too raises serious issues about conflicts between the rights of the individual and the protection of children's rights.

One other suggestion for prevention has to do with a potentially important proactive role for school attendance officers in identifying MBPS cases early. It could be very useful for school attendance officers to identify children with significant numbers of school absences due to "illness." If an identified school health officer had the time and interest to contact the pediatricians of individual children to compare notes on the child's health problems and school attendance,

---

[2]Viets (1990) reports on a highly regarded social worker who was found guilty of poisoning one foster child who died of sodium bicarbonate overdose and endangering a second foster child a year later. Despite conviction and a 5-year jail term, she later moved to another state and served as a contract medical social worker for several years! The state's screening system failed to identify her criminal background when she applied for a license, but she was eventually recognized and revealed by a local reporter who had read about the case.

this might serve as an early warning sign to the physician that a child's care at home was an exaggerated response to trivial medical problems or that a child was missing substantial school time while being taken to a variety of specialists.[3] However, it is clear that this kind of a project would require considerable expense for a school district as well as a relatively sophisticated investigator and the cooperation of the parents and physicians.

THE LONG-TERM QUESTION: WHAT ABOUT REUNIFICATION?

The major question that remains in these unsettling cases after the discovery of severe abuse and the child's temporary placement away from the parent is, What do we do with the children? As can be expected with a syndrome so new and complex, and one moreover that can arouse such passionate disbelief, the outcomes vary enormously and there is little in the way of extended follow-up data to assist us in our decision making about the long-term placement of the children. It is an important issue not only in each individual juvenile court process, but also because of the comorbidity found in siblings (Bools, Neale, & Meadow, 1992; Meadow, 1990), and the possibility of serial abuse (Alexander, Smith, & Stevenson, 1990; DiMaio & Bernstein, 1974). As we have noted several times, even child protective services workers with extensive experience in sexual and/or physical abuse can be sluggish in responding to the initial pleas of clinicians very experienced in the problem. Their ability to provide for the *long*-term protection of the children is at times even more problematic.

Mental health consultants are asked critical but very difficult questions concerning the long-term prognosis for reunification of mother with the child who has been victimized as well as the safety of siblings and future unborn children. Meadow (1990b) summarized his extensive experience in this area:

> The agencies concerned have taken varying courses of action. Some have thought that the abuse was so gross and so violent that it must

---

[3]In a case we recently heard about in Florida, the child's pediatrician unfortunately missed some important clues when school authorities, suspecting that something was wrong, required the child's mother to provide letters from the physician to explain the child's frequent absences. (These were later used by mother to try and "prove" her case.)

signify a degree of breakdown in the parent–child relationship that makes it unsafe for the child to be with that mother again. Others, on hearing the mother's full confession and sometimes after a change in her life, such as a new partner, a new job, or new help, have believed that she should be given the chance to look after that child or a new baby again. Although one understands that such mothers may "continue this killing unless stopped or until she runs out of children" . . ., it is not necessarily so, and as with other forms of child abuse, the mother may be capable of satisfactory care for a subsequent infant despite having harmed another. Only two of the children reported in this article were reunited with their natural mothers in the short term. (p. 356)

Meadow suggested that a child is more at risk when certain factors are present. These factors include severe abuse (such as suffocation or poisoning); abuse of a child younger than 5; previous unexplained sibling deaths; mother's lack of understanding of her behavior; a poor outlook for help for mother and family; mothers with adult Munchausen syndrome; mothers with other major problems such as substance abuse; and the persistence of fabrication even after confrontation has occurred (Meadow, 1985). He and his colleagues (Neale, Bools, & Meadow, 1991) have since refined their position on factors contributing to long-term outcome, based on an extended follow-up of between 2 and 14 years' duration:

> We judged the outcome mainly by the emotional, physical and educational development of the children and the success, or otherwise, of their placement. Particularly poor outcomes were found in those cases where there had been long delays before intervention, multiple placements in care, and where continuing involvement with the mother ocurred without firm professional support. Overall, those children physically abused as part of MSP [Munchausen Syndrome by Proxy], and taken into long term care at an early age without access from their mother, fared best. Those who were subject to long term uncontrolled involvement with their mothers fared worst. The overall impression from our follow-up study has been that the adverse effects of Munchausen by Proxy abuse are more severe than expected and include the impairment of the child's physical, emotional and educational development. Where children maintain contact with their mother, either through rehabilitation or access, long-term professional involvement and vigilance are of great importance. Those involved need to be aware not only of the dangers to the index child, and to both younger and older brothers and sisters, but also to future babies born to the abusing mother. (p. 332)

There is also little uniformity in the judicial treatment of mothers for abuse of their children. In England mothers are rarely required to serve actual jail terms. Though often sentenced, they are usually granted probation of between 2 and 4 years. The variability in jurisdictions in the United States is great. For severe endangerment, mothers often get probation if psychological treatment is involved, though for killing a child there have been murder convictions and one mother convicted of manslaughter is now serving a 5 to 25 year sentence.

Little in the literature allows us to feel comfortable with the inconsistent treatment of these cases. McGuire and Feldman (1989) describe a case in which the social services agency finally began supervision of the mother of a 3-year-old girl whose intractable vomiting led to multiple hospitalizations from birth—though the staff was divided on the necessity for it. The child's symptoms improved dramatically, but soon after her brother was born he was admitted for bloody enteritis and lethargy. At 4 months of age, he was hospitalized, and was described as a "wary, wide-eyed child . . . agitated and fussy when fed by his mother" (p. 290). Though he improved while the mother wandered around the rest of the hospital gleefully telling other parents her child had cancer, child protective services returned him to home for "lack of proof." The family then moved from the area. The reports of McGuire and Feldman (1989) and others (Sneed & Bell, 1976; Waller, 1983; Woolcott, Aceto, Rutt, Bloom, & Glick, 1982; Rogers et al., 1976; Chan, Salcedo, Atkins, & Ruley, 1986; Genofsky, 1986) on the psychological ill effects on the children are sobering, to say the least. McGuire and Feldman (1989) conclude:

> Several factors suggest that extreme care must be taken in deciding to leave these children with the family. First, the abuser tends to be skilled in manipulating the system to [a great] extent. . . . Second, in our experience, abuse continued after confrontation of the mother, after involvement of children's protective services, after discovery of abuse of a sibling, and while being closely observed in the hospital. (pp. 291–292)

They also point out that a high level of parental denial and psychiatric problems also suggest a poor prognosis for psychotherapy with Munchausen by Proxy parents.

These views leave us with major dilemmas, particularly as mental health professionals committed to a belief in the value of family integrity and individual and family rehabilitation.

Kinscherff and Famularo (1991) make a strong plea for the value of filing immediate petitions for permanent termination of parental rights in cases of extreme, life-threatening MBPS. They conclude that these cases pose a chronic and lethal danger to the child because there are no reliably effective treatments for the perpetrator. The child may continue to be victimized even during monitoring of the family, and the courts are unable to provide adequate long-term planning and protection for these children. They point to the ignorance in the court system, the "compelling presentation of the parent and her denials," the shifting parties in the legal and child protective systems, and the great variation in experience and turnover in the court systems as factors that further complicate adequate management of MBPS cases. They conclude:

> There are myriad opportunities for current or subsequent workers and courts to err by modifying earlier orders or agreements to permit unsupervised contact or placement with the parent. Simply put, any possibility of contact with the perpetrator carries high risks of death, physical and psychological morbidity, continued victimization, and loss to supervision should the family flee the jurisdiction. Current child protective and legal systems cannot reliably provide the necessary degree of protection for a child absent termination of contact and parental rights. (p. 46)

While undoubtedly a reasonable approach, their advice provides little help in cases of less extreme abuse.[4] Rendering responsible mental health consultation on such serious and permanent matters as termination of parental rights is particularly difficult because courts prefer to decide in 6 months or a maximum of 18 months about permanent reunification or separation of a child and his or her parent, thereby increasing pressure on therapists to make very difficult judgments. A therapist treating a mother is susceptible to the patient's dynamics and convincing denials and protestations. We have usually found that the child's therapist, though also susceptible to some overidentification with his or her patient, can offer a more objective view of the best interests of the child than can the parent's therapist. When there are active and stable court-appointed legal guardian programs available to represent children's interests, their input can also greatly enhance the consultant's ability to make practical recommendations to the court about long-term prospects for reunification.

As we noted in Chapter 9 therapeutic work with Munchausen

---

[4]One social worker found it difficult to "keep up the necessary level of concern when she felt such a 'fraud' visiting a normal family with no clear evidence of abuse, merely a history of the mother inventing stories about the child stopping breathing." But Neale, Bools, and Meadow (1991, p. 332) note that "such false apnoea attacks are a common prelude to suffocation."

patients usually does not go into very much depth (largely due to the nature of the mother's dynamics); indeed, the therapy often seems to consist of a kind of marking time. As Kinscherff and Famularo (1991) point out, the assessment of "progress" in the treatment of MBPS lacks clear correlates such as the urine screening used for substance abusers, for example, or even some physiologic measures of sexual abusers. Unfortunately, sometimes the assessment of future risk of victimization of the child requires the parent to be allowed continued contact. Kinscherff and Famularo feel that stipulated agreements and court orders for monitoring and follow-up are often useless due to overloaded caseworkers, turnover of social service personnel, and the mendacity, hostility, and mobility of the Munchausen families. As we have learned from reports of long-term follow-up now being published (Neale, Bools, & Meadow, 1991), with dedicated supervision, the more subtle forms of doctor shopping, fabrication, and less overt means of abuse will at times continue undetected. We must rely heavily on the excellent work done by this British group of researchers because so little other follow-up data exists. Additional research on MBPS families reunification and outcome will be extremely valuable to those of us faced with these difficult decisions.

As complicated as these issues are in cases where serious abuse has taken place, even thornier problems occur with lesser forms of abuse. As we have described, lesser forms of Munchausen by Proxy behavior are not necessarily indicative of the degree of compulsion involved in the process, or of the prognosis for change. Even in cases of less dramatic abuse, decisions about the potential for parent rehabilitation, assessment of the success of parent's psychotherapeutic treatment, and judgments about continued risk to the child of reunification with the Munchausen parent can be very troubling. Solid longitudinal research is desperately needed in these areas so that just, therapeutic, and nonarbitrary decisions are made on such critical questions of family stability and child safety.

Our clinical experience and the available literature point to several fundamental conditions that should serve as a starting point in decision making about reunification of a victimized child (and siblings) with the parent. Assuming that Meadow's (1985) basic risk factors are *not* present, we propose several additional criteria that should be met before serious consideration of parent and child reunification is considered:

• The victimized child does not also have any serious, bona fide medical problems that would require complex or extended contact with the medical system after reunification. This could seriously complicate the efforts of monitoring agents to determine if the MBPS behavior has resolved.

• The parent should have achieved some insight and a meaningful explanatory system for understanding the nature of her MBPS behavior and the needs she was attempting to meet through the use of the child as proxy.

• The parent should have developed some alternative coping strategies to use when under stress and have demonstrated awareness of significant stress factors in her own life.

• The parent's spouse, partner, or extended family should have accepted the reality of the abusing parent's MBPS and demonstrated a sincere commitment to the future protection of the child(ren).

• The parent's therapist as well as a more objective consulting psychologist/psychiatrist experienced with MBPS patients should be in agreement that the parent has made progress during psychotherapy.

• The parent should not also exhibit additional serious psychopathology such as a thought disorder, affective disorder, organicity, or the like.

• There should be no evidence that the parent continues to claim that her child has unsubstantiated medical problems or that she is continuing to distort facts or somaticize her own problems.

• The parent should be able to demonstrate adequate basic parenting skills, genuine warmth for the child, and increased empathic understanding of the child's experiences.

• The court should mandate that the child's medical providers are kept to a minimum and coordinated by a single physician familiar with and committed to stopping the MBPS behavior.

• The social services arm of the court should provide long-term follow-up of the family's reunification over a period of several years rather than months. Follow-up does not simply mean periodic home visits and visual inspection of the child, but also regular communication with the child's pediatrician and school (to examine patterns of absence and medical utilization).

• Provision should be made either for restrictions on the family's ability to move to new jurisdictions or at least a transfer of long-term follow-up responsibilities to educated authorities in new jurisdictions.

This list, in conjunction with Meadow's (1985) suggestions, is long, demanding, and represents an ideal set of conditions unlikely to be met in many cases due to legal and practical constraints. Given what we know from the reports of psychotherapy with these parents, most are unlikely to achieve this level of insight, understanding, or empathy, and few courts are willing to institute such rigorous controls on these families. Thus we offer these guidelines as goals to guide us in our optimal management of these cases. When not fulfilled, they serve as warning signs that need to inform our clinical judgments and our community practices with these cases.

The bottom line, however, is that we remain very far from having a comprehensive understanding of all the risk factors and individual determinants of a successful or unsuccessful reunification of child and parents. But given the severe and life-threatening extent to which some of these parents will go in their pursuit of a relationship with the medical system, we urge major caution on the part of the legal system in pressing forward with reunification. This is certainly one condition where in order to provide for physical and psychological safety, the parties charged with that task must suspend deeply held belief systems concerning the family and rely on the most current data and expertise available.

Epilogue

In December 1992 as this book is being sent to the publishers, we are encountering a spate of reports of alleged Manchausen by Proxy syndrome cases in several major U.S. cities. We have been interviewed for three news magazine television programs, a popular dramatic series just aired a two-part program on the issue, and we have been approached repeatedly by network talk shows to see if we would agree to appear alongside a Munchausen by Proxy mother. As a friend put it, "You're hot," meaning, of course, that the syndrome has suddenly caught the eye of the media and the fascination of the public.

We view this scene with ambivalence. Making the case, as we do in this book, that there is a need to educate the medical and legal professions and the general public about the presentation and ravages of this disorder, we welcome the opportunity to "get the word out." But we fear the propensity of the media (including unfortunately even the print media) to simplify and sensationalize serious problems, to over publicize them, and then to drop them entirely once the public becomes "bored" by media overload. We worry about their treatment of such a profoundly complex and disturbing subject (one program declined to present one case of a child who had died because it was "too sad").

We remain concerned about the possibility that the disorder, however more common than previously suspected, will be misrepresented as being as common as child neglect and child abuse. We also worry that media attention might lead to many cases of unjustified suspicion of MBPS involving appropriately upset parents dealing with children with complex bona fide medical problems. We are concerned about how easily an abbreviated, simplified version of these complex social and psychological issues could readily be turned into yet another assault on "modern" mothers or on our over-burdened and imperfect child protection systems.

We hope that in this book we have shunned none of these difficult issues. We publish this work after years of careful deliberation, knowing that there is more to be learned than is now known, and that not only nuance and subtlety, but larger reconsiderations lie ahead. But we hold the firm belief that enough is known through our work and that of many others to make a first effort at unraveling this truly fascinating and perplexing disorder.

APPENDICES

Bibliographic References to MBPS Signs and Symptoms[1]

Signs/Symptoms	Reference number
Abdominal pain	4, 208, 231, 280, 365, 408
Abuse dwarfism	139, 254, 257, 258, 285, 360
Anorexia	101, 205, 323, 390
Apnea	4, 15, 26, 33, 65, 76, 111, 126, 127, 155, 175, 177, 192, 202, 209, 213, 223, 231, 238, 250, 265, 300, 319, 326, 327, 342, 369, 417, 419
Arthralgia (painful joints)	145
Arthritis (swollen joints)	145
Asthma	26, 65, 215, 330
Ataxia (dyscoordination)	101, 145, 222, 223, 227, 319, 323, 408, 442
Bacteriuria (bacteria in urine)	55, 225, 280
Biochemical chaos	227
Bleeding from ears	34, 300, 422
(Bleeding from ears due to abuse)	121
Bleeding from mouth	5
Bleeding from other sites (NG tube, ileostomy)	210
Bleeding tendency	54, 145, 231, 344, 422

(cont.)

[1]Updated version adapted from "Web of deceit: A literature review of Munchausen Syndrome by Proxy" by D. Rosenberg, 1987, *Child Abuse and Neglect, 11*, p. 553. Copyright 1987 by Pergamon Press Ltd. Adapted by permission.

Signs/Symptoms	*Reference number*
Bleeding from upper respiratory tract	177
Bleeding from vagina, rectum	185, 186
Bradycardia (slow heartbeat)	326
Catheter contamination, sepsis	33
Central catheter sepsis	105, 332
Chest pain	156, 187
Cerebral palsy	381, 403
Cutaneous abscesses	173, 323
Cyanosis (turning blue)	26, 111, 155, 192, 323, 326
Cystic fibrosis	275, 362
Contaminated/altered urine	244
Coma	196
Dehydration	2, 4, 20, 49, 136, 193, 213, 293, 323, 390
Delirium	155
Diabetes	41, 224, 268, 344
Diaphoresis (sweating)	323
Diarrhea	2, 19, 20, 49, 54, 59, 89, 94, 95, 101, 126, 151, 155, 190, 193, 210, 213, 219, 222, 223, 244, 272, 288, 341, 390, 395, 411, 430, 433, 436
Dermatitis artefacta (lesions, scratches, bruises)	15, 153, 374
Difficulty breathing	208
Easy bruising	414
Eczema	272
Edema (peripheral)	272
Epistaxis (nosebleeds)	227
Esophageal burns	178, 179
Ear infections	430
External otitis	444
Feculent vomiting	227
Failure to thrive	95, 200, 222, 391, 395, 422
Feeding difficulties	381, 391, 403
Fetal distress	118
Fevers	33, 71, 101, 134, 145, 173, 192, 213, 227, 249, 328, 334, 408, 430, 432
Food allergy	157, 216, 231, 418
Glycosuria (sugar in urine)	145, 227, 268, 408
Headache	206, 330, 408, 432
Hearing loss	4, 158
Hallucinations	96
Hematemesis (vomiting blood)	4, 34, 111, 126, 136, 181, 227, 249, 414, 435
Hematochezia or melena (blood in stool)	34, 54, 101, 210, 227, 249, 414, 435
Hematuria (blood in urine)	26, 34, 145, 225, 227, 272, 279, 337, 414

(cont.)

Signs/Symptoms	*Reference number*
Hemoptysis (coughing blood)	227, 414
Hyperactivity	96, 145
Hypernatremia (high blood Na+)	225, 288, 323, 433, 442
Hypertension	55
Hypoglycemia (low blood sugar)	20, 217, 244, 295, 343
Hypokalemia (low blood K+)	49, 323
Hyponatremia (low blood Na+)	49, 323
Hypothermia	20, 272
Hypotonia	27, 151
Hypochromic microcytic anemia	90
Immunodeficiency	130, 138, 173, 192, 299
Insomnia	96
Irritability	26, 27, 101, 249
Leaking urine	133
Lethargy	19, 20, 94, 101, 125, 135, 187, 204, 205, 222, 225, 323, 361
Leukopenia (low white blood cell count)	55
Morning stiffness	145
Mouth lesions	136
Muscle aches	204
Nocturia	408
Nystagmus (jerking eye movements)	323, 419
Obstetrical or pregnancy complications[2]	118
Painful urination	187
Personality change	26, 231
Polydipsia	145, 408
Polymicrobial bacteremia	130, 138, 192, 280, 299, 328, 332
Polyphagia (eating a lot)	145
Polyuria	49, 145, 272, 408
Prolonged sleep	71, 347
Pyuria (pus in urine)	225, 279, 280
Poisoning (includes MBPS and intentional poisonings)	57, 63, 72, 84, 109, 135, 136, 145, 155, 178, 179, 193, 196, 200, 205, 217, 219, 223, 230, 244, 266, 276, 295, 294, 297, 302, 323, 341, 342, 347, 361, 395, 408, 411, 419, 422, 430, 431, 436, 442
Rash	101, 145, 153, 227
Renal failure (acute)	302
Renal stones	365
Respiratory distress	136

(cont.)

[2]References received too late to be published in bibliography:
Goss, P. W., & McDougall, P. N. (1992). Munchausen syndrome by proxy, a cause of preterm delivery. *Medical Journal of Australia, 157*(11–12), 814–817.
Jureidini, J. (1993). Obstetric factitious disorder and Munchausen syndrome by proxy. *Journal of Nervous and Mental Disease, 181*(2), 135–137.

Signs/Symptoms	*Reference number*
Respiratory symptoms	204, 215
Seizures	2, 4, 15, 61, 63, 71, 76, 111, 125, 129, 135, 141, 145, 155, 175, 202, 213, 222, 224, 227, 231, 266, 280, 288, 295, 300, 328, 331, 342, 347, 419, 431, 433, 435, 442
Septic arthritis (infected joint)	173, 299
Shock	288, 433
Stupor	155, 193, 431
Unconsciousness	20, 101, 178, 179, 196, 217, 223, 227, 266, 297, 316, 323, 326, 342, 347, 419, 442
Vaginal discharge	133
Vaginal irritation	187
Unimicrobial bacteremia	130, 192
Urination from umbilical micropenis	252
Difficulty urinating	341
Urine gravel	408
Ventricular tachycardia	187, 361, 419
Vomiting	4, 20, 27, 49, 54, 59, 84, 94, 101, 126, 138, 151, 155, 190, 193, 200, 202, 213, 219, 222, 223, 225, 244, 272, 288, 300, 328, 341, 395, 414, 422, 430, 433, 436, 442
Weakness	323
Weight loss	162, 187, 207, 293, 408

The Genene Jones Case

> . . . A woman with a strange attraction to medicine, unable to distinguish between true illness and imagined calamity, is drawn to employment as a nurse. So powerful is her attraction that she needlessly subjects herself to invasive medical procedures. She is set loose in a hospital to care for the most helpless of human beings, where all the warning signs are ignored: her firing from Methodist Hospital, her history of telling lies, her on-the-job errors, her inability to admit mistakes, her unwillingness to follow orders, her exaggerated sense of her abilities, her need to be in control, her desperate craving for attention. For a while, Genene Jones would be satisfied to point out medical problems that didn't exist. It was only a mater of time before that would no longer be enough.
>
> —Elkind (1989, p. 58)

We summarize here many of the fascinating details of the case of Genene Jones from Peter Elkind's (1989) book *The Death Shift* because they reflect and support many of the findings discussed in this book.

Genene Jones was one of four adopted children, whose father, a gambler "wheeler-dealer" type died when she was a teenager, as did her brother. She was jealous of her sister, who she felt was favored, and felt herself to be unwanted by her parents. She always looked to her father for comfort, and within days of his death she began talking about marriage.

After graduation from a licensed vocational nursing program she initially obtained work as an LVN, but was soon fired for upsetting a patient. Dismissed from a second job for having elective surgery while she was supposed to be working, and unable to obtain work in an adult hospital, she took a position in a pediatric intensive care unit (ICU). She was entrusted with the lives of seriously ill children "after a less rigorous screening than a bank would give to an applicant for a job of a teller" (Elkind, 1989, p. 41). She was noted to have made eight mistakes in her 1st year and had two serious incidents of insubordination in which she appeared at the ICU at inappropriate times, once inebriated.

Genene was a person who enjoyed being the center of attention, and she told colorful stories about her life and exaggerated illnesses of her friends and children. She had the ability to convince people of her abilities and avoided reprimand for serious infractions by gaining the support of the head nurse. "Drawn compulsively to the hospital, Genene developed excuses to become a patient herself. During her first 27 months of employment, she made 30 visits to the county's outpatient clinic or emergency room where she presented an extraordinary assortment of complaints" (Elkind, 1989, p. 56). On March 10, 1981, she was admitted to the county hospital, but was discharged after 8 days because they were unable to find a cause of her illness. Between June and December that year she was hospitalized four more times. A psychiatrist found her to be quite normal, aware of conflicts, and conscious of her depression over the death of her partner of several years (though the partner had not in fact died)!

Soon after the hospitalization, back at work, she began requesting the sickest patients to care for. Whenever a child stopped breathing and needed cardiopulmonary resuscitation (CPR), Genene was there. "She seemed to thrive on the excitement and 'wounded' by every death" (Elkind, 1989, p. 60). Yet she often volunteered to take the babies to the morgue.

She had desperately wanted children but was unable to attend counseling sessions for her own 9-year-old child because she was "too busy." However, she began attaching herself to the children in the hospital who were totally under her control. After the death of one of Genene's charges, a death she had been predicting for weeks (she even called and told the parents he had passed away when he was very much alive), the ICU experienced a rash of unexpected and bizarre deaths with symptoms like hemorrhaging and cardiac arrest. Used to 3 to 4 resuscitations a month, in August alone the hospital experienced 9, and in September 13. Many were deaths where recovery would normally have been expected. All the incidents occurred during the 3:00–11:00 shift and *all* were Genene's patients!

Yet the hospital did not act. Her supervisor saw her as somewhat odd but caring, and as someone who got along well with the families of her patients.

As the deaths continued substantial circumstantial evidence accumulated concerning inappropriate doses of a medicine that is used to decrease the ability of the blood to clot. But the nursing administrative staff rallied to protect Genene against the doctors, who were becoming suspicious.

The babies continued to have unexplained arrests despite Genene's knowledge that she was being investigated. Even when an investigation was announced and she had a chance to leave, she did not, declaring, "after all, babies were *dying!*"

After the investigation Genene was asked to leave the ICU but only along with *all* other ICU LVNs. Indeed, anyone who called the personnel office at the medical center hospital would have been told that Genene was eligible to reapply for appointment. Soon after the removal of Genene and the other LVNs the rash of unexplained deaths in the ICU ceased.

Genene was then hired by one of the pediatric residents, Dr. H., who was opening a private office in a small town some distance from the hospital. This particular physician had supported her during the angry protestations at the hospital for her removal. At the opening of the office, Genene proudly paraded around with a name tag identifying herself as a "pediatric clinician," a position usually reserved for RNs with advanced training. Very soon after the opening of the office a pattern set in in which children began having respiratory arrests at the clinic. Though the clinic had seen only 2 to 3 patients a day over the first few weeks of opening, it sent four children to the hospital in an ambulance because of serious respiratory problems. Dr. H. *did not remember* the exaggeration of minor symptoms, the respiratory arrests, and the unexplained seizures of the hospital patients where both had previously worked. One day a patient who had mysteriously arrested and been saved while directly in Genene's care in Dr. H.'s office, returned with a brother who was ill. Dr. H. decided to give the girl her routine inoculations since she appeared to be quite well. Genene administered these injections while holding the child on her lap. Soon after she was breathing with grave difficulties. However, 9 minutes later when she arrived at the emergency room of the local hospital, she appeared fine. The doctor decided to send her on to San Antonio for an investigation of this strange malady. Eight miles into the trip riding with Genene in the ambulance, she had a cardiac arrest. Though rushed to a nearby hospital, she died. The parents took out an ad in the paper to thank, among others, Dr. H. and Genene.

The medical community in the small town finally grew suspicious and confronted Dr. H. She remembered a missing vial of Anectine (a drug that causes muscle paralysis and respiratory arrest). Genene said she had found it, that the cap was off, but that there were no needle marks in the rubber stopper. Finally able to bring herself to check, Dr. H. discovered that there were indeed needle marks and finally confronted Genene.

In terms of the hypotheses of this book, there is a painful irony that may explain why Dr. H. was so susceptible to Genene's manipulations. There may have been strong parallels in their childrearing. She herself was a child of alcoholic parents who lost her father at 13 years of age. Although she seemed headed for trouble, she became a clerk typist in the basement of a public library. She was described as lacking in ambition and self-esteem, until she gave ". . . herself to an aggressive intellectual, with ambition for both of them" (Elkind, 1989, p. 115). Her background issues of childhood neglect and submerged strivings for authority are similar to the dynamics of a MBPS patient. How ironic that Dr. H.'s effort to break out of the mold of letting others tell her what to do was her insistence on having Genene Jones work for her, against the advice of others!

Genene was eventually tried on two counts of murder and was convicted and sentenced to 60 years in prison. Charges were contemplated but never filed against the medical center. Even after judgment and sentencing, Genene reveled in the spotlight. In the days following her trial, she chatted happily to reporters for hours about the very events that she had been unwilling to discuss in court. A succession of media visitors found her in fine spirits; just days after collapsing in tears upon her conviction, she was mugging for the photographers. "I'm not afraid of jail, because I'm innocent," Genene declared. "If I had to spend 99 years in solitary, I could live with myself because I didn't do anything" (Elkind, 1989, p. 327).

In August a Texas Department of Corrections official, noting Genene's nursing background, wrote to the Bexar County Hospital District to ask if there was any problem with inmate Jones being assigned to work in the prison hospital's dispensary.

Development of Protocols for Clinical Warning Signs

We need to develop *clinical profiles* that will help distinguish true illness from induced episodes. For example, Meadow (1990b), in writing about induced apnea versus SIDS, has suggested that "repetitive suffocation has a characteristic clinical presentation that should allow identification before brain damage or death occurs" (p. 352). Cristoffel (1985) argues that autopsies should be done on all infants whose deaths are not entirely explained, pointing out that this is the only way to distinguish true SIDS from other forms of suffocation

Each medical pediatric subspecialty should develop a list of "red flags" for factitious disorders such as the one begun by Meadow (1990b) for chronic apnea:

Chronic apnea	MBPS	SIDS
More than one episode and older than 6 months	55%	<15%
Dead siblings	48%	2%
Previously unexplained disorder	44%	<15%

More intensive monitoring of young patients can also yield valuable guidelines for differentiating true apnea from induced episodes. Southall et al. (1987) combined video surveillance with multichannel monitoring of several physiological variables in two patients where maternal smothering was suspected. The characteristic pattern they found during smothering included the sudden onset of large body movements during regular breathing, a series of large breaths at about 1 minute after onset of suffocation, a prolonged expiratory phase at a slow rate, severe sinus tachycardia, and at about 1 minute after episode onset, large slow waves and a subsequent isoelectric baseline on the EEG typical of hypoxia.

If Rosenberg (1987) is correct that the majority of actual illness-inducing behavior occurs in the hospital, this should give us ample opportunity not only to observe the relationship of the mother to the clinical turns-for-the-worse, but to begin setting up information-gathering processes.

Additional research identifying and distinguishing specific characteristics of induced illness of all kinds will be extremely valuable for physicians involved in documenting MBPS abuse of their young patients.

References

1. Abe, K., Shinozima, K., Okuno, A., Abe, T., & Ochi, H. (1984). Munchausen's syndrome in children: Bizarre clinical and laboratory features. *Acta Paediatrica Japan, 26,* 539–543.
2. Ackerman, N. B., & Strobel, C. T. (1981). Polle syndrome: Chronic diarrhea in Munchausen's child. *Gastroenterology, 81,* 1140–1142.
3. Adelson, L. (1964). Homicide by pepper. *Journal of Forensic Science, 9,* 391–395.
4. Alexander, R., Smith, W., & Stevenson, R. (1990). Serial Munchausen syndrome by proxy. *Pediatrics, 86*(4), 581–585.
5. Amegavie, L., Marzouk, O., Mullen, J., Sills, J., and Gauthier Le Tendre, J.B.M. (1986). Munchausen's syndrome by proxy: A warning for health professionals. *British Medical Journal, 193,* 855–856.
6. American Association of University Women Educational Foundation. (1992). *How schools shortchange girls.* Washington, DC: AAUW Educational Foundation and National Education Association.
7. American Psychiatric Association. (1991). *DSM-IV options book: Work in progress.* Washington, DC: Author.
8. Amir, J. (1989). Polymicrobial bacteremia and child abuse (Letter to the editor). *American Journal of Diseases of Children, 143,* 444.
9. Anderson, P. C., & McCaffree, M. K. (1966). Pseudo DNA autosensitivity. A factitial disease. *Journal of the American Medical Association, 196*(1), 224–225.
10. Andrews, V. C. (1979). *Flowers in the Attic.* New York: Pocket Books.
11. Anonymous. (1983). Meadow and Munchausen. *Lancet, i,* 456.
12. Anonymous. (1991, October). My sister-in-law was starving her baby. *Good Housekeeping,* pp. 26–29.
13. Arlow, J. (1971). Character perversion. In J. Marcus (Ed.), *Currents in Psychoanalysis.* New York: International Universities Press.

14. Asher, R. (1951). Munchausen's syndrome. *Lancet, i,* 339–341.
15. Atoynatan, T. H., O'Reilly, E., & Loin, L. (1988). Munchausen syndrome by proxy. *Child Psychiatry and Human Development, 19,* 3–13.
16. Bach, S. (1991). On sadomasochistic object relations. In G. I. Fogel & W. A. Myers (Eds.), *Perversions and near perversions in clinical practice.* New Haven: Yale University.
17. Barker, J. C. (1962). The syndrome of hospital addiction: A report on the investigation of seven cases. *Journal of Mental Sciences, 108,* 167–182.
18. Bass, M., Kravath, R. E., & Glass, L. (1986). Death-scene investigation in sudden infant death. *New England Journal of Medicine, 315*(2), 100–105.
19. Baugh, J. R., Krug, E. F., & Weir, M. R. (1983). Punishment by salt poisoning. *Southern Medical Journal, 76,* 540–541.
20. Bauman, W. A., & Yalow, R. S. (1981). Child abuse: Parenteral insulin administration. *Journal of Pediatrics, 99,* 588–591.
21. Beal, S. M., & Blundell, H. K. (1988). Recurrence incidence of sudden infant death syndrome. *Archives of Disease in Childhood, 63,* 924–930.
22. Benedek, E. P. (1985). Children and psychic trauma: A brief review of contemporary thinking. In S. Eth & R. S. Pynoos (Eds.), *Postraumatic Stress Disorder in Children.* Washington, DC: American Psychiatric Press.
23. Benjamin, J. (1990). The alienation of desire: Women's masochism and ideal love. In C. Zanardi (Ed.), *Central papers on the psychology of women.* New York: New York University Press.
24. Bentovim, A. (1985). Munchausen's syndrome and child psychiatrists (Letter to the editor). *Archives of Disease in Childhood, 60,* 688
25. Bepko, C. (1989). Disorders of power: Women and addiction in the family. In M. McGoldrick, C. M. Anderson, & F. Walsh (Eds.), *Women in families: A framework for family therapy.* New York: W. W. Norton.
26. Berger, D. (1979). Child abuse simulating "near miss" sudden infant death syndrome. *Journal of Pediatrics, 95,* 554–556.
27. Berkner, P., Kastner, T., & Skolnick, L. (1988). Chronic ipecac poisoning in infancy: A case report. *Pediatrics, 82*(3), 384–386.
28. Black, D. (1981). The extended Munchausen syndrome: A family case. *British Journal of Psychiatry, 138,* 466–469.
29. Blix, S., & Brack, G. (1988). The effects of a suspected case of Munchausen's syndrome by proxy on a pediatric nursing staff. *General Hospital Psychiatry, 10,* 402–409.
30. Bograd, M. (1990). Scapegoating mothers: Conceptual errors in systems formulations. In M. P. Mirkin (Ed.), *The social and political contexts of family therapy,* Boston: Allyn & Bacon.
31. Bools, C. (1991). *Munchausen syndrome by proxy behaviour: A psychiatric study of perpetrating mothers.* Unpublished manuscript.
32. Bools, C., Neale, B., & Meadow, R. (1992). Co-morbidity associated with fabricated illness (Munchausen syndrome by proxy). *Archives of Disease in Childhood, 67,* 77–79.

33. Boros, S. J., & Brubaker, L. C. (1992). Munchausen syndrome by proxy case accounts. *FBI Law Enforcement Bulletin, 61*(6), 16–20.
34. Bourchier, D. (1983). Bleeding ears: Case report of Munchausen syndrome by proxy. *Australian Paediatric Journal, 19,* 256–257.
35. Braverman, L. (1989). Beyond the myth of motherhood. In M. McGoldrick, C. M. Anderson, & F. Walsh (Eds.), *Women in families: A framework for family therapy.* New York: W. W. Norton.
36. Brazelton, T. B., & Cramer, B. G. (1990). *The Earliest Relationship.* Reading, MA: Addison-Wesley.
37. Brody, S. (1959). Value of group psychotherapy in patients with "polysurgery addiction." *Psychiatric Quarterly, 33,* 260–283.
38. Brown, L. M., & Gilligan, C. (1992). *Meeting at the crossroads: Women's psychology and girl's development.* Cambridge, MA: Harvard University Press.
39. Burd, L., & Kerbeshian, J. (1986). Letter to the editor. *Ophthalmology, 93*(10), 1368.
40. *Burdeau v. McDowell.* (1921). 256 U.S. 465.
41. Burman, D., & Stevens, D. (1977). Munchausen family. *Lancet, ii,* 456.
42. Bursten, B. (1973). Some narcissistic personality types. *International Journal of Psycho-Analysis, 54,* 287–299.
43. Byard, R. W. (1992). Factitious patients with fictitious disorders: A note on Munchausen's syndrome (Letter to the editor). *Medical Journal of Australia, 156,* 507–508.
44. Caffey, J. (1972). On the theory and practice of shaking infants. Its potential residual effects of permanent brain damage and mental retardation. *American Journal of Diseases of Children, 124*(2), 161–169.
45. Cantwell, H. (1984). Child protective services in parenteral mismanagement of diabetes. *Diabetes Educator, 10,* 41–43.
46. Carrell, S. (1984, March). Texas nurse found guilty of killing child. *American Medical News,* pp. 1–27.
47. Cassell, J. (1987). On control, certitude and the "paranoia" of surgeons. *Culture, Medicine, and Psychiatry, 11,* 229–249.
48. Chadwick, D. L. (1992). The diagnosis of inflicted injury in infants and young children. *Pediatric Annals, 21*(8), 477–483.
49. Chan, D. A., Salcedo, J. R., Atkins, D. M., & Ruley, E. J. (1986). Munchausen syndrome by proxy: A review and case study. *Journal of Pediatric Psychology, 11,* 71–80.
50. Child Neurology Society. (1989). *International director of child neurologists.* St. Paul, MN: Author.
51. Chin, P. & Breu, G. (1991, December 16). The murder that never was. *People Magazine,* pp. 111–116.
52. Christoffel, K. K., Zieserl, E. J., & Chiaramonte, J. (1985). Should child abuse and neglect be considered when a child dies unexpectedly? *American Journal of Diseases of Children, 139,* 876–880.
53. Christopher, K. L., Wood, R. P., Eckert, R. C., Blayer, F. B., Raney, R. A., & Souhrada, J.-T (1983). Vocal-cord dysfunction presenting as asthma. *New England Journal of Medicine, 308,* 1566–1570.

54. Clark, G. D., Key, J. D., Rutherford, P. R., Bithoney, W. G. (1984). Munchausen's syndrome by proxy (child abuse) presenting as apparent autoerythrocyte sensitization syndrome: An unusual presentation of Polle syndrome. *Pediatrics, 74,* 1100–1102.

55. Clayton, P. T., Counahan, R., & Chantler, C. (1978). Munchausen syndrome by proxy. *Lancet, i,* 102–103.

56. Cleary, E. W. (Ed.). (1984). *McCormick on evidence* (3rd ed.). St. Paul, MN: West Publishing.

57. Cohle, S. D., Trestrail, J. D., Graham, M. A., Oxley, D. W., Walp, B., & Jachimczyk, J. (1988). Fatal pepper aspiration. *American Journal of Diseases of Children, 142,* 633–636.

58. Colin, R. (1985). 493 A.2d 1083 (Md. App. 1985).

59. Colletti, R. B., & Wasserman, R. C. (1989). Recurrent infantile vomiting due to intentional ipecac poisoning. *Journal of Pediatric Gastroenterology and Nutrition, 8,* 394–396.

60. Cramer, B., Gershberg, M. R., Stern, M. (1971). Munchausen syndrome: Its relationship to malingering, hysteria, and the physician-patient relationship. *Archives of General Psychiatry, 24,* 573–578.

61. Croft, R. D., & Jervis, M. (1989). Munchausen's syndrome in a 4-year old. *Archives of Disease in Childhood, 64,* 740–741.

62. Crouse, K. A. (1992). Munchausen syndrome by proxy: Recognizing the victim. *Pediatric Nursing, 18*(3), 249–252.

63. Crumpacker, R. W., & Kriel, R. L. (1973). Voluntary water intoxication in normal infants. *Neurology, 23,* 1251–1255.

64. Curran, J. P. (1973). Hysterical dermatitis factitia. *American Journal of Diseases of Children, 125,* 564–567.

65. Cursi, M. (1992, April 13). Malpractice case invokes memory of bizarre baron. *Recorder,* p. 1.

66. De Angelis, C. (1992). Clinical indicators of child abuse. In D. H. Schetky, & E. P. Benedek (Eds.), *Clinical handbook of child psychiatry and the law.* Baltimore: Williams & Wilkins.

67. Dershewitz, R., Vestal, B., Maclaren, N. K., & Corblath, M. (1976). Transient hepatomegaly and hypoglycemia. *American Journal of Diseases of Children, 130,* 998–999.

68. Deutsch, H. (1955). The imposter. Contribution to ego psychology of a type of psychopath. *Psychoanalytic Quarterly, 24,* 483–505.

69. DiMaio, V.J.M. (1988). SIDS or murder? *Pediatrics, 81,* 747–748.

70. DiMaio, V.J.M., & Bernstein, C. G. (1974). A case of infanticide. *Journal of Forensic Science, 19,* 745–754.

71. Dine, M. S. (1965). Tranquilizer poisoning: An example of child abuse. *Pediatrics, 36,* 782–785.

72. Dine, M. S., & McGovern, M. E. (1982). Intentional poisoning of children, an overlooked category of child abuse: Report of seven cases and review of the literature. *Pediatrics, 70,* 32–35.

73. Dirckx, J. (1992, Jan–Feb). Medical language. *Journal of the American Association of Medical Transcription,* p. 16.

74. Douchain, F. (1987). Lithiase urinaire "factice": Syndrome de Munchausen par procuration? *La Presse Medicale, 16,* 179.
75. Drell, M. J. (1988). More on Munchausen by proxy (Letter to the editor). *Journal of the American Academy of Child and Adolescent Development, 27,* 140.
76. Dubail, J. (1991, January 6). Did abuse pose as love? Boys' deaths, mother's behavior raise questions. *Sun-Sentinel* [Broward, FL], p. 1, 23A.
77. Duffy, T. P. (1992). The Red Baron. *New England Journal of Medicine, 327*(6), 408–410.
78. Egginton, J. (1990). *From cradle to grave: The short lives and strange deaths of Marybeth Tinning's nine children.* New York: Jove Books.
79. Ehrenreich, B., & English, D. (1978a). *Complaints and disorders: The sexual politics of sickness.* New York: Feminist Press.
80. Ehrenreich, B., & English, D. (1978b). *For her own good.* New York: Doubleday.
81. Ekman, P., & O'Sullivan, M. (1991, September). Who can catch a liar? *American Psychology,* pp. 913–920.
82. Elkind, P. (1989). *The death shift: The true story of nurse Genene Jones and the Texas baby murders.* New York: Viking Penguin.
83. Ellerstein, N. S. (1979). The cutaneous manifestations of child abuse and neglect. *American Journal of Diseases of Children, 133,* 906–909.
84. Embry, C. K. (1987). Toxic cyclic vomiting in an 11-year-old girl. *Journal of the American Academy of Child and Adolescent Development, 26,* 447–448.
85. Emery, J. E., Gilbert, E, & Zugibe, F. (1988). Three crib deaths, a babysitter and probable infanticide. *Medicine, Science and Law, 28,* 205–211.
86. Emery, J. L. (1985). Infanticide, filicide, and cot death. *Archives of Disease of Childhood, 60,* 505–507.
87. Emery, J. L. (1986). Families in which two or more cot deaths have occurred. *Lancet, i,* 313–315.
88. Engstrom, I. (1991). Parental distress and social interaction in families with children and adolescents with inflammatory bowel disease. *Journal of the American Academy of Child and Adolescent Psychiatry, 30*(6), 904–913.
89. Epstein, M., Markowitz, R. L., Gallo, D. M., Holmes, J. W., & Gryboski, J. D. (1987). Munchausen syndrome by proxy: Consideration in diagnosis and confirmation by video surveillance. *Pediatrics, 80,* 220–224.
90. Ernst, T. N., & Philip, M. (1986). Severe iron deficiency anemia. An example of covert child abuse (Munchausen by proxy). *Western Journal of Medicine, 144,* 358–359.
91. Estelle v. McGuire. (1991). 501 U.S.—116 L Ed 2d 385, 112 S.Ct.
92. Feenstra, J., Merth, I. T., & Treffers, P.D.A. (1988). Een geval van het syndroom van Munchhausen bij proxy. *Tijdschr Kindergeneeskd, 56*(4), 148–153.

93. Feldman, K., & Robertson, W. O. (1979). Salt poisoning: Presenting symptom of child abuse. *Veterinary and Human Toxicology, 21,* 341–343.

94. Feldman, K. W., Christopher, D. M., & Opheim, K. B. (1989). Munchausen syndrome/bulimia by proxy: Ipecac as a toxin in child abuse. *Child Abuse and Neglect, 13,* 257–261.

95. Fenton, A. C., Wailoo, M. P., & Tanner, M. S. (1988). Severe failure to thrive and diarrhoea caused by laxative abuse. *Archives of Disease in Childhood, 63,* 978–979.

96. Fialkov, M. J. (1984). Peregrination in the problem pediatric patient. *Clinical Pediatrics, 23,* 571–575.

97. Fiatal, R. A. (1989). Lights, camera, action. Video surveillance and the fourth amendment. (Part 1). *FBI Law Enforcement Bulletin, 58*(1), 23–31.

98. Finkelhor, D. (1984). *Child sexual abuse.* New York: New Theory and Research Free Press.

99. Fischler, R. S. (1983). Poisoning: A syndrome of child abuse. *American Family Physician, 28,* 103–108.

100. *Fitzgerald v. Stanford University Hospital* (1992). Cal. Sup Court 694922.

101. Fleisher, D., & Ament, M. E. (1977). Diarrhea, red diapers, and child abuse. *Clinical Pediatrics, 17,* 820–824.

102. Ford, C. V., King, B. H., & Hollender, M. H. (1988). Lies and liars: Psychiatric aspects of prevarication. *American Journal of Psychiatry, 14*(5), 554–562.

103. Fox, R. (1957). Training for uncertainty. In R. Merton, G. Reader, & P. Kendall (Eds.), *The student physician.* Cambridge: Harvard University Press.

104. Fras, J. (1978). Factitial disease: An update. *Psychosomatics, 19*(2), 119–122.

105. Frederick, V., Luedtke, G. S., Barrett, F. F., Hixson, S. D., & Burch, K. (1990). Munchausen syndrome by proxy: Recurrent central catheter sepsis. *Pediatric Infectious Diseases Journal, 9*(6), 440–442.

106. Freedman, M. R., Rosenberg, S. J., & Schmalling, K. B. (1991). Childhood sexual abuse in patients with paradoxical vocal cord dysfunction. *Journal of Nervous and Mental Disease, 179*(5), 245–248.

107. Freud, A. (1936). *The ego and mechanisms of defense.* New York: International University Press.

108. Frost, J. D., Glaze, D. G., & Rosen, C. L. (1988). Munchausen's syndrome by proxy and video surveillance. *American Journal of Diseases of Children, 142,* 917–918.

109. Gairdner, D. (1980). Commentary. *Archives of Disease in Childhood, 55,* 646.

110. Garbarino, J., Dubrow, N., Kostelny, K., & Pardo, C. (1992). *Children in danger. Coping with the consequences of community violence.* San Francisco: Jossey-Bass.

111. Geelhoed, G. C., & Pemberton, P. (1985). SIDS, seizures or 'sophageal reflux? *Medical Journal of Australia, 143,* 357–358.

112. Gilbert, R. W., Pierse, P. M., & Mitchell, D. P. (1987). Cryptic otalgia: A case of Munchausen syndrome in a pediatric patient. *Journal of Otolaryngology, 16*(4), 231–233.

113. Ginies, J. L., Goulet, O., Champion, G., Larchet, M., Granry, J. C., Coupris, L., Tekete, C., Ricour, C., & Limal, J. M. (1989). Syndrome de Numchausen par procuration et pseudo-obstruction intestinale chronique. *Archives Françaises de Pediatrie, 46,* 267–269.

114. Glasser, M. (1986). Identification and its vicissitudes as observed in the perversions. *International Journal of Psycho-Analysis, 67,* 9–16.

115. Godding, V., & Kruth, M. (1991). Compliance with treatment in asthma and Munchausen syndrome by proxy. *Archives of Disease in Childhood, 66*(8), 956–960.

116. Goldner, V. (1985). Feminism and family therapy. *Family Process, 24,* 31–47.

117. Goldstein, W. N. (1991). Clarification of projective identification. *American Journal of Psychiatry, 148*(2), 153–161.

118. Goodlin, R. C. (1985). Pregnant females with Munchausen syndrome. *American Journal of Obstetrics and Gynecology, 153,* 207–210.

119. Goodwin, J., Cauthorne, C. G., Rada, R. T. (1980). Cinderella syndrome: Children who simulate neglect. *American Journal of Psychiatry, 137*(10), 1223–1225.

120. Gordon, L. (1988). *Heroes of their own lives: The politics and history of family violence.* New York: Viking Penguin.

121. Grace, A., Kalinkiewicz, M., & Drake-Lee, A. B. (1984). Covert manifestations of child abuse. *British Medical Journal, 289,* 1041–1042.

122. Green, M., & Solnit, A. J. (1964). Reactions to the threatened loss of a child: A vulnerable child syndrome. *Pediatrics, 34,* 58–66.

123. Greenacre, P. (1958). The relationship of the impostor to the artist. *Psychoanalytic Quarterly, 27,* 359–382.

124. Greenacre, P. (1969). The fetish and the transitional object. *Psychoanalytic Study of the Child, 24,* 144–164.

125. Greene, J. W., Craft, L. T., & Ghishan, F. (1983). Acetaminophen poisoning in infancy. *American Journal of Diseases of Children, 137,* 386–387.

126. Griffith, J. L. (1988). The family systems of Munchausen syndrome by proxy. *Family Process, 27,* 423–437.

127. Griffith, J. L., & Slovik, L. S. (1989). Munchausen syndrome by proxy and sleep disorders medicine. *Sleep, 12,* 178–183.

128. Grinker, R. (1961). Imposture as a form of mastery. *Archives of General Psychiatry, 5,* 449–452.

129. Guandolo, V. L. (1985). Munchausen syndrome by proxy: An outpatient challenge. *Pediatrics, 75,* 526–530.

130. Halsey, N. A., Tucker, T. W., Redding, J., Frentz, J. M., Sproles, T., & Dawm, R. S. (1983). Recurrent nosocomial polymicrobial sepsis secondary to child abuse. *Lancet, ii,* 558–560.

131. Hanon, K. A. (1991). Child abuse: Munchausen's syndrome by proxy. *FBI Law Enforcement Bulletin, 60*(12), 8–11.

132. Herman, J. (1981). *Father-daughter incest.* Cambridge: Harvard University Press.
133. Herman-Giddens, M. E., & Berson, N. L. (1989). Harmful genital care practices in children. A type of child abuse. *Journal of the American Medical Association, 261*(4), 577–579.
134. Herzberg, J. H., & Wolff, S. M. (1972). Chronic factitious fever in puberty and adolescence: A diagnostic challenge to the family physician. *Psychiatric Medicine, 3,* 202–212.
135. Hickson, G. B., Greene, J. W., & Craft, L. T. (1983). Apparent intentional poisoning of an infant with acetaminophen. *American Journal of Diseases of Children, 137,* 917.
136. Hill, R. M., Barer, J., Hill, L. L., Butler, C. M., Harvey, D. J., & Horning, M. G. (1975). An investigation of recurrent pine oil poisoning in an infant by the use of gas chromatographic-mass spectrometric methods. *Journal of Pediatrics, 87,* 115–118.
137. Hobbs, C. J. (1983). Unusual syndromes of child abuse and neglect. *Nursing Times, 79*(1), 21–23.
138. Hodge, D., Schwartz, W., Sargent, J., Bodurtha, J., & Starr, S. (1982). The bacteriologically battered baby: Another case of Munchausen by proxy. *Annals of Emergency Medicine, 11,* 205–207.
139. Holborow, P. L. (1985). A variant of Munchausen's syndrome by proxy. *Journal of the American Academy of Child Psychiatry, 24,* 238.
140. Hopwood, J. S. (1927). Child murder and science. *Journal of Mental Science, 73,* 95–108.
141. Hosch, I. A. (1987). Munchausen syndrome by proxy. *MCN American Journal of Maternal/Child Nursing, 12,* 48–52.
142. Howe, G. L., Jordan, H. W., Lockert, E. W., & Walton, M. (1983). Munchausen's syndrome or chronic factitious illness: A review and case presentation. *Journal of the National Medical Association, 75*(2), 175–181.
143. Hoyer, T. V. (1959). Pseudologia fantastica. *Psychiatric Quarterly, 33,* 203–220.
144. Hughes, M. C. (1984). Recurrent abdominal pain and childhood depression: Clinical observations of 23 children and their families. *American Journal of Orthopsychiatry, 54*(1), 146–155.
145. Hvizdala, E. V., & Gellady, A. M. (1978). Intentional poisoning of two siblings by prescription drugs. *Clinical Pediatrics, 17,* 480–482.
146. Imber-Black, E. (1989). Women's relationships with larger systems. In M. McGoldrick, C. M. Anderson, & F. Walsh (Eds.), *Women in families: A framework for Family Therapy.* New York: W. W. Norton.
147. Inbau, F. E., & Reid, J. E. (1953). *Lie Detection and Criminal Investigation.* Baltimore: Williams & Wilkins.
148. Jacobi, A. (1895). Hyperthermy in a man up to 148° F. (64.4° c.). *Transactions of the Association of American Physicians, 10,* 159–191.
149. Jamieson, R., McKee, E., & Roback, H. (1979). Munchausen's syndrome: An unusual case. *American Journal of Psychotherapy, 33*(4), 616–621.

150. *Matter of Jessica Z.* (1987, January 27). 515 N.Y.S. 2d 370.
151. Johnson, J. E., Carpenter, B.L.M., Benton, J., Cross, R., Eaton, L. A., & Rhoads, J. M. (1991). Hemorrhagic colitis and pseudomelanosis coli in ipecac ingestion by proxy. *Journal of Pediatric Gastroenterology and Nutrition, 12,* 501–506.
152. Johnston, J. R., Campbell, L.E.G., Mayes, S. S. (1985). Latency children in post-separation divorce disputes. *Journal of the American Academy of Child Psychiatry, 24,* 563–574.
153. Jones, D.P.H. (1983). Dermatitis artefacta in mother and baby as child abuse. *British Journal of Psychiatry, 143,* 199–200.
154. Jones, D.P.H. (1987). The untreatable family. *Child Abuse and Neglect, 11,* 409–420.
155. Jones, J. G., Butler, H. L., Hamilton, B., Perdue, J. D., Stern, H. P., & Woody, R. C. (1986). Munchausen syndrome by proxy. *Child Abuse and Neglect, 10,* 33–40.
156. Kahan, B. B., & Yorker, B. C. (1990). Munchausen syndrome by proxy. *Journal of School Health, 60*(3), 108–110.
157. Kahan, B. B., & Yorker, B. C. (1991). Munchausen syndrome by proxy: Clinical review and legal issues. *Behavioral Sciences and the Law, 9,* 73–83.
158. Kahn, G., & Goldman, E. (1991). Munchausen syndrome by proxy: Mother fabricates infant's hearing impairment. *Journal of Speech and Hearing Research, 34*(4), 957–959.
159. Kaminer, Y., & Robbins, D. R. (1989). Insulin misues: A review of an overlooked psychiatric problem. *Psychosomatics, 30*(1), 19–24.
160. Kaplan, L. J. (1991). *Female perversions: The temptations of Emma Bovary.* New York: Doubleday.
161. Katz, J. (1984). *The silent world of doctor and patient.* New York: Free Press.
162. Katz, R. L., Mazer, C., & Litt, I. F. (1985). Anorexia nervosa by proxy. *Journal of Pediatrics, 107*(2), 247–248.
163. Kaufman, K., Coury, D., Pickrell, E., & McCleery, J. (1989). Munchausen syndrome by proxy: A survey of professionals' knowledge. *Child Abuse and Neglect, 13,* 141–147.
164. Kaufman, K. L., Pickrell, E., Baus, J., McCleary, J., Gutches, L., & Johnson, C. F. (1987). *Hospital management of Munchausen syndrome by proxy: Identification, procedures, and costs.* Unpublished manuscript.
165. Kempe, C. H. (1971). Paediatric implications of the battered baby syndrome. *Archives of Disease in Childhood, 46,* 28–37.
166. Kempe, C. H. (1975). Uncommon manifestations of the battered child syndrome. *American Journal of Diseases in Children, 129,* 1265.
167. Kempe, C. H., Silverman, F. N., Steele, B. F., Droegemueller, W., & Silver, H. K. (1962). The battered-child syndrome. *Journal of the American Medical Association, 181,* 17–24.
168. Kempf, S. (1990). Munchausen syndrome by proxy: An overview for attorneys. Unpublished Manuscript.

169. Kinscherff, R., & Famularo, R. (1991). Extreme Munchausen syndrome by proxy: The case for termination of parental rights. *Juvenile and Family Court Journal, 40,* 41–53.

170. Klein M. (1946). Notes on some schizoid mechanisms. *International Journal of Psychoanalysis, 27,* 99–110.

171. Klein, M. (1955). On identification. In M. Klein, P. Heimann, & R. E. Money-Kyrle (Eds.), *New Directions in Psychoanalysis.* New York: Basic Books.

172. Klonoff, E. A., Youngner, S. J., Moore, D. J., & Hershey, L. A. (1983). Chronic factitious illness: A behavioral approach. *International Journal of Psychiatry in Medicine, 13*(3), 173–183.

173. Kohl, S., Pickering, L. K., & Dupree, E. (1978). Child abuse presenting as immunodeficiency disease. *Journal of Pediatrics, 93,* 468.

174. Korbin, J. E. (1989). Fatal maltreatment a proposed framework. *Child Abuse and Neglect, 13,* 481–489.

175. Kravitz, R. M., & Wilmott, R. W. (1990). Munchausen syndrome by proxy presenting as factitious apnea. *Clinical Pediatrics, 29*(10), 587–592.

176. Krener, P., & Adelman, R. (1988). Parent salvage and parent sabotage in the care of chronically ill children. *American Journal of Diseases of Children, 142,* 945–951.

177. Kurlandsky, L., Lukoff, J. Y., Zinkham, W. H., Brody, J. P., & Kessler, R. W. (1979). Munchausen syndrome by proxy: Definition of factitious bleeding in an infant by ^{51}Cr labelling erythrocytes. *Pediatrics, 63,* 228–231.

178. Lansky, L. L. (1974). An unusual case of childhood chloral hydrate poisoning. *American Journal of Diseases of Children, 127,* 275–276.

179. Lansky, S. B., & Erickson, H. M. (1974). Prevention of child murder. *Journal of the American Academy of Child Psychiatry, 13,* 691–698.

180. Lazoritz, S. (1987). Munchausen by proxy or Meadow's syndrome? *Lancet, ii,* 631.

181. Lee, D. A. (1979). Munchausen syndrome by proxy in twins. *Archives of Disease in Childhood, 54,* 646–647.

182. Leeder, E. (1990). Supermom or child abuser? Treatment of the Munchausen mother. *Women and Therapy, 9*(4), 69–88.

183. Leonard, K. F., & Farrell, P. A. (1992). Munchausen's syndrome by proxy: A little-known type of abuse. *Postgraduate Medicine, 91*(5), 197–204.

184. Lerer, R. J. (1990). For three years I treated the wrong patient. *Medical Economics, 67*(3), 54, 56, 58–59.

185. Lesnik-Oberstein, M. (1986a). "Munchausen syndrome by proxy" in de kindergeneeskunde. *Ned Tijdschr Geneeskd, 130*(5), 221–222.

186. Lesnik-Oberstein, M. (1986b). Munchausen syndrome by proxy (Letter to the editor). *Child Abuse and Neglect, 10,* 133.

187. Libow, J. A., & Schreier, H. A. (1986). Three forms of factitious illness in children: When is it Munchausen syndrome by proxy? *American Journal of Orthopsychiatry, 56,* 602–611.

188. Lidz, T., Miller, J. M., Padget, P., & Stedem, A.F.A. (1949). Muscular

atrophy and pseudologica fantastica associated with islet cell adenoma of the pancreas. *Archives of Neurology and Psychiatry, 62,* 304–313.

189. Light, M. J., & Sheridan, M. S. (1990). Munchausen syndrome by proxy and apnea—A survey of apnea programs. *Clinical Pediatrics, 29*(3), 162–168.

190. Lim, L.C.C., Yap, H. K., & Lim, J. W. (1991). Munchausen syndrome by proxy. *Journal of the Singapore Paediatric Society, 33*(1,2), 59–62.

191. Lipsett, D. R. (1986). The factitious patient who sues. (1986). *American Journal of Psychiatry, 143*(11), 1482.

192. Liston, T. E., Levine, P. L., & Anderson, C. (1983). Polymicrobial bacteremia due to Polle syndrome: The child abuse variant of Munchausen by proxy. *Pediatrics, 72,* 211–213.

193. Livingstone, R. (1987). Maternal somatization disorder and Munchausen syndrome by proxy. *Psychosomatics, 28*(4), 213–217.

194. Lorber, J. (1978b). Unexplained coma in a two-year-old. *Lancet ii,* 680.

195. Lorber, J. (1978a). Unexplained episodes of coma in a two-year old. *Lancet, ii,* 472–473.

196. Lorber, J., Reckless, J.P.D., & Watson, J.B.G. (1980). Nonaccidental poisoning: The elusive diagnosis. *Archives of Disease in Childhood, 55,* 643–646.

197. Lovejoy, F. H., Marcuse, E. K., & Landrigan, P. J. (1971). Two examples of purpura factitia. *Clinical Pediatrics, 10*(3), 183–184.

198. Lowenhaupt-Tsing, A. (1990). Monster stories: Women charged with perinatal endangerment. In F. Ginsberg & A. Lowenhaupt-Tsing (Eds.), *Uncertain terms, negotiating gender in American culture.* Boston: Beacon Press.

199. Luepnitz, D. A. (1988). *The family interpreted: Feminist theory in clinical practice.* New York: Basic Books.

200. Lyall, E. G., Stirling, H. F., Crofton, P. M., & Kelnar, C. J. (1992). Albuminuria growth failure. A case of Munchausen syndrome by proxy. *Acta Paediatrica, 81*(4), 373–376.

201. Lyell, A. (1979). Cutaneous artifactual disease. A review, amplified by personal experience. *Journal of the American Academy of Dermatology, 1*(5), 391–407.

202. Lyons-Ruth, K., Kaufman, M., Masters, N., & Wu, J. (1991). Issues in the identification and long-term management of Munchausen by proxy syndrome within a clinical infant service. *Infant Mental Health Journal, 12*(4), 309–320.

203. Maccoby, E. E., & Jacklin, C. N. (1974). *The psychology of sex differences.* Stanford, CA: Stanford University Press.

204. MacDonald, T. M. (1989). Myalgia encephalomyelitis by proxy. *British Medical Journal, 299,* 1030–1031.

205. Mahesh, V. K., Stern, H. P., Kearns, G. L., & Stroh, S. E. (1988). Application of pharmacokinetics in the diagnosis of chemical abuse in Munchausen syndrome by proxy. *Clinical Pediatrics, 27*(5), 243–246.

206. Mahomed, F. A. (1881). Remarks on a case with paradoxical temperatures. *Lancet, ii,* 790–791.

207. Mahowald, M. W., Schenck, C. H., Rosen, G. R., and Hurwitz, T. D. (1992). The role of a sleep disorder center in evaluating sleep violence. *Archives of Neurology, 49*(6), 604–607.

208. Main, D. J., Douglas, J. E., & Tamanika, H. M. (1986). Munchausen syndrome by proxy. *Medical Journal of Australia, 145,* 300–301.

209. Makar, A. F., & Squier, P. J. (1990). Munchausen syndrome by proxy: Father as a perpetrator. *Pediatrics, 85*(3), 370–373.

210. Malatack, J. J., Wiener, E. S., Gartner, J. C., Zitelli, B. J., & Brunetti, E. (1985). Munchausen syndrome by proxy: A new complication of central venous catheterization. *Pediatrics, 75,* 523–525.

211. Mann, J. (1979). Feigned bereavement. (letter to the editor). *British Journal of Psychiatry, 134,* 127.

212. Manning, S. C., Casselbrandt, M., & Lammers, D. (1990). Otolaryngolic manifestations of child abuse. *International Journal of Pediatric Otolaryngology, 20,* 7–16.

213. Manthei, D. J., Pierce, R. L., Rothbaum, R. J., Manthei, U., & Keating, J. P. (1988). Munchausen syndrome by proxy: Covert child abuse. *Journal of Family Violence, 3*(2), 131–140.

214. Markantonakis, A. (1989). Munchausen syndrome by proxy (Letter to the editor). *British Journal of Psychiatry, 155,* 130–131.

215. Masterson, J., Dunworth, R., & Williams, N. (1988). Extreme illness exaggeration in pediatric patients: A variant of Munchausen by proxy? *American Journal of Orthopsychiatry, 58*(2), 188–195.

216. Masterson, J., & Wilson, J. (1987). Factitious illness in children: The social worker's role in identification and management. *Social Work in Health Care, 12*(4), 21–30.

217. Mayefsky, J. H., Sarnaik, A. P., & Postellon, D. C. (1982). Factitious hypoglycemia. *Pediatrics, 69,* 804–805.

218. Mayo, J. P., & Haggerty, J. J. (1984). Long-term psychotherapy of Munchausen syndrome. *American Journal of Psychotherapy, 38*(4), 571–578.

219. McClung, H. J., Murray, R., Braden, N. J., Fyda, J., Myers, R. P., & Gutches, L. (1988). Intentional ipecac poisoning in children. *American Journal of Diseases of Children, 142,* 637–639.

220. McDonald, A., Kline, S. A., & Billings, R. F. (1979). The limits of Munchausen's syndrome. *Canadian Journal of Psychiatry, 24,* 323–328.

221. McGoldrick, M. (1989). Women through the family life cycle. In M. McGoldrick, C. M. Anderson, & F. Walsh (Eds.), *Women in families: A framework for family therapy.* New York: W. W. Norton.

222. McGuire, T. L., & Feldman, K. W. (1989). Psychologic morbidity of children subjected to Munchausen syndrome by proxy. *Pediatrics, 83*(2), 289–292.

223. McKinley, I. (1986). Munchausen's syndrome by proxy (Letter to the editor). *British Medical Journal, 293,* 1308.

224. McSweeney, J. J., & Hoffman, R. P. (1991). Munchausen's syndrome by proxy mistaken for IDDM. *Diabetes Care, 14*(10), 928–929.

225. Meadow, R. (1977). Munchausen syndrome by proxy: The hinterland of child abuse. *Lancet, ii,* 343–345.

226. Meadow, R. (1980). Munchausen syndrome by proxy. *Archives of Disease in Childhood, 55,* 731–732.

227. Meadow, R. (1982a). Munchausen syndrome by proxy. *Archives of Disease in Childhood, 57,* 92–98.

228. Meadow, R. (1982b). Munchausen syndrome by proxy and psuedo-epilepsy. *Archives of Disease in Childhood, 57,* 811–812.

229. Meadow, R. (1982c). When a doctor turns detective. *Nursing Mirror, 154*(6), 17–20.

230. Meadow, R. (1984a). Factitious illness: The hinterland of child abuse. In R. Meadow (Ed.), *Recent advances in paediatrics.* Edinburgh, Scotland: Churchill Livingstone.

231. Meadow, R. (1984b). Fictitious epilepsy. *Lancet, ii,* 25–28.

232. Meadow, R. (1984c). Munchausen by proxy and brain damage. *Developmental Medicine and Child Neurology, 26,* 669–676.

233. Meadow, R. (1985). Management of Munchausen syndrome by proxy. *Archives of Disease in Childhood, 60,* 385–393.

234. Meadow, R. (1987). Video recording and child abuse. *British Medical Journal, 294,* 1629–1630.

235. Meadow, R. (1989a). ABC of child abuse Munchausen syndrome by proxy. *British Medical Journal, 299,* 248–250.

236. Meadow, R. (1989b). Not so sudden infant death (abstract). *Archives of Disease in Childhood, 64,* 1216–1217.

237. Meadow, R. (1989c). Recurrent cot death and suffocation (Letter to the editor). *Archives of Disease in Childhood, 64,* 179–180.

237. Meadow, R. (1990a). One hundred twenty years on: Voices on child abuse. *British Medical Journal, 301,* 714–716.

238. Meadow, R. (1990b). Suffocation, recurrent apnea and sudden infant death. *Journal of Pediatrics, 117,* 351–357.

239. Meadow, S. R. (1990c). Letter to the editor. *Child Abuse and Neglect, 14,* 289–290.

240. Meadow, R. (1991a). Neurological and developmental variants of Munchausen syndrome by proxy. *Developmental Medicine and Child Neurology, 33*(3), 270–272.

241. Meadow, S. R. (1991b). Commentary (Letter to the editor). *Archives of Disease in Childhood, 66*(8), 956–960.

242. Meadow, R. (1992). Difficult and unlikable patients. *Archives of Disease in Childhood, 67,* 697–702.

243. Meadow, R., & Lennert, T. (1984). Munchausen by proxy or Polle syndrome: Which term is correct? *Pediatrics, 74,* 554–556.

244. Mehl, A. L., Coble, L., & Johnson, S. (1990). Munchausen syndrome by proxy: A family affair. *Child Abuse and Neglect, 14,* 577–585.

245. Meloy, R. (1988). *Psychopathic minds: Origins, dynamics, and treatment.* Northvale, NJ: Jason Aronson.

246. Menninger, K. (1934). Polysurgery and polysurgical addiction. *Psychoanalytic Quarterly, 3,* 173–199.

247. Meropol, N. J., Ford, C. V., & Zaner, R. M. (1985). Factitious illness: An exploration in ethics. *Perspectives in Biology and Medicine, 28*(2), 269–281.

248. Meyers, H. C. (1991). Perversion in fantasy and furtive enactments. In G. I. Fogel & W. Myers (Eds.), *Perversions and near perversions in clinical practice.* New Haven: Yale University Press.

249. Mills, R. W., and Burke, S. (1990). Gastrointestinal bleeding in a 15 month old male. A presentation of Munchausen's syndrome by proxy. *Clinical Pediatrics, 29*(8), 474–477.

250. Minford, A.M.B. (1981). Child abuse presenting as apparent "near miss": Sudden infant death syndrome. *British Medical Journal, 282,* 521.

251. Mirkin, M. P. (1990). Eating disorders: A feminist family therapy perspective. In M. P. Mirkin (Ed.), *The social and political contexts of family therapy.* Boston: Allyn & Bacon.

252. Mitchels, B. (1983). Munchausen syndrome by proxy: Protecting the child. *Journal of Forensic Science, 23,* 105–111.

253. Mitchels, B. (1983). Munchausen syndrome by proxy: Protection or correction? *New Law Journal, 133,* 165–168.

254. Money, J. (1977). The syndrome of abuse dwarfism (psychosocial dwarfism or reversible hyposomatotropism). *American Journal of Diseases of Children, 131,* 508–513.

255. Money, J. (1982). Child abuse: Growth failure, IQ deficit and learning disability. *Journal of Learning Disabilities, 15,* 583–586.

256. Money, J. (1986). Munchausen's syndrome by proxy: Update. *Journal of Pediatric Psychology, 11*(4), 583–584.

257. Money, J. (1989). Paleodigms and paleodigmatics: A new theoretical construct applicable to Munchausen's syndrome by proxy, child abuse dwarfism, paraphilias, anorexia nervosa, and other syndromes. *American Journal of Psychotherapy, 43*(1), 15–24.

258. Money, J., Annecillo, C., & Hutchison, J. W. (1985). Forensic and family psychiatry in abuse dwarfism: Munchausen's syndrome by proxy, atonement and addiction to abuse. *Journal of Sex and Marital Therapy, 11,* 30–40.

259. Money, J., & Lamacz, M. (1987). Genital examination and exposure experienced as nosocomial sexual abuse in childhood. *Journal of Nervous and Mental Disease, 175*(12), 713–721.

260. Money, J., & Werlwas, J. (1976). Folie à deux in the parents of psychosocial dwarfs: Two cases. *Bulletin of the American Academy of Psychiatry and the Law, 4*(4), 351–362.

261. Money, J., & Werlwas, J. (1982). Paraphilic sexuality and child abuse: The parents. *Journal of Sex and Marital Therapy, 8*(1), 57–64.

262. Money, J., & Wolff, G. (1974). Late puberty, retarded growth and reversible hyposomatotropinism (psychosocial dwarfism). *Adolescence, 9*(33), 121–134.

263. Money, J., Wolff, G., & Annecillo, C. (1972). Pain agnosia and self-injury in the syndrome of reversible somatotropin deficiency (psy-

chosocial dwarfism). *Journal of Autism and Child Schizophrenia, 2*(2), 127–139.

264. Moore, K., & Reed, D. (1988). *Deadly medicine.* New York: St. Martin's Press.

265. Morris, B. (1985). Child abuse manifested as factitious apnea. *Southern Medical Journal, 78*(8), 1013–1014.

266. Mortimer, J. G. (1980). Acute water intoxication as another unusual manifestation of child abuse. *Archives of Disease in Childhood, 55,* 401–403.

267. Nadelson, T. (1979). The Munchausen spectrum: Borderline character features. *General Hospital Psychiatry, 1,* 11–17.

268. Nading, J. H., & Duval-Arnould, B. (1984). Factitious diabetes mellitus confirmed by ascorbic acid. *Archives of Disease in Childhood, 59,* 166–167.

269. Neale, B., Bools, C., & Meadow, R. (1991). Problems in the assessment and management of Munchausen syndrome by proxy abuse. *Children and Society, 5*(4), 324–333.

270. Newberger, E. H. (1992). Intervention in child abuse. In D. H. Schetky & E. P. Benedek (Eds.), *Clinical handbook of child psychiatry and the law.* Baltimore: Williams & Wilkins.

271. Ney, P. G. (1988). Transgenerational child abuse. *Child Psychiatry and Human Development, 18*(3), 151–168.

272. Nicol, A. R., & Eccles, M. (1985). Psychotherapy for Munchausen syndrome by proxy. *Archives of Disease in Childhood, 60,* 344–348.

273. North American Society for Pediatric Gastroenterology & Nutrition. (1990–1991). [Membership directory]. Cincinnati, OH: Author.

274. Oren, J., Kelly, D. H., & Shannon, D. C. (1987). Familial occurrence of sudden infant death syndrome and apnea of infancy. *Pediatrics, 80*(3), 355–358.

275. Orenstein, D. M., & Wasserman, A. L. (1986). Munchausen syndrome by proxy simulating cystic fibrosis. *Pediatrics, 78,* 621–624.

276. Osborne, J. P. (1976). Non-accidental poisoning and child abuse. *British Medical Journal, 1,* 1211.

277. O'Shea, B. M., Lowe, N. F., McGennis, A. J., & O'Rourke, M. H. (1982). Psychiatric evaluation of a Munchausen's Syndrome. *Irish Medical Journal, 75*(6), 200–202.

278. O'Shea, B., & McGennis, A. (1982). The psychotherapy of Munchausen's syndrome. *Irish Journal of Psychotherapy, 1,* 17–19.

279. Outwater, K. M., Lipnick, R. N., Luban, N.L.C., Ravenscroft, K., & Ruley, E. J. (1981). Factitious hematuria: Diagnosis by minor blood group typing. *Journal of Pediatrics, 98,* 95–98.

280. Palmer, A. J., & Yoshimura, G. J. (1984). Munchausen syndrome by proxy. *Journal of the American Academy of Child Psychiatry, 23,* 503–508.

281. Pankratz, L. (1981). A review of the Munchausen syndrome. *Clinical Psychology Review, 1,* 65–78.

282. Pankratz, L., & Lezak, M. D. (1987). Cerebral dysfunction in the Munchausen syndrome. *Hillside Journal of Clinical Psychiatry, 9*(2), 195–206.

283. Paperny, D., Hicks, R., & Hammar, S. L. (1980). Munchausen's syndrome. *American Journal of Diseases of Children, 134,* 794–795.
284. Partridge, J. C., Payne, M. L., Leisgang, J. J., Randolph, J. F., & Rubinstein, J. H. (1981). Water intoxication secondary to feeding mismanagement. *American Journal of Diseases of Children, 135,* 38–41.
285. Patton, R. G., & Gardner, L. I. (1962). Influence of family environment on growth: The syndrome of "maternal deprivation." *Pediatrics, 70,* 957–962.
286. *People v. Frye.* (1923). 293 F.1013.
287. *People v. Gorshen.* (1959). 51 Cal. 2d.
288. *People v. Phillips.* (1981). 122 Cal. App. 3d.
289. *People v. Tinning.* (1988). 536 N.Y.S. 2d.
290. Peters, J. M. (1989). Criminal prosecution of child abuse: Recent trends. *Pediatric Annals, 18*(8), 505–509.
291. Peterson, D. R., Chinn, N. M., & Fischer, L. D. (1980). The sudden infant death syndrome: Repetitions in families. *Journal of Pediatrics, 97*(2), 265–267.
292. Phares, V. (1992). Where's poppa? The relative lack of attention to the role of fathers in child and adolescent psychopathology. *American Psychologist, 47*(5), 656–664.
293. Pickel, S., Anderson, C., & Holliday, M. A. (1970). Thirsting and hypernatremic dehydration: A form of child abuse. *Pediatrics, 45,* 54–59.
294. Pickering, D. (1964). Salicylate poisoning: The diagnosis when its possibility is denied by the parents. *Acta Paediatrica, 53,* 501–504.
295. Pickering, D. (1968). Neonatal hypoglycaemia due to salicylate poisoning. *Proceedings of the Royal Society of Medicine, 61,* 1256.
296. Pickering, D. (1976). Salicylate poisoning as a manifestation of the battered child syndrome. *American Journal of Diseases of Children, 130,* 675–676.
297. Pickering, D., Moncrieff, M., & Etches, P. C. (1976). Nonaccidental poisoning and child abuse. *British Medical Journal, 1,* 1210–1211.
298. Pickering, L. K., & Hogan, G. R. (1971). Voluntary water intoxication in a normal child. *Journal of pediatrics, 78*(2), 316–318.
299. Pickering, L. K., & Kohl, S. (1981). Munchausen syndrome by proxy. *American Journal of Diseases of Children, 135,* 288–289.
300. Pickford, E., Buchanan, N., & McLaughlin, S. (1988). Munchausen syndrome by proxy: A family anthology. *Medical Journal of Australia, 148,* 646–650.
301. Pope, H. G., Jonas, J. M., & Jones, B. (1982). Factitious psychosis: Phenomenology, family history, and long-term outcome of 9 patients. *American Journal of Psychiatry, 139*(11), 1480–1486.
302. Proesmans, W., Sina, J., Debucquoy, P., Renoirte, M., & Eeckels, R. (1981). Recurrent acute renal failure due to non-accidental poisoning with glafenin in a child. *Clinical Nephrology, 16,* 207–210.
303. Putnam, F. W. (1991). Recent research on multiple personality disorder. *Psychiatric Clinics—North America, 14*(3), 489–502.

304. Pynoos, R. S., & Eth, S. (1985). Children traumatized by witnessing acts of personal violence: Homicide, rape or suicide behavior. In S. Eth & R. S. Pynoos (Eds.), *Postraumatic stress disorder in children*. Washington, DC: American Psychiatric Association Press.

305. Rahilly, P. M. (1991). The pneumographic and medical investigation of infants suffering apparent life-threatening episodes. *Journal of Paediatrics and Child Health, 27*(6), 349–353.

306. Rand, D. C. (1989). Munchausen syndrome by proxy as a possible factor when abuse is falsely alleged. *Issues of Child Abuse Accusations, 1*(4), 32–34.

307. Rand, D. C. (1990). Munchausen syndrome by proxy: Integration of classic and contemporary types. *Issues in Child Abuse Accusations, 2*(2), 83–89.

308. Rand, D. C. (1992). In *Solomon's dilemma: False allegations in divorce custody*. C. C. Thomas.

309. Rappoport, J. (1989). *Obsessive-compulsive disorder in children and adolescents*. Washington, DC: American Psychiatric Press.

310. Raspe, R. E. (1944). *The surprising adventures of Baron Munchausen*. New York: Peter Pauper.

311. Rauh, J. L. (1976). Self-induced subcutaneous emphysema in an adolescent. *Journal of Pediatrics, 88*(4), 690–691.

312. Ravenscroft, K., Jr., & Hochheiser, J. (1980, October). *Factitious hematuria in a six-year-old girl: A case example of Munchausen syndrome by proxy*. Paper presented at the annual meeting of the American Academy of Child Psychiatry, Chicago.

313. Raymond, C. A. (1987). Munchausen's may occur in younger persons. *Journal of the American Medical Association, 257*(24), 3332.

314. Reece, R. M. (1990). Unusual manifestations of child abuse. *Psychiatric Clinics of North America, 37*(1), 905–921.

315. Reich, P., Lazarus, M., Kelly, M. J., & Rogers, M. P. (1977). Factitious feculent urine in an adolescent boy. *Journal of the American Medical Association, 238*, 420–421.

316. Rendle-Short, J. (1978). Nonaccidental barbiturate poisoning of children. *Lancet, ii*, 1212.

317. Renik, O. (1993). Countertransference, enactment and the psychoanalytic process. In M. Horowitz, O. Kernberg, & E. Wineshel (Eds.), *Psychic structure and the psychic change*. Madison, CT: International Universities Press.

318. Rich, S. (1992, June 22). U.S. medical "credit card" proposed. *San Francisco Chronicle*, p. 1.

319. Richardson, G. F. (1987). Munchausen syndrome by proxy. *American Family Physician, 36*(1), 119–123.

320. Richtsmeier, A. J., & Waters, D. B. (1984). Somatic symptoms as family myth. *American Journal of Diseases of Children, 138*, 855–857.

321. Roberts, I. F., West, R. J., Ogilvie, D., & Dillon, M. J. (1979). Malnutrition in infants receiving cult diets: A form of child abuse. *British Medical Journal, 1*, 296–298.

322. Robins, P. M., & Sesan, R. (1991). Munchausen syndrome by proxy: Another women's disorder? *Professional Psychology: Research and Practice, 22*(4), 285–290.

323. Rogers, D., Tripp, J., Bentovim, A., Robinson, A., Berry, D., & Goulding, R. (1976). Nonaccidental poisoning: An extended syndrome of child abuse. *British Medical Journal, 1,* 793–796.

324. Rosaldo, R. (1989). *Culture and truth: The remaking of social analysis.* Boston: Beacon Press.

325. Rosen, B., & Stein, M. (1980). Women who abuse their children. Implications for pediatric practice. *American Journal of Diseases of Children, 134,* 947–950.

326. Rosen, C. L., Frost, J. D., Bricker, T., Tarnow, J. D., Gillette, P. C., Dunlavy, S. (1983). Two siblings with cardiorespiratory arrest: Munchausen syndrome by proxy or child abuse? *Pediatrics, 71,* 715–720.

327. Rosen, C. L., Frost, J. D., & Glaze, D. G. (1986). Child abuse and recurrent infant apnea. *Journal of Pediatrics, 109,* 1065–1067.

328. Rosenberg, D. (1987). Web of deceit: A literature review of Munchausen syndrome by proxy. *Child Abuse and Neglect, 11,* 547–563.

329. Rosenberg, D. (1992). Munchausen syndrome by proxy. In R. Reece (Ed.), *Child abuse: Medical diagnosis and management.* Philadelphia: Lea & Febiger.

330. Roth, D. (1990). How "mild" is mild Munchausen syndrome by proxy? *Israel Journal of Psychiatry and Related Sciences, 27*(3), 160–167.

331. Roueche, B. (1986, May 12). Annals of medicine: The dinosaur collection. *New Yorker,* pp. 102–111.

332. Rubin, L. G., Angelides, A., Davidson, M., & Lanzkowsky, P. (1986). Recurrent sepsis and gastrointestinal ulceration due to child abuse. *Archives of Disease in Childhood, 61,* 903–905.

333. Ruddick, S. (1980). Maternal thinking. *Feminist Studies 6*(2), 342–368.

334. Rumans, L. W., & Vosti, K. L. (1978). Factitious and fraudulent fever. *American Journal of Medicine, 65,* 745–755.

335. Rypma, J. S. (1990). *Munchausen syndrome by proxy: detection and prosecution.* Unpublished manuscript.

336. Sadler, J. Z. (1987). Ethical and management considerations in factitious illness: One and the same. *General Hospital Psychiatry, 9,* 31–36.

337. Salmon, R. F., Arant, B. S., Baum, M. G., & Hogg, R. J. (1988). Factitious hematuria with underlying renal abnormalities. *Pediatrics, 82*(3), 377–379.

338. Samuels, M. P., McClaughlin, W., Jacobson, R. R., Poets, C. F., & Southall, D. P. (1992). Fourteen cases of imposed upper airway obstruction. *Archives of Disease in Childhood, 67,* 162–170.

339. Samuels, M. P., & Southall, D. P. (1992). Munchausen syndrome by proxy. *British Journal of Hospital Medicine, 47*(10), 759–762.

340. Sanders, M. (1991, October). *Munchausen syndrome by proxy: Diagnostic and treatment considerations.* Paper presented at the annual convention of the American Association of Child and Adolescent Psychiatry, San Francisco.

341. Santangelo, W. C., Rickey, J. E., Rivera, L., & Fordtran, J. S. (1989). Surreptitious ipecac administration simulating intestinal pseudo-obstruction. *Annals of Internal Medicine, 110*(12), 1031–1032.

342. Saulsbury, F. T., Chobanian, M. C., & Wilson, W. G. (1984). Child abuse: Parenteral hydrocarbon administration. *Pediatrics, 73,* 719–722.

343. Scarlett, J. A., Mako, M. E., Rubenstein, A. H., Blix, P. M., Goldman, J., Horwitz, D. L., Tager, H., Jaspan, J. B., Stjerholm, M. R., & Olefsky, J. M. (1977). Factitious hypoglycemia. Diagnosis by measurement of serum C-peptide immunoreactivity and insulin-binding antibodies. *New England Journal of Medicine, 297*(10), 1029–1032.

344. Schade, D. S., Drumm, D. A., Eaton, R. P., & Sterling, W. A. (1985). Factitious brittle diabetes mellitus. *American Journal of Medicine, 78,* 777–784.

345. Schechter, S. (1982). *Women and male violence.* Boston: South End Press.

346. Schetky, D. H., & Benedek, E. P. (Eds.). (1992). *Clinical handbook of child psychiatry and the law.* Baltimore: Williams & Wilkins.

347. Schnaps, Y., Frand, M., Rotem, Y., & Tirosh, M. (1981). The chemically abused child. *Pediatrics, 68,* 119–121.

348. Schoenfeld, H., Margolin, J., & Baum, S. (1987). Munchausen syndrome as a suicide equivalent: Abolition of syndrome by psychotherapy. *American Journal of Psychotherapy, 41*(4), 604–612.

349. Schreier, H. A. (1992). The perversion of mothering: Munchausen syndrome by proxy. *Bulletin of the Menninger Clinic, 56*(4), 421–437.

350. Schreier, H. A., & Libow J. A. (1993). Munchausen by proxy syndrome: Diagnosis and prevalence. *American Journal of Orthopsychiatry, 63*(2), 318–321.

351. Schreier, H. A., & Libow, J. A. (1988). *Munchausen syndrome by proxy in a father.* Unpublished manuscript.

352. Senner, A., & Ott, M. J. (1990). Munchausen syndrome by proxy. Unpublished manuscript.

353. Shaywitz, B. A., Siegel, N. J., & Pearson, H. A. (1977). Megavitamins for minimal brain dysfunction. *Journal of the American Medical Association, 238,* 1749–1750.

354. Sheridan, M. (1989). Munchausen syndrome by proxy. *Health and Social Work, 14*(1), 53–58.

355. Short, I. A. (1955). Munchausen syndrome (letter). *British Medical Journal, IV,* 1206–1207.

356. Siegel, P. T. (1990, August). How to interview a mother suspected of Munchausen syndrome by proxy. *Paper presented at the 98th Annual Convention of the American Psychological Association.* Boston.

357. Sigal, M., Carmel, I., Altmark, D., & Silfen, P. (1988). Munchausen syndrome by proxy: A psychodynamic analysis. *Medicine and Law, 7,* 49–56.

358. Sigal, M., Gelkopf, M., & Levertov, G. (1990). Medical and legal aspects of the Munchausen by proxy perpetrator. *Medicine and Law, 9,* 739–749.

359. Sigal, M., Gelkopf, M., & Meadow, S. R. (1989). Munchausen by

proxy syndrome: The triad of abuse, self-abuse and deception. *Comprehensive Psychiatry, 30*(6), 527–533.

360. Silver, H. K., & Finkelstein, M. (1967). Deprivation dwarfism. *Journal of Pediatrics, 70*(3), 317–324.

361. Simon, F. A. (1980). Uncommon type of child abuse. *Journal of Pediatrics, 96,* 785.

362. Single, T., & Henry, R. L. (1991). An unusual case of Munchausen syndrome by proxy. *Australia and New Zealand Journal of Psychiatry, 25,* 422–425.

363. Smith, N. J., & Ardern, M. H. (1989). More in sickness than in health. A case study of Munchausen by proxy in the elderly. *Journal of Family Therapy, 11*(4), 321–334.

364. Smith, S. M., & Hanson, R. (1974). One hundred thirty-four battered children: A medical and psychological study. *British Medical Journal, 3,* 666–670.

365. Sneed, R. C., & Bell, R. F. (1976). The dauphin of Munchausen: Factitious passage of renal stones in a child. *Pediatrics, 58,* 127–129.

366. Sobel, R., & Margolis, J. A. (1965). Repetitive poisoning in children: A psychosocial study. *Pediatrics, 35,* 641–651.

367. Sofinowski, R. E., & Butler, P. M. (1991). Munchausen syndrome by proxy: A review. *Texas Medicine, 87*(10), 66–69.

368. Solyom, C., & Solyom, L. (1990). A treatment program for functional paraplegia/Munchausen syndrome. *Journal of Behavior Therapy and Experimental Psychiatry, 21*(3), 225–230.

369. Southall, D. P., Stebbens, V. A., Rees, S. V., Lang, M. H., Warner, J. O., & Shinebourne, E. A. (1987). Apnoeic episodes induced by smothering: Two cases identified by covert video surveillance. *British Medical Journal, 294,* 1637–1641.

370. Sperling, M. (1959). Equivalents of depression in children. *Journal of Hillside Hospital, 8,* 138–147.

371. Spiro, H. R. (1968). Chronic factitious illness. *Archives of General Psychiatry, 18,* 569–79.

372. Stacey, J. (1990). *Brave new families.* New York: Basic Books.

373. Stancin, T. (1990, August). *Educating medical personnel about Munchausen syndrome by proxy.* Paper presented at the 98th Annual Convention of the American Psychological Association. Boston, MA.

374. Stankler, L. (1977). Factitious skin lesions in a mother and two sons. *British Medical Journal, 97,* 217–219.

375. Steele, B. F., & Pollack, C. A. (1968). A psychiatric study of parents who abuse children. In R. Helfer and C. H. Kempe (Eds.), *The Battered Child.* Chicago: University of Chicago Press.

376. Steinem, G. (1992). *Revolution from within.* Boston: Little, Brown.

377. Steinschneider, A. (1972). Prolonged apnea and the sudden infant death syndrome: Clinical and laboratory observations. *Pediatrics, 50,* 646–654.

378. Stephenson, J.B.P. (1990). Specific syncopes and anoxic seizure types.

In *Fits and Faints,* Clinics in Developmental Medicine no. 109. Philadelphia: J. B. Lippincott.

379. Stern, D. N. (1985). *The interpersonal world of the infant: A view from psychoanalysis and developmental psychology.* New York: Basic Books.

380. Stern, E. S. (1948). The Medea complex: The mother's homicidal wishes to her child. *Journal of Mental Science, 94,* 321–331.

381. Stevenson, R., & Alexander, R. (1990). Munchausen syndrome by proxy presenting as a developmental disability. *Journal of Developmental and Behavioral Pediatrics, 11*(5), 262–264.

382. Stoller, G. (1991). The term perversions. In G. T. Fogel & W. Myers (Eds.), *Perversions and near perversions in clinical practice.* New Haven, CT: Yale University Press.

383, Stoller, R. J. (1975). *Perversion.* New York: Pantheon.

384. Stone, F. (1989). Munchausen-by-proxy syndrome: An unusual form of child abuse. *Social Casework: The Journal of Contemporary Social Work,* 243–246.

385. Stone, M. H. (1977). Factitious illness. *Bulletin of the Menninger Clinic, 41*(3), 239–254.

386. Strandvik, B. (1987). Psychosocial stressors and gastrointestinal disorders in childhood and adolescence. *Scandinavian Journal of Gastroenterology, 128*(Suppl.), 128–131.

387. Strassburg, H. M., & Peuckert, W. (1984). Not "Polle Syndrome" please. *Lancet, i,* 166.

388. *Study of National Incidence and Prevalence of Child Abuse and Neglect.* (1988). Washington, DC: U.S. Department of Health and Human Services.

389. Sturm, L., & Roberts, D. (1991, August). *A cross-agency model for clinical protocols and collaborative research, parental falsification of pediatric symptoms: Munchausen Syndrome by Proxy.* Paper presented at the American Psychological Association Symposium, San Francisco, CA.

390. Sugar, J. A., Belfer, M., Israel, E., & Herzog, D. B. (1991). A 3-year-old boy's chronic diarrhea and unexplained death. *Journal of the American Academy of Child and Adolescent Psychiatry, 30*(6), 1015–1021.

391. Sullivan, C. A., Francis, G. L., Bain, M. W., & Hartz, J. (1991). Munchausen syndrome by proxy: 1990. A portent for problems? *Clinical Pediatrics, 30*(2), 112–116.

392. Summit, R. C. (1983). The child sexual abuse accommodation syndrome. *Child Abuse and Neglect, 7,* 177–193.

393. Sussman, N., Borod, J. C., Canselmo, J. A., & Braun, D. (1987). Munchausen syndrome: A reconceptualization of the disorder. *The Journal of Nervous and Mental Diseases, 175*(11), 692–695.

394. Suskind, R. M., & Lewinter-Suskind, L. (Eds.). (1990). *The malnourished child.* New York: Raven Press.

395. Sutphen, J. L., & Saulsbury, F. T. (1988). Intentional ipecac poisoning: Munchausen syndrome by proxy. *Pediatrics, 82*(3, pt. 2), 453–456.

396. Taylor, E. (1989). *Prime time families. Television culture in post war America.* Berkeley and Los Angeles: University of California Press.

397. Taylor, E. M., & Emery, J. L. (1982). Two-year study of the causes of perinatal deaths classified in terms of preventability. *Archives of Disease in Childhood, 57,* 668–673.

398. Taylor, L., & Newberger, E. H. (1979). Child abuse in the international year of the child. *New England Journal of Medicine, 301,* 1205–1212.

399. Tee, L. (1975). Precursers of Munchausen's syndrome in childhood (Letter to the editor). *American Journal of Psychiatry, 132*(7), 757.

400. Terr, L. (1990). *Too scared to cry—Psychic trauma in childhood.* New York: Harper & Row.

401. Tojo, A., Nanba, S., Kimura, K., Hirata, Y., Matsuoka, H., Sugimoto, T., Watanabe, N, & Ohkubo, A. (1990). Factitious proteinuria in a young girl. *Clinical Nephrology, 33*(6), 299–302.

402. Trolliet, P. B., Francois, R., & Bondon, P. (1986). Identification d'une lithiase urinaire factice par l'analyse des calculs en spectrophotometrie infrarouge. *Presse Medicale, 15,* 2019.

403. Turk, L. J., Hanrahan, K. M., & Weber, E. R. (1990). Munchausen syndrome by proxy: A nursing overview. *Issues in Comprehensive Pediatric Nursing, 13,* 279–288.

404. Turow, J. (1989). *Playing doctor—television, storytelling and medical power.* New York: Oxford University Press.

405. United States Department of Health and Human Services. (1988). *Study of the national incidence and prevalence of child abuse and neglect.* Washington, DC: U.S. Government Printing Office.

406. Vaisrub, S. (1978). Baron Munchausen and the abused child. *Journal of the American Medical Association, 239,* 752.

407. Vaughan, V. C., & Brazelton, T. B. (1976). *The family—Can it be saved?* Chicago: Year Book Medical.

408. Verity, C. M., Winckworth, C., & Burman, D. (1979). Polle syndrome: Children of Munchausen. *British Medical Journal, 2,* 422–423.

409. Victor, R. G. (1972). Self-induced phlebotomy as cause of factitious illness. *American Journal of Psychotherapy, 26,* 425–431.

410. Viets, J. (1990, October 11). Marin murder case catches up with woman in South Carolina. *San Francisco Chronicle,* p. A5.

411. Volk, D. (1982). Factitious disorder in two children. *American Journal of Diseases of Children, 136,* 1027–1028.

412. Von Leo, E. E. Lighthart, R., & Verhulst, F. C. (1990). Das Munchausen-syndrom. Welcher name verdient den vorzug? "Munchausen's syndrome by proxy" oder "Münchausen's syndrome-e-proximo." *Der Kinderarzt, 21*(8), 1110–1114.

413. Wahl, C. W., & Golden, J. S. (1966). The psychodynamics of a polysurgical patient: Report of sixteen patients. *Psychosomatics, 7,* 65–72.

414. Waller, D. A. (1983). Obstacles to the treatment of Munchausen by proxy syndrome. *Journal of the American Academy of Child Psychiatry, 22,* 80–85.

415. Wallerstein, R. (1988, March 8). *New perspectives on psychoanalysis and psychotherapy*. Paper delivered at Herrick Hospital Ground Rounds. Berkeley, CA.

416. Wangh, M. (1962). The "evocation of a proxy." A psychological maneuver, its use as a defense, its purpose and genesis. In *Psychoanalytic study of the child*, vol. 17. New York: International University Press.

417. Waring, W. W. (1992). The persistent parent. *American Journal of Diseases of Children, 146*(6), 753–756.

418. Warner, J. O., & Hathaway, M. J. (1984). Allergic form of Meadow's syndrome (Munchausen by proxy). *Archives of Disease in Childhood, 59,* 151–156.

419. Watson, J.B.G., Davies, J. M., & Hunter, J.L.P. (1979). Nonaccidental poisoning in childhood. *Archives of Disease in Childhood, 54,* 143–144.

420. Weber, S. (1987). Munchausen syndrome by proxy. *Journal of Pediatric Nursing, 2*(1), 50–54.

421. Welldon, E. V. (1988). *Mother, madonna, whore. The idealization and denigration of motherhood.* London: Free Association Books.

422. White, S. T. (1985). Surreptitious warfarin ingestion. *Child Abuse and Neglect, 9,* 349–352.

423. Willging, J. P., Bower, C. M., & Cotton, R. T. (1992). Physical abuse of children. A retrospective review and an otolaryngology perspective. *Archives of Otolaryngology—Head and Neck Surgery, 118*(6), 584–590.

424. Williams, C. (1986). Munchausen syndrome by proxy: A bizarre form of child abuse. *Family Law, 16,* 32–34.

425. Williams, C., & Bevan, V. T. (1988). The secret observation of children in hospital. *Lancet, i,* 780–781.

426. Winchester, P. D., Todd, J. K., & Roe, M. H. (1977). Bacteremia in hospitalized children. *American Journal of Diseases of Children, 131,* 753–758.

427. Winerip, M. (1991, September 15). Aftermath of an emergency: A mistaken charge of child abuse takes its toll. *New York Times Sunday Magazine,* p. 53.

428. Winnicott, D. W. (1958). Transitional objects and transitional phenomena. In *Collected papers: Through pediatrics to psycho-analysis.* New York: Basic Books.

429. Witt, M. E., & Ginsberg-Fellner, F. (1981). prednisone-induced Munchausen syndrome. *American Journal of Diseases of Children, 135,* 852–853.

430. Wood, P. R., Fowlkes, J., Holden, P., & Castro, D. (1989). Fever of unknown origin for six years: Munchausen syndrome by proxy. *Journal of Family Practice, 28*(4), 391–395.

431. Woody, R. C., & Jones, J. G. (1987). Neurologic Munchausen-by-proxy syndrome. *Southern Medical Journal, 80*(2), 247–248.

432. Woolcott, P., Aceto, T., Rutt, C., Bloom, M., & Glick, R. (1982). Doctor shopping with the child as proxy patient: A variant of child abuse. *Journal of Pediatrics, 101,* 297–301.

433. Wright, N. (1984). *A mother's trail.* New York: Bantam Books.

434. Yassa, R. (1978). Munchausen's syndrome: A successfully treated case. *Psychosomatics, 19,* 242–243.
435. Yomtovian, R., & Swanger, R. (1991). Munchausen syndrome by proxy documented by discrepant blood typing. *American Journal of Clinical Pathology, 95*(2), 232–233.
436. Yorker, B. C., & Kahan, B. B. (1990). Munchausen's syndrome by proxy as a form of child abuse. *Archives of Psychiatric Nursing, 4*(5), 313–318.
437. Yorker, B., & Kahan, B. (1991). The Munchausen syndrome by proxy variant of child abuse in the family courts. *Journal of Juvenile and Family Court Judges, 42*(3), 51–38.
438. Yorker, B. C., Kahan, B. B., & Jewart, R. D. (1992). *A gender-sensitive understanding of the Munchausen syndrome by proxy form of child abuse.* Unpublished manuscript.
439. Yudkin, S. (1961). Six children with coughs: The second diagnosis. *Lancet, ii,* 561–563.
440. Zeanah, C. H. (1989). Implications of research on infant development for psychodynamic theory and practice. *Journal of the American Academy of Child and Adolescent Psychiatry, 28*(5), 657–668.
441. Zinner, J., & Shapiro, R. L. (1989). Projective identification as a mode of perception and behavior in families of adolescents. In J. S. Scharff (Ed.), *Foundations of object relations family therapy.* Northvale, NJ: Jason Aronson.
442. Zitelli, B. J., Seltman, M. F., & Shannon, R. M. (1987). Munchausen syndrome by proxy and its professional participants. *American Journal of Diseases of Children, 141,* 1099–1102.
443. Zitelli, B. J., Seltman, M. F., & Shannon, R. M. (1988). Reply to Frost letter (Letter to the editor). *Archives of Disease in Childhood, 142*(9), 917–918.
444. Zohar, Y., Avidan, G., Shvili, Y., & Laurian, N. (1987). Otalaryngologic cases of Munchausen's syndrome. *Laryngoscope, 97,* 201–203.
445. Zumwalt, R. E., & Hirsch, C. S. (1980). Subtle fatal child abuse. *Human Pathology, 11*(2), 167–174.

Index